Freedom Is a Constant Struggle

The Mississippi Civil Rights Movement and Its Legacy

KENNETH T. ANDREWS

THE UNIVERSITY OF CHICAGO PRESS   Chicago and London

KENNETH T. ANDREWS is assistant professor of
sociology at the University of North Carolina at Chapel Hill.

The University of Chicago Press, Chicago 60637
The University of Chicago Press, Ltd., London
© 2004 by The University of Chicago Press
All rights reserved. Published 2004
Printed in the United States of America

13 12 11 10 09 08 07 06 05 04   1 2 3 4 5

ISBN: 0-226-02040-1 (cloth)
ISBN: 0-226-02043-6 (paper)

Library of Congress Cataloging-in-Publication Data

Andrews, Kenneth T.
    Freedom is a constant struggle : the Mississippi civil rights
movement and its legacy / Kenneth T. Andrews.
        p. cm.
    Includes bibliographical references (p.) and index.
        ISBN 0-226-02040-1 (cloth : alk. paper) — ISBN
        0-226-02043-6 (pbk. : alk. paper)
        1. Civil rights movements—Mississippi—History—
20th century. 2. African Americans—Civil rights—
Mississippi—History—20th century. 3. Mississippi—Race
relations—History—20th century. I. Title.

E185.93.M6A85 2004
976.2'063—dc22

                        2003025013

⊗ The paper used in this publication meets the minimum
requirements of the American National Standard for
Information Sciences—Permanence of Paper for Printed
Library Materials, ANSI Z39.48-1992.

For Marne

They say that freedom is a constant struggle,

They say that freedom is a constant struggle,

They say that freedom is a constant struggle,

O Lord, we've struggled so long,

We must be free, we must be free.

"Freedom Is a Constant Struggle," SNCC Freedom Singers

Contents

Tables and Figures

Acknowledgments

WRITING THIS book and conducting the research for it have been rich and rewarding experiences, and one of the major reasons for this is the generosity of friends, family, and colleagues.

The study of social movements and politics has grown rapidly in recent years and has also maintained a scholarly community that is intellectually engaging. Many scholars have been generous with their time and insights about the civil rights movement and social movements. John Dittmer, James Loewen, Doug McAdam, Ron Pagnucco, and Jill Quadagno provided helpful advice at early stages on identifying sources and developing the project. In the summer of 2000, I participated in a workshop at the Center for Advanced Study in the Behavioral Sciences organized by Doug McAdam and Charles Tilly with an interdisciplinary faculty that provided a great opportunity to develop the arguments and analysis in this book. In writing this book, many others have commented on chapters or provided feedback at conferences and through correspondence, including Edwin Amenta, Elisabeth Clemens, David Cunningham, Christian Davenport, Bob Edwards, Jenny Irons, Jim Jasper, Doug McAdam, John McCarthy, David Meyer, Aldon Morris, Frances Fox Piven, Kurt Schock, and Jackie Smith.

At Harvard University, many colleagues read drafts of chapters or discussed the research with me informally, including Michael Biggs, Irene Bloemraad, Bayliss Camp, Mariko Chang, David Frank, Marshall Ganz, Lowell Hargens, Jason Kaufman, Stan Lieberson, Peter Marsden, Ziad Munson, Orlando Patterson, Barbara Reskin, and Chris Winship. I also benefited from feedback from participants in a workshop on social movements and politics that I organized at Harvard, where I presented multiple chapters and refined my arguments and analyses from this project and learned a tremendous amount in particular through conversations with Michael Biggs, Irene Bloemraad, Marshall Ganz, and Ziad Munson.

This project began in the Department of Sociology at suny–Stony Brook, where I received critical feedback and support from friends as the research took shape and developed. Some read drafts of numerous preliminary drafts. I am thankful to Melissa Bolyard, Drew Fish, Lisa Handler, Anna Linders, Pat Moynihan, Sally Naetzker, Shuva Paul, Alex Trillo, and Charlie Zicari. Many faculty at Stony Brook contributed through discussion, meetings, and departmental forum.

My committee of Michael Schwartz, Les Owens, Mary Vogel, and Bob Zussman provided wide latitude to pursue my questions about the consequences of the civil rights struggle in Mississippi, and they pushed me to strengthen the project at every step. Michael Schwartz contributed to the design and implementation of the study, and he pressed me to extract the broader lessons buried in statistical output, archival documents, and oral histories. This project began in one of Mary Vogel's graduate seminars, and she played an essential role throughout.

Research for the project, especially the interviews and some of the archival research, was supported by a National Science Foundation Dissertation Improvement Grant. At Harvard, funding from internal grants allowed me to employ two outstanding research assistants—Julie Paik and Chris Park—who collected and analyzed extensive data.

While conducting the research, I spent two years as a member of the Department of Sociology at Millsaps College, in Jackson, Mississippi. I owe many thanks to my colleagues Frances Coker, Ming Tsui, and George Bey for providing a superb base for my research. Jenny Irons, Melanie Peele, and Robyn Ryle worked as research assistants on the project during those two years, and they contributed substantially to this project by collecting key pieces of the archival data. I am especially appreciative of Jenny Irons, who provided detailed feedback on the penultimate draft of the manuscript.

While working at a number of archives in Mississippi and beyond, I benefited directly and indirectly from the many archivists and research librarians who have built and sustained the rich body of documentary evidence on the civil rights movement. In particular, I am indebted to the archivists at the Library of Congress, the Mississippi Department of Archives and History, Moorland-Spingarn Research Center at Howard University, Freedom Information Service (maintained by Jan Hillegas), the Information Services Library of Jackson State University (formerly the R&D Center), the National Archives and Records Administration, the

Schomburg Center for the Study of Black Culture, the State Historical Society of Wisconsin, Tougaloo College (Clarence Hunter), the Oral History Collection at the University of Southern Mississippi, and the library of the United States Commission on Civil Rights.

The activists and community leaders I interviewed for this study were generous with their time and insights. The chance to collect firsthand accounts from the people who were on the front line of the civil rights struggle was an invaluable opportunity. As I began this project, Ed King provided contacts and copies of his own writing on the Mississippi movement. As I began conducting case studies, Hollis Watkins and L. C. Dorsey played an important role by suggesting contacts for interviews. By doing so, they facilitated my research. L. C. Dorsey, a grassroots activist from Bolivar County and professor at Jackson State University, opened her address book to connect me to a dense network of movement participants in the Mississippi Delta. After many years of trying to understand this important social movement, I remain inspired by the people I met and the lessons I learned from studying the civil rights movement in Mississippi.

Finally, I owe many thanks to Marne for her support, friendship, and love.

Acronyms and Descriptions for Organizations

ACBC (Association of Communities of Bolivar County): local movement-based CAP in Bolivar County

BCCAP (Bolivar County Community Action Program, Inc.): local CAP in Bolivar County

CAP (community action program): OEO program with local delegate agencies that administer poverty programs; also referred to as CAA (community action agency)

CDGM (Child Development Group of Mississippi): early Head Start program in Mississippi that had heavy movement participation

CMI (Central Mississippi, Inc.): local CAP covering six Mississippi counties including Holmes

COFO (Council of Federated Organizations): umbrella organization that coordinated movement activity in Mississippi from 1961–64

CORE (Congress of Racial Equality): national civil rights organization

MAP (Mississippi Action for Progress): Head Start program that challenged CDGM beginning in 1966; included more moderate movement leaders

MCUP (Madison County Union for Progress): local movement organization in Madison County

MFDP (Mississippi Freedom Democratic Party; also FDP): statewide independent political party that began in 1964

NAACP (National Association for the Advancement of Colored People)

OEO (Office of Economic Opportunity): federal agency coordinating poverty programs

SCLC (Southern Christian Leadership Conference)

SNCC (Student Nonviolent Coordinating Committee)

VEP (Voter Education Project): program of the Southern Regional Council that funded voter registration projects throughout the South

CHAPTER ONE

Introduction

Do SOCIAL movements matter? When people come together to challenge inequalities and face powerful authorities and opponents, what hope can they have of bringing about significant changes? This question has puzzled movement participants and observers throughout history. There are numerous examples to inspire confidence in the power of social movements, and there are equally plentiful cases to support a pessimistic assessment that movements are more likely to fail, invite repression, become co-opted, or produce polarization and violence than to achieve success.

The civil rights movement has raised the same questions for its participants and subsequent observers. John Lewis, one of the early SNCC leaders from Nashville, argues that "so many things are undeniably better. . . . But there is a mistaken assumption among many that these signs of progress mean that the battle is over, that the struggle for civil rights is finished, that the problems of segregation were solved in the '60s and now all we have to deal with are economic issues" (1998, 490). Mary King is critical of a flippant view, writing:

> Those who sardonically claim "not much has changed for American blacks" must not know how bad it was. Such a comment reveals . . . that the speaker was not on the front lines in the southern civil rights movement and never experienced the brutality that was directed against blacks and their supporters at that time. (1987, 544)

Others have painted a less optimistic assessment, pointing to the limited gains, continuing inequality and injustices, and the costs that were suffered through the fierce struggles of the movement. Annie Devine, a legendary activist from Canton, Mississippi, wonders whether "all we may have done through the civil rights movement is open Pandora's box" (quoted in Dent 1997, 347).

L. C. Dorsey, a civil rights leader from Bolivar County, observes that "to the optimist, things are beautiful and even the small changes take on grand dimensions. For the pessimist, the changes may seem miniscule when viewed from eyes that expect the rubble from the fallen walls of racism already to be cleared away" (1977, 41). From the perspective of the activist, change can be measured relative to the goals that were sought or against the conditions that prevailed before the movement began. In this study, I use the tools of historical and social scientific analysis to shed new light on the legacy of the civil rights movement.

Many scholars of social movements assume that movements are, at least under certain conditions, effective agents of social change, especially for poor and powerless groups. This belief in the efficacy of protest and collective action underlies much of the scholarship by historians and social scientists on social movements. This is especially true for scholars of the civil rights movement. In fact, many studies of the origins and development of the movement have been justified by pointing to its success in challenging and transforming the southern system of racial domination. For example, Aldon Morris, in *The Origins of the Civil Rights Movement*, argues that the movement had "a profound impact on American society" (1984, 266). Similarly, Dennis Chong points to the movement as "the quintessential example of public-spirited collective action in our time" that "spark[ed] radical changes in American society" (1991, 1). Although these and many other scholars make strong assertions about the success of the civil rights movement, they do not examine this basic question. Surprisingly, we know more about the origins and early development of the civil rights movement than about the role the movement played in transforming the institutions and social relations of the South.

Adding to the confusion are disagreements about how movements influence social change. Some scholars locate the power of movements in disruptions and threats that force concessions from powerful opponents and authorities. In contrast, other scholars see movements as engaged in a form of persuasive communication designed to bring about change by appealing to the "hearts and minds" of bystanders. In this view, effective protest can win influential allies and secure much-needed resources. Finally, another line of argument claims that movements are efficacious when they adopt the organizational forms, institutionalized tactics, and rhetorical frameworks of interest groups and abandon the "politics of protest." Professionalization and moderation are the necessary steps to winning new advantages as groups make the transition from outsiders to insiders. These alternatives were well represented within the civil rights movement as leaders debated the strengths and weaknesses of strategies built around the basic mechanisms of disruption, persuasion, and negotiation as tools of social change.

In this study, I address these long-standing questions about the impacts of social movements through a multilayered study of the Mississippi civil rights movement. Mississippi stood most firm in its resistance to the civil rights movement and federal efforts to enforce racial equality. Tom Dent, a native of New Orleans who worked in the Mississippi movement for many years, tells us that "if racial change and justice meant anything anywhere, change in Mississippi, to the degree it existed, would be . . . the surest barometer of progress in the American South" (1997, 338). By examining this historically important case, I clarify our broader understanding of the ways in which movements transform social and political institutions as well as the constraints and obstacles that movements face when they try to do so. Through this analysis, I shed light on the movement building that took place in Mississippi and the resilience of the movement in the face of massive repression. I trace the movement's development beginning in the early 1960s, and I analyze its impact and setbacks during the 1970s and 1980s. This time period includes the expansion of voting rights and gains in black political power, the desegregation of public schools and the emergence of "white flight" academies, and the rise and fall of federally funded antipoverty programs. I chart the movement's engagement in each of these arenas as well as the tactical interaction between local civil rights movements and white power holders.

Research on the civil rights movement has focused primarily on the period up to the passage of the Voting Rights Act in 1965, often regarded as the final chapter of the southern phase of the black movement. However, many important struggles took place after 1965 as local movements tried to shape electoral politics, increase access to and improve the quality of public schools, and secure public resources like Head Start and community action programs.

Furthermore, historians of the civil rights movement have focused most heavily on the national leaders, the major civil rights organizations, and a handful of key protest campaigns. These are, of course, appropriate topics for research. However, this disproportionate focus on the national level of the movement obscures the depth and breadth of the civil rights struggle. Moreover, this focus locates the potential impacts of the movement in major court decisions and legislative reforms without asking whether or to what extent these legal changes were realized in the institutions throughout the South. The major legal reforms of the civil rights era only beg the question of whether the implementation of new laws and policies made the functioning of politics, schools, and social policies more equitable in the post–civil rights South.

Movements rarely, if ever, achieve all of their goals, but they can and do generate enduring consequences. Sidney Tarrow notes that "protest cycles do not simply end and leave nothing but lassitude or repression in their wake; they have indirect and long-term effects that emerge when the initial excitement is over and disillusionment passes" (1994, 172). Tarrow's observation is widely regarded as accurate by scholars of social movements and contentious politics. This study broadens and refines our understanding of movement impacts. Underlying this study is an argument that explains how movements have long-term and short-term impacts. I claim that focusing at the local level provides the best opportunity and the most important barometer for examining the consequences of social movements. In addition, I show that there is continuity between the heyday of movement activity and the period of movement decline.

Clayborne Carson, one of the leading historians of the civil rights movement, wrote an incisive essay about the historical scholarship on the movement, making three major criticisms that have influenced my argument. Carson observes that "because the emergent goals of American social movements have usually not been fulfilled, scholars have found it difficult to determine their political significance" (1986, 19). From this complexity and causal ambiguity, some scholars assume that movements are important and others assume that they are inconsequential. Some scholars assume that professional interest groups and routine political processes are the key actors because they are more likely to persist once mass mobilization wanes.[1] Second, there is the assumption "that the black struggle can best be understood as a protest movement, orchestrated by national leaders in order to achieve national civil rights legislation" (Carson 1986, 23). This assumption leads to an inaccurate view of the tactics, organizations, leaders, goals, and impacts of the movement. Throughout the civil rights movement, campaigns and tactics targeted change at the local level. In a small handful of campaigns such as in Birmingham and Selma, there was a complex effort to use local mobilization to leverage federal action. These highly visible cases represent a small fraction of the broader civil rights struggle. The assumption of a national movement effecting national legislation leads to a third error—"the prevailing scholarly conception . . . that [the movement] ended in 1965" with the passage of the Voting Rights Act (Carson 1986, 27). Rather, Carson argues that there is substantial continuity alongside transformation in the broader struggle by blacks after the Voting Rights Act.

Clayborne Carson's insights are a key starting point for this study of the continuity and transformation of the Mississippi civil rights movement from the early 1960s through the early 1980s. This focus allows us to better understand the consequences of social movements. In short, to understand the history of the black freedom struggle, we must examine in detail the ongoing conflicts after the major legislative victories of the civil rights movement. The question here is a rather direct and obvious one, and it grows out of a straightforward concern on the part of social movement participants and observers to understand the consequences of social movements. While the question is generally acknowledged to be important, research and theory remain sparse.[2] Many barriers stand in the way of insightful research on the impacts of movements—both methodological and conceptual. In the next section, I describe the research that has allowed me to address these challenges and develop my analysis of the impact of the civil rights movement.

Overview of the Study

The argument developed through this study demonstrates the importance of movement dynamics for explanations of political change. In addition to the actions of elites, courts, legislatures, and countermovements, social movements can and sometimes do play a key role in the process of social change. I show how the Mississippi movement built indigenous organizations and facilitated the growth of new leadership. I call this combination of leaders, indigenous resources, and local organizations the "movement infrastructure," and I demonstrate that long-term patterns of institutional change are shaped by variations in the emergence and continuity of a community's movement infrastructure. The cultivation of local leadership and the building of effective organizations are crucial steps in developing the capacity for ongoing social change efforts.

I advance strong claims about the central importance of the civil rights movement, but I also find that the movement was itself in an ongoing and dynamic relationship with opponents and authorities. The movement was transformed through these interactions, including the efforts of whites to repress or undermine the movement and of federal actors to intervene in local conflicts and advance government programs and legal changes. One must examine this dynamic interaction to fully account for the ways that the southern communities changed following the peak of civil rights mobilization. This approach connects to the broader effort to shift from more static to dynamic analyses of movements and other forms of contentious politics, and the focus on the intersections between movements, opponents, and authorities broadens the scope beyond a narrower movement-centered analysis (McAdam, Tarrow, and Tilly 2001).

My central arguments emerge from two sets of comparisons. First, I compare the institutional changes that occur in communities with different levels of movement activity. How do communities with greater or lesser movement strength differ in terms of their long-term development? This set of comparisons allows me to assess the patterns of political and institutional development in Mississippi following the civil rights movement and the role that the movement played in shaping those patterns. Second, I compare across the different types of outcomes reflecting the movement's broad and ambitious change agenda—electoral participation, social welfare policies, school desegregation, and black office holding. Did the civil rights movement have greater impacts in some arenas than others? And, if so, why? For each of these arenas, I argue that the patterns of change (including the timing, form, and magnitude of change) can only be explained by examining the interaction of three factors: (1) movement infrastructure and strategy, (2) white countermobilization, and (3) federal intervention (specifically, the extent to which implementation efforts are receptive to movement mobilization). By comparing across communities and arenas, I argue that broad patterns of political change derive from numerous political conflicts taking place across many localities. These local conflicts are consequential in shaping the overall patterns of change. This is a fundamentally different set of causal argument about the impact of the civil rights movement in particular and social movements in general than is advanced by many scholars because I focus on the cumulative and bottom-up dynamics of change.

In this study, I employ two major research strategies to examine the trajectory and impact of local civil rights movements in Mississippi. First, I have assembled a quantitative county-level data set to examine the movement's impacts on electoral politics, primary and secondary schools, and social policies. Second, I completed intensive examination of three communities using archival data and informant interviews to examine *how* movements matter and the interaction of movements, opponents, and authorities. These strategies are complementary, and both are essential if we are to understand the complex dynamics of the civil rights movement and its legacy. The quantitative analysis allows for precise estimates of movement impacts and other forces shaping change, such as the social and economic characteristics of the community, the role of violence by whites, and the intervention of federal agencies and courts. The comparisons of all counties by level of movement activism present the broad patterns. The quantitative data described above carries the burden of making systematic comparisons across communities by summarizing major relationships, including patterns over time and among variables. The qualitative case studies explore the process of movement building, the tactical interaction between movements and countermovements, and many other dynamics that cannot be measured quantitatively across all counties. The case studies examine variations among counties, all of which had high levels of activism in the early 1960s, and demonstrate what these changes looked like and how they came about in specific contexts. The key strength of the case studies is to illustrate major characteristics of communities and organizations, to provide insight into the motivations and social relationships within those communities, and to demonstrate processes of change or mechanisms through which change occurs. (See appendix A for a more detailed description of the research design.) The following map (fig. 1.1) shows the patterning of movement activity in Mississippi and identifies the three case studies. Mississippi counties are grouped into three major categories of sustained, episodic, and non-movement counties based on indicators of movement activity and organization in the early 1960s. (The indicators used for these comparisons are described in detail in chapter 4.)

The case studies represent three distinct patterns of movement-outcome relationships. Each case had an active civil rights movement in the early and mid-1960s, but they vary in the extent to which the movement was sustained and influential. The first case examines a county where a strong local movement resulted in substantial gains in office holding and social policies. The second and third cases were less successful in the electoral arena. Specifically, the second case examines the effects of extended repression on movement infrastructure. In contrast, the third case examines the obstacles to movement development in counties with major structural obstacles to mobilization—including the rapid mechanization of farming and pervasive black poverty.

FIGURE I.I: Map of Movement Counties

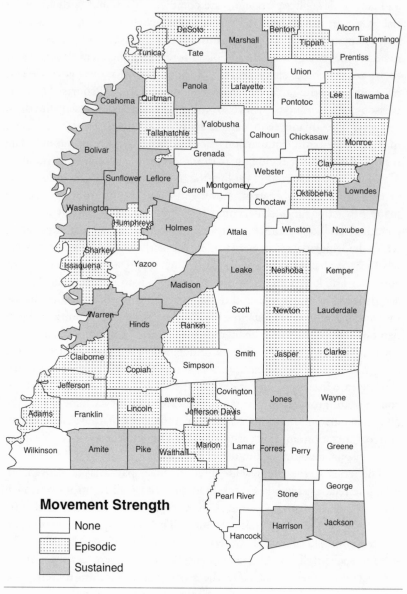

Movement Strength

- None
- Episodic
- Sustained

The Legacy of Political Struggle in Mississippi

The questions that inform this study engage recent scholarship by sociologists and political scientists concerning the dynamics and consequences of social movements. However, I also contribute to the scholarship by historians on the civil rights struggle. Clayborne Carson has argued that the civil rights movement should be reconceptualized as one part of a broader "black freedom struggle." He states that "contrary to the oft-expressed view that the civil rights movement died during the mid-1960s, we find that many local activists stressed the continuity between the struggle to gain political rights for southern blacks and the struggles to exercise them in productive ways" (1986, 27). By examining a small slice of that struggle, I illuminate broader dynamics of conflict and change that have been the core of the African American experience.

This study challenges the periodization of the civil rights movement as beginning in the mid-1950s and ending in 1965. There are substantial flaws in the standard narrative of the civil rights movement in which protest culminates in two major pieces of national legislation—the Civil Rights Act of 1964 and the Voting Rights Act of 1965. In fact, given the wide variation in the implementation of these legislative gains, local movements had to spend significant energy to ensure that the changes implied by the new legislation would be realized. These struggles developed over many years following this burst in national legislative change.

The political context after 1965 was different in important ways for local movements. Not surprisingly, strategies used by whites to resist the civil rights movement changed as well. This forced movements to develop new strategies for countering the efforts to dilute significant social change. In the arena of electoral politics, white resistance crystallized in legislation passed during a special session of the Mississippi legislature. Local variation in white resistance corresponded partially to the characteristics of the local social structure. However, white strategies developed through a process of tactical interaction responding to black mobilization (real or anticipated) and to the perceived successes of the civil rights movement. To study the impacts of movements, we must examine the tactical interaction between movements and countermovements and the way resistance changes over time.

This focus on countermobilization helps explain why even the most well-organized and tactically astute movements do not achieve everything they seek. Movements, especially those striving for far-reaching changes, encounter organized resistance. Furthermore, the fundamental transformations sought by social movements and the limited range of resources available to those movements point to other reasons why movements rarely, if ever, get everything they want. However, these insights should not deter us from explaining the relatively greater impact of some movements over others, or the relatively greater impact of movements in some arenas than others. The civil rights movement was far from monolithic, varying widely in its distribution, strength, and subsequent impacts.

Looking Ahead

In chapter 2, I build a theoretical framework for analyzing movement outcomes. This argument incorporates key insights from the work of sociologists and political scientists on social movements, conflict, democratic participation, politics, and policy. The theoretical framework pays close attention to indigenous movements (their organizations, tactical repertoires, leadership), other key actors and institutions (including countermovements, local elites, and government actors), and, finally, the characteristics of local social and political institutions and structures.

In chapter 3, I present a brief statewide history of the Mississippi movement as a broader context for my study of the impacts of movements at the local level. This history emphasizes the development of an organizing model in Mississippi, the broad pattern of repression and resistance to the movement, and the role of federal actors and policies. I conclude this chapter by summarizing the major historical developments in terms of electoral politics, social policies, and school desegregation. In chapter 4, I focus on local variations in movement building before and after the Voting Rights Act and the War on Poverty, presenting an overview of the three case studies. I illustrate the tactical dilemmas and strategies employed at the local level, and I show how movement building varied depending on the social context and the interaction between civil rights groups and local power holders.

Chapters 5 through 8 are organized around the major outcome arenas—electoral participation, social welfare policies, school desegregation, and black office holding. In each chapter, I draw on quantitative data to show how the pattern of institutional change varied by the level of movement activity, and I assess the role of countermobilization, federal intervention, and community characteristics in shaping the pattern of change. I present material from the case studies to demonstrate the role played by local movements in these long-term changes, and I examine the transformation of the movement's organization, leadership, and strategies through its engagement with electoral politics, poverty programs, and school desegregation.

Chapter 5 covers the electoral arena, where I analyze black participation in electoral politics after the Voting Rights Act, including increases in voter registration and campaigns by black candidates for local and statewide office. I examine efforts by local civil rights groups, and I also show how these efforts were shaped by violent repression. I find that the Voting Rights Act determined the timing of change and that local movements influenced the amount of change in black electoral participation.

In chapter 6, I examine developments in social welfare policies, focusing especially on the short-lived War on Poverty. These federal policy initiatives presented local movements with distinct and at times contradictory dilemmas. Movements were reluctant to become involved with poverty programs, fearing co-optation and dependence. Many movements attempted to operate outside the constraints of federal bureaucracies to establish economic autonomy for black communities. However, movements did participate in and shape poverty programs in Mississippi. I examine whether and to what extent movements influenced the distribution of funding and the programmatic focus of poverty programs.

Chapter 7 delineates the struggles surrounding primary and secondary education. Here, we find sporadic and unfocused mobilization by civil rights organizations. As was the case in the electoral arena, litigation and federal enforcement play an important intervening role in shaping the direction of change. The key period of court action took place in the late 1960s and early 1970s. However, courts are limited in their capacity to implement and direct the process of institutional change. This means that whites were uniquely positioned to resist by obstructing institutional change locally and by establishing white counterinstitutions, that is, private academies.

In chapter 8, I return to the question of movement influence on black electoral politics in Mississippi by examining the election and influence of black elected officials. This chapter picks up where the analysis of black electoral participation left off in chapter 5. Although local movements shaped the extent of black political participation in the immediate aftermath of the Voting Rights Act, the emerging black vote had very minimal substantive impact on policy or the election of black candidates during the late 1960s. This relationship changed over time as litigation successfully dismantled barriers to black political power. In counties with strong movement infrastructures, local organizations and networks of activists were able to gain increasing positions of influence in municipal and county government, leading to modest changes in the enactment of policies.

In the concluding chapter, I return to the broad historical and sociological themes of this study. I highlight the key conclusions and implications of this study for the Mississippi case and for the civil rights movement generally. Around the globe, the civil rights movement continues to serve as an inspiration and the basis for broader insight concerning the power of the powerless to create significant long-term change. I reflect on the lessons that can be learned from the civil rights movement for our understanding of social movements more broadly.

CHAPTER TWO

Explaining the Consequences of Social Movements

THIS CHAPTER presents the conceptual framework that I use to explain the impacts of social movements. I bring substantial attention to the role of social movements in explanations of broad patterns of change. Most often, scholars have asked about the origins of social movements—why and how did this individual or group engage in protest or conflict. Instead, I address questions about the consequences of sustained periods of conflict. To answer these questions, I focus on the interaction of three factors: the movement's infrastructure and strategies, the forms of resistance and repression by movement opponents, and the structure and activities of federal actors—including courts, government agencies, and law enforcement. The movement infrastructure includes organizations, leadership, and resources that support initiatives to challenge existing institutional arrangements. This concept informs my analysis of whether and, if so, how movements bring about enduring institutional changes.

In this chapter, I begin by presenting a conceptualization of movement outcomes. I identify then propose solutions to the major challenges to defining and studying the consequences of social movements. Then I present the movement infrastructure model by identifying the key dimensions of a movement's leadership, organizational structure, and resources that influence its persistence and efficacy. I differentiate this approach from three major alternatives that focus disproportionately on the role of disruption, persuasion, or negotiation. Finally, I examine two additional factors—countermobilization and the social and political context—that influence the dynamics of movements and the broader pattern of change.

Conceptualizing Outcomes

The two basic challenges to studying the impacts of social movements are (1) defining success and other relevant benchmarks for movement impact, and (2) determining whether the movement played any role in generating change. The key challenge for identifying the possible impacts of movements is the wide range of alternative indicators and conflicts among participants and observers about them. Even when we reach consensus about the appropriate indicators of a movement's impact (e.g., passage of legislation or a change in public opinion), there are many other factors that could have played a contributing role in producing change. In fact, factors beyond the movement could be much more influential, effectively reducing the significance of movements to a sideshow. Whenever social scientists attempt to identify the connection between a potential cause (movement strength) and a possible outcome (legislative change), we face the possibility that the relationship is spurious—that some other factor is the real cause of change. Fortunately, we can turn to theory and prior research to identify alternative explanations, and we can develop careful research strategies to increase the plausibility of causal claims. I discuss each of these challenges in greater detail and identify the best strategies for overcoming these obstacles.

There are two main possibilities for conceptualizing the consequences of movements. Perhaps the most obvious strategy is to study whether a movement achieves its stated goals—whether it succeeds or fails. William Gamson's *The Strategy of Social Protest* ([1975] 1990) remains the most influential study of the success of social movements. Gamson examines a sample of fifty-three American "challenging groups" between 1800 and 1945, and he assesses the ability of movement organizations to achieve "acceptance" (i.e., to be seen as the representative of legitimate interests) and to gain "new advantages" (i.e., to achieve the particular goals sought by the group). Gamson finds that many of the factors within a movement's control—such as tactics, the use of violence, and organizational structure—played a role in determining whether a movement achieved its goals.[1] In a reanalysis of Gamson's data, Jack Goldstone (1980a, 1980b) argues that historical timing is the key factor predicting the success of a social movement. During periods of crisis like the Great Depression, movements are more likely to achieve their goals. Simplifying it somewhat, the debate between Gamson and Goldstone concerns whether mobilization or the political environment is the key causal force. A recent examination of Gamson's data shows that both environmental factors (e.g., periods of crisis) and organizational factors (e.g., factionalism) predict the success of protest groups (Frey, Dietz, and Kalof 1992).

Gamson's study shows the intellectual payoff to studying success, and this is an important component of any effort to understand the legacy of social movements. However, there are some significant limitations to this strategy. Often there is a conflict among leaders, participants, and external observers about the goals of a movement. Whose goals should set the standard for success or failure? In addition, the goals of activists change dramatically over time. Many movements begin with modest objectives that become radical if not revolutionary. These problems are not insurmountable. We could, for example, examine the impact of a movement using a variety of publicly stated objectives that use several criteria for success. However, it is clear that success is not a simple dichotomy, and we must think carefully about how to measure success.

Concrete examples provide insight into the subtleties involved in measuring the impacts of movements. Following the Freedom Rides in 1961, the Kennedy administration was concerned about the volatile aspects of direct-action strategies in the civil rights movement. The leaders of the major civil rights organizations were invited to a meeting in which the Kennedy administration proposed focusing on voter registration and promised funding from liberal foundations to support the work. From the administration's perspective, voter registration promised to be less confrontational, and it had the additional advantage of increasing the number of black voters to offset the defection of white southerners from the Democratic Party. James Forman, executive secretary of SNCC, observed in retrospect that

> SNCC's goal was to lay bare the injustice perpetrated on black people—among them the denial of the vote—in the hope that this would lead to greater mass action. . . . And the United States, through the Kennedy Administration, was interested in trying to register voters for the sake of the Democratic Party. . . . We would be walking a thin line of contradiction in the American system, but we felt able to do it. (1972, 265)

The Voter Education Project, which provided funding for voter registration work throughout the South, eventually withdrew financial support from SNCC's projects in Mississippi because of limited success in registering black voters (Carson 1981). Thus, SNCC's early work in Mississippi had little immediate effect that could be measured in terms of new registered voters. But, if we take SNCC's goal seriously, of creating indigenous leadership and local bases of opposition, it becomes less clear whether

SNCC "failed." As Forman's analysis suggests, movements often have public goals and "real" goals. Other SNCC leaders would have placed greater emphasis on the desegregation of public facilities. Moving beyond SNCC, national civil rights groups would have focused on a variety of additional goals, such as the enactment of major legislation, the expansion of economic opportunities, or undermining negative stereotypes and racial animosity. The goals of movement leaders and organizations can tell us about the priorities of movements, but they rarely converge around a singular conception of success. In addition, publicly stated goals may capture a small part of a movement's broader objectives. Thus, movement goals only provide a partial basis for understanding the impacts of social movements.

The success of the U.S. women's suffrage movement and the failure of the modern women's movement to pass the Equal Rights Amendment illustrate these challenges further. Suffrage campaigns would seem to provide an excellent case where a straightforward assessment of success or failure is appropriate. Recent works by Lee Ann Banaszak and Holly McCammon on the suffrage movement have added considerably to our understanding of the impact of social movements. Banaszak shows that the differential success of the women's suffrage movements in the United States and Switzerland

> was not a simple byproduct of overall economic and cultural conditions. Rather, it was an object of prolonged struggle. . . . These movements mobilized resources, found allies and enemies, discovered opportunities or faced obstacles, and took or failed to take advantage of their opportunities. Out of such struggles women were enfranchised—sooner or later—at different moments in the national and subnational histories of the United States and Switzerland. (1996, 5)

McCammon and her colleagues have studied the state-level passage of suffrage legislation prior to the Nineteenth Amendment, and they find that the success of the movement was patterned by the movement's efforts and the broader social and political context—especially the openness of the political system and "women's growing presence in the public sphere" (2002, 64).

A puzzle remains: many suffrage leaders and organizations saw the vote as a first step necessary to accomplish broader political or social change, but the passage of the Nineteenth Amendment seems to have encouraged the retrenchment of the movement rather than an expansion of the movement or the accomplishment of broad policy changes. In *Votes without Leverage*, Anna Harvey (1998) argues that the organizations designed to win suffrage were not well equipped to engage in electoral politics through the political parties. As a result, the existing parties were able to mobilize women as Republicans and Democrats, effectively sidetracking the broader agenda of suffrage leaders and groups. It was only in the 1970s, as the party system began to decline and public interest organizations became more central, that women's organization could become influential in the policy process. Although it would make little sense to talk about the "failure" of the suffrage movement, it is clear that a simple discussion of success or failure can be a barrier to a deeper understanding of the impact or lack of impact of movements.

The campaign for the Equal Rights Amendment poses similar challenges for thinking about the impacts of social movements. Jane Mansbridge's *Why We Lost the ERA* (1986) is the most comprehensive study of a major movement "failure" (though it was a major "success" for the STOP ERA movement). Even though the campaign for the ERA failed, Mansbridge identifies several major consequences of the campaign, arguing that the ERA "raised consciousness, helped women organize politically, and stimulated legislative and judicial action" (188). Again, we see that our understanding of social change will be richer if we examine the broader consequences of movements.

With these challenges in mind, some scholars have conceptualized movement influence more broadly than simply as success, instead focusing on impacts, consequences, or outcomes (Amenta and Young 1999; Andrews 1997; Giugni 1998; Tilly 1999). The concept of "outcomes" or equivalent terms such as "consequences" or "impact" provides greater flexibility because scholars can assess the influence of the movement in many different domains of activity and examine intended and unintended impacts of the movement. This conceptualization also allows for the possibility that a movement could have counterproductive effects—for example, if a campaign led to increasing surveillance or imprisonment of activists or bystanders. Edwin Amenta and Michael Young state that "it is possible for challengers to do worse than merely fail to achieve goals" (1999, 26).

I argue that researchers must move beyond a success/failure dichotomy because movements often have conflicting, multiple, and changing goals. In her analysis of "feminism within American institutions," Mary Katzenstein shows how feminists mobilized within the Catholic Church. Initially activists organized around the issue of ordination in 1975, but by 1983 the movement had broadened its analysis and goals to include issues like "running shelters for homeless women, doing prison work, organizing in the sanctuary movement, joining in protests against U.S. intervention in Central America . . ." (1990, 41). This expansion of the movement's goals was paralleled by an expansion of the movement's infrastructure, which multiplied the points of potential impact. On the issue of ordination, the movement had clearly failed, but the movement had substantial influence in many other domains. James Button's study of the civil rights movement in six Florida communities is instructive here as well. Button studied a wide range of outcomes in the public and private sectors, allowing him to examine variations between towns and among outcomes. He argues that "at the local level the civil rights movement did not evoke a unilinear process of change" (1989, 211).

There is another limitation to focusing narrowly on success or failure. Many movements have unanticipated consequences. Other movements, countermovements, and state actors shape the course of struggle by responding to the presence and action of movements. These responses and the ensuing dynamic interaction between movements, opponents, allies, and authorities are what make movements interesting and, also, difficult to predict by a simple and static analysis of the movement's characteristics or goals (McAdam, Tarrow, and Tilly 2001). The dilemma, then, for analyzing the consequences of social movements is to carefully examine the factors that generate different patterns of conflict and the enduring consequences of those conflicts.

Countermobilization, if extensive enough, can overwhelm the apparent gains of a social movement. For example, James Alt (1994), in his analysis of black and white voter registration, documents the massive increases in white voter registration that accompanied the widely celebrated increases in black registration. When these patterns of mobilization and countermobilization shape local institutions, they reveal the underlying political nature of those structures (James 1989; Paul, Mahler, and Schwartz 1997). In other words, institutional arrangements do not simply evolve. Rather, they have embedded within them the outcomes of prior struggles (Royce 1985). Analysis of a movement's impact must examine changes relative to the demands of other groups, including the movement's opponents.

The temporal pattern of mobilization, countermobilization, and institutional change is important for understanding outcomes. Edwin Amenta, Bruce Caruthers, and Yvonne Zylan's (1992) research on the Townsend movement finds that, at the national level, the impact of the movement on congressional action mirrored shifts in the internal strength of the movement over the 1930s and 1940s with the movement's strength and impact peaking in 1939. However, the impact of movements may lag behind the peaks of mobilization, so that effects are seen only after the movement has declined. In contrast, a movement may generate changes that subsequently are eroded (Button 1978; Quadagno 1994; Salamon 1979). Analyses of the outcomes of social movements must plot the shifting levels of mobilization against the varying impacts of the movement over a broad time span (Andrews 1997; Rasler 2000).

Given these challenges, where should we begin? I propose the following guidelines for selecting appropriate outcomes:

1. Identify broad arenas where movements have made claims and become involved in collective struggles. Select arenas inductively based on the domains where movements act, but do not limit analysis to the stated objectives of movements within those domains.
2. Examine multiple outcomes in each domain. Measuring different types of outcomes provides a more fine-grained assessment of a movement's impacts, and multiple outcomes can be used to assess influence at different thresholds, avoiding the problem of setting the bar of success too high or too low by using a single indicator.
3. Select criteria that constitute collective benefits (or collective costs) to a movement's constituency. Determining what constitutes a collective benefit and defining a movement's constituency pose additional, but not insurmountable, challenges.
4. Expand analysis beyond absolute impacts to examine relative impacts. For example, are movement gains in one arena undermined by losses in another arena? Do movements have greater impacts in some locales than others?
5. Examine the movement's impact on outcomes over a long time period—well beyond the assumed decline of the movement. This allows one to assess the durability of movement influence and to identify consequences that do not emerge at the peak of movement conflict.

These guidelines for conceptualizing and analyzing outcomes are preferable to studying "success" because they allow us to examine intended and unintended consequences of social movements. Furthermore, they allow us to accommodate shifts over the course of struggle in movement goals. By studying multiple arenas, we can assess differential impacts across domains of activity, allowing for more refined statements about movement impact. In this tradition, David Snyder and William Kelly state:

> This "single-outcome-as-goal" model also characterizes all quantitative studies of the consequences of protest or violence. . . . In fact, movement organizations (as do all groups) routinely experience relative success or failure on various dimensions as a consequence of their everyday activities. (1979, 218–19)

This insight—that movements are neither monolithic nor uniform in their distribution, strength, or impact—opens up new areas for exploring the outcomes that movements do generate.[2] Much of the research on the impact of the civil rights movement, especially its impact on electoral politics, would support Button's claim. For example, Button finds variation across his cases, with some towns achieving black political control, and he finds variation across outcomes, such as greater gains in public sector than in private sector employment. This broad strategy outlined here clarifies my approach to outcomes.

Many of the examples that I use focus on political changes, including agenda setting, policy enactment and implementation, and the acquisition of political power. Nevertheless, this discussion applies to social and cultural impacts as well because these types of changes are intertwined with and can mediate between social movements and changes in political institutions (Rochon 1998; Wirt 1997). The general framework I propose for conceptualizing and selecting outcomes and the main challenges to studying the impact of social movements are the same regardless of whether one is studying political, social, or cultural impacts.[3] These claims also extend to studies aimed at studying "spillover effects" of movements on other movements (Isaac and Christiansen 2002; Meyer and Whittier 1994; Minkoff 1997).

Having defined potential outcomes, we face the additional challenge of determining whether movements have played a significant causal role in generating changes. With few exceptions, mobilization has been conceptualized as a dependent variable, the object of analysis. Theorists have focused on the origins of movements, positing that some set of factors (e.g., grievances, societal breakdown, resources, networks) accounts for the emergence of the movement. Edwin Amenta and colleagues note that "in the strongest form of this argument, [political] opportunity structures determine both movement formation and what may be perceived as gains won by the movement" (1992, 310). Some scholars move from this methodological problem to make the broader claim that "movements succeed or fail as the result of forces outside their control" (Tarrow 1998, 24; see also Kitschelt 1986). If mobilization is the outcome of exogenous factors, this may undermine any claims about the *independent effects* of the movement on patterns of change. For example, if the civil rights movement emerged in response to electoral realignments and urbanization, then any changes could be attributable to these initial causes of movement activity.

The challenge for scholars is to disentangle these factors and examine how they interact in a complex historical sequence. This process of determining whether movements (or any other factor) played a causal role in social change has two steps in this study. First, quantitative data are used to conduct multivariate analyses. These analyses allow one to examine the relationship between movement strength and social change while also considering the role of other contributing factors. When these analyses provide evidence for movement influence, the case studies are used to determine how this occurs by specifying the underlying causal mechanisms. Many quantitative social scientists stop after the first step, leaving the causal process ambiguous at best. This is especially problematic where multiple interpretations are available. For example, a movement may have been influential through disruption or persuasion. Many qualitative studies are unable to address the problem of alternative explanations and skip straight to a narrative account of movement dynamics that attributes change to movement without seriously examining alternative explanations.

Before moving forward, we should consider a broad but inaccurate assumption about studying the consequences of social movements. It is common to argue that studying the impacts of social movements involves a distinctive and more difficult challenge than is the case for explaining other dimensions of social movements. For example, Amenta and Young claim that "the relative lack of attention . . . is due also to conceptual and methodological problems peculiar to the subject" (1999, 22). However, there is nothing inherent in studying the consequences of movements that is different from any other causal claims (about social movements or anything else). For example, studying participation in movements faces the same challenges of conceptualizing participation and accounting for many plausible factors that might explain patterns of individual participation. Participation can be conceptualized many different ways, and scholars face the same challenge of comparing across different movements where participation can take radically different forms.[4] One possible difference is that a claim about the influence of movements on legal change, for example, must engage possible explanations beyond the normal domain of scholarship on social movements.[5] Explanations of movement characteristics (e.g., participation, emergence, factionalism, tactical orientation) are nested in a literature and debates of scholars who share common assumptions about the importance of social movements (even when they disagree about everything else), and the main audience for this scholarship is other people who study social movements. Studying the consequences of social movements requires that one engage with the many other disciplines, subfields, theoretical approaches, and empirical traditions that have their own explanations of cultural, social, or political change.[6] For any of the outcomes discussed in this study—electoral participation, federal policy funding and implementation, school desegregation and the founding of private schools, and the election of black candidates to office—there is extensive scholarship in areas such as law, education, public policy, and political science. Studies that examine the impacts of movements on cultural changes such as values, identities, or public opinion or on social changes such as social networks or civic and voluntary groups face the same challenge. Rather than an obstacle, this engagement should be seen as an opportunity to create bridges between work on social movements—which is often quite insular—and other areas of social science inquiry.

Dimensions of Movement Infrastructure

I propose a movement infrastructure model for examining whether and, if so, how movements have enduring impacts. Three components of a movement's infrastructure must be examined to explain a movement's influence on social change: leadership, organizational structure, and resources. Strategies and tactics are shaped by the configuration of a movement's leadership, organization, and resource capacities. Leaders and organizations often carry particular repertoires of action and ideologies that influence the ability of movements to have lasting impacts. Infrastructures that allow the movement to employ multiple mechanisms of influence including disruption, persuasion, and bargaining will have the greatest impact across outcomes because movements must engage a complex and changing environment. This ability is crucial because, as Daniel Cress and David Snow argue, most of the impacts that movements have operate through "multiple pathways rather than through one surefire pathway or set of conditions" (2000, 1096). At a general level, I claim that the autonomy and continuity of the infrastructure are key factors explaining the long-term viability and impact of the movement, sustaining a movement through shifts in the broader political environment (Andrews 1997; Rupp and Taylor 1987). A strong movement infrastructure can spur political elites to initiate policy concessions in response to the perceived threat of the movement. Often that threat rests on the belief that a movement has the capacity to institute more substantial change through parallel, autonomous institutions (Clemens 1998; Schwartz 1976).

This argument dovetails with the work of scholars who have focused on the organizational survival of social movements (Edwards and Marullo 1995). I focus on the process by which organizational consolidation is achieved in one locale and organizational collapse occurs in another. This is based on the assumption that organizational survival is a key intervening link that allows activism to be sustained during periods of limited opportunity (Clemens 1998; Minkoff 1993; Tarrow 1994; Taylor 1989). As Debra Minkoff notes, "The very existence of associations in which people can participate should have some discernible, if not easily measurable, impact on society and, ultimately, social change" (1993, 905). The key limitation of the research on organizational persistence is the assumption that survival is associated with later influence—a claim that is rarely demonstrated.

In my argument, leadership is important for movement impact in ways that differ from most conventional accounts of organizational leadership. Rather than the individual properties of leaders, I give greater attention to the social relations of leaders to one another, to movement participants, and to the institutions targeted by the movement (for a general discussion of leadership in movements, see Aminzade, Goldstone, and Perry 2001). I draw on the arguments advanced by Aldon Morris and Belinda Robnett about civil rights leadership that emphasize the linkage between leaders and community institutions. For Morris (1984), successful movement leadership is rooted in "indigenous" organizations. This link makes leaders more responsive and less easily co-opted when they negotiate with authorities and opponents. Hence, the structural location of black ministers within community institutions made them an effective leadership base during many civil rights campaigns.

Leaders and organizations must be embedded in indigenous, informal networks. In her study of gender and leadership in the civil rights movement, Robnett (1996) distinguishes between formal leaders (e.g., ministers) and an intermediate layer of "bridge leaders" who stand at nodal points within the informal networks of a community. Movements with a simple structure of formal leaders and mass base are unlikely to be successful because bridge leaders are needed to expand participation throughout the community. Bridge leaders make co-optation of formal leaders less likely because bridge leaders can effectively connect to the demands and expectations of a movement's broader constituency. This type of leadership structure can generate ongoing tension within the movement. However, it also can provide advantages, such as innovation (Stepan-Norris and Zeitlin 1995). A differentiated leadership structure allows for communication to various audiences, including participants, potential recruits, opponents, and state actors (Klandermans 1997). A leadership structure with a diversity of skills and experiences will be better able to use mass-based tactics as well as routine negotiation with other groups, including authorities (Ganz 2000; Gerlach and Hine 1970).

The critical role of preexisting organizations and resources has been established in the emergence of social movements. To persist over time, movements must forge new organizational forms and establish independent resource flows (McAdam 1982; Schwartz 1976). In the mobilization process, the informal structure of relationships among activists and organizations must be expansive across communities and subgroups. In the policy-making process, formal organizations become a necessary vehicle for advancing a group's claims. Organizational structures can alter the routine operation of the political process when they are perceived as legitimate and/or threatening by established political actors (Clemens 1997; Gamson 1990).

Movements that rely primarily on the mobilization of people rather than on externally generated financial resources are more likely to continue using protest tactics (Schwartz and Paul 1992). As a result, their strategic and tactical options are often broader (Ganz 2000). Ultimately, movements require substantial contributions of participants to maintain organizations and launch protest campaigns. This is seen most clearly at the local level, where movement organizations are less likely to maintain a paid professional staff.

The importance of indigenous resources does not preclude the possibility that external resources can facilitate the movement or its efficacy. However, dependence on external resources makes movements vulnerable to shifts in the discretion of external actors (Jenkins and Eckert 1986; McAdam 1982). In addition, external resources often entail obligations that can constrain the movement's strategy and tactics and increase the chance of co-optation.

In the movement infrastructure model, strategy and tactics depend to a large degree on a movement's leadership, organization, and resources. This contrasts with alternative explanations that view effective protest and formal organization in conflict with one another or ignore the role of organization. Strategy and tactics are conceptualized broadly in the infrastructure model and range from protest to the building of counter-institutions. Consistent with this line of argument, Marshall Ganz (2000) has shown how the United Farm Workers were able to organize California farmworkers where more resource-rich organizations failed. According to Ganz, the UFW's leadership and organizational structure generated greater strategic capacity "if a leadership team includes insiders and outsiders, strong and weak network ties, and access to diverse, yet salient, repertoires of collective action and also if an organization conducts regular, open authoritative deliberation, draws resources from multiple constituencies, and roots accountability in those constituencies" (2000, 1005; see also Delaney, Jarley, and Fiorito 1996). Ganz's argument refers to the characteristics of a single organization, but these characteristics can also be properties of a broader field of organizations. For most social movements, the impact of the movement will be more closely tied to the collective properties of multiple organizations rather than a single challenger.[7] As a property of a single organization or set of groups, strategic capacity facilitates the ability of movements to develop creative solutions to collective problems.

In sum, strong movement infrastructures have diverse leaders and a complex leadership structure, multiple organizations, informal ties that cross geographic and social boundaries, and a resource base that draws substantially on contributions from their members for both labor and funds. These characteristics provide movements with greater flexibility that allows them to influence the policy process through multiple mechanisms including disruption, persuasion, and negotiation. This argument differs from the main alternatives among sociologists and political scientists. I will briefly outline three major alternatives by highlighting areas of convergence and divergence with the movement infrastructure argument.

Disruption: Securing Concessions from Threat

One of the most common ways of conceptualizing movement efficacy focuses on the short-term potential of protest to win victories. The first two models of movement efficacy focus on protest, but they specify alternative mechanisms through which protest influences change—disruption and persuasion. In both arguments, mobilization has the momentary potential through an "action-reaction" process to leverage change by mobilizing political elites, electoral coalitions, or public opinion.

In the first argument, movements are dramatic, disruptive, and threatening to elites, which prompts a rapid response—typically either concessions and/or repression. Frances Fox Piven and Richard Cloward have been the primary proponents of this view, arguing that "the most useful way to think about the effectiveness of protest is to examine the disruptive effects on institutions of different forms of mass defiance, and then to examine the political reverberations of those disruptions" (1977, 24). The independent influence of protest is constrained by its role in a sequence of events. In *Poor People's Movements* (1977), Piven and Cloward raise questions about the independent impact of protest because it "wells up in response to momentous changes in the institutional order. It is not created by organizers and leaders" (36). Protest is one link in a sequence, and once the sequence is initiated, protesters have little control over the policy response. The authors conclude that "whatever influence lower-class groups occasionally exert in American politics does not result from organization, but from mass protest and the disruptive consequences of protest" (36).[8]

Organizations, particularly mass-based membership organizations, are doomed to failure because powerless groups can never mobilize as effectively as dominant groups in a society. As a result, organizations can only lessen the disruptive capacity and efficacy of protest (Piven and Cloward 1984, 1992; also see Gamson and Schmeidler 1984; A. Morris 1984). Elite reaction is ultimately focused in a self-interested way on ending protest. Analyzing urban policy changes in the 1960s, Ira Katznelson argues that "the targets of these public policies were not objects of compassion, but of fear born of uncertainty" (1981, 3). Policy makers caught off guard by protest attempt to quickly assemble a strategy of repression, concessions, or a combination of the two that will end the protest wave (Tarrow 1993). Disruption models focus on the limitations of protest on policy making beyond the agenda-setting stage.

Persuasion: Generating Support through Symbolic Protest

In the second model, movements are dramatic and generate support from sympathetic individuals and groups that take up the cause of the movement. The intervening role of "third parties," "bystander publics," or "conscience constituents" is critical. In a classic essay, Michael Lipsky argues that "the 'problem of the powerless' in protest activity is to activate 'third parties' to enter the implicit or explicit bargaining arena in ways favorable to protesters" (1968, 1145). Lipsky claims that "if protest tactics are not considered significant by the media . . . protest organizations will not succeed. Like the tree falling unheard in the forest, there is no protest unless protest is perceived and projected" (1151; also see Benford and Hunt 1992).[9]

David Garrow (1978) argues that civil rights campaigns, especially in Selma, Alabama, generated momentum for the 1965 Voting Rights Act. For some theorists, repression is an intervening link. For example, Garrow contends that attacks by southern officials on civil rights activists further solidified the support of bystanders. Paul Burstein (1985) shows that the movement did not reverse the direction of public opinion on race and civil rights. He argues instead that movements are probably unable to have such a substantial impact on opinion. Rather, protest increased the salience of the civil rights issue through protest, demonstrating the injustice of southern racism and violence. As civil rights became more important in the eyes of the American public, political representatives acted on louder and clearer signals from their constituents (Burstein 1999). In this view, protest is a form of communication, and persuasion is the major way that movements influence policy (Lohmann 1993; Mansbridge 1994).

The first two arguments focus on similar aspects of movements, but they differ on key points. The disruption model emphasizes disruptive and often violent action forcing a response from political elites, and the persuasion model proposes that protest can mobilize sympathetic third parties that advance the movement's agenda by exerting influence on political elites (see also McAdam and Su 2002 on disruptive and persuasive movement activity). Both of these action-reaction arguments share the assumption that (1) large-scale dramatic events shape the process of change by (2) mobilizing more powerful actors to advance the movement's cause, and (3) that (implicitly) movements have little or no direct influence beyond this initial point. In both models, the primary focus is on the communicative aspects of public protest events rather than on organizational form or capacity within a movement.

Negotiation: The Routinization of Protest

The negotiation model, a third major approach, argues that the determinant of movement efficacy is the acquisition of routine access to the polity through institutionalized tactics. This approach typically describes a drift toward less disruptive tactics, such as electoral politics, coalitions, lobbying, and litigation. Organization and leadership figure prominently in this model. Organizational changes parallel the tactical shift, including increasing centralization and bureaucratization of movement organizations. In order to achieve influence, social movements generate organizations that evolve into interest groups. In the negotiation model, the organizational and tactical shifts are accompanied by an increase in influence over relevant policy arenas. In contrast, the action-reaction model would predict that movement influence declines as tactics become routinized and organizations become incorporated. Most important, the access-influence model argues that disruptive tactics have little independent impact on institutional change. Rufus P. Browning, Dale Rogers Marshall, and David H. Tabb, in their study of the impacts of black and Hispanic political mobilization on a variety of policy outcomes, argue that protest and electoral strategies were used together effectively, but "demand-protest strategies by themselves produced limited results in most cities" (1984, 246).

Negotiation models also assert that securing insider status is more consequential than pursuing a single, specific policy objective. Thomas Rochon and Daniel Mazmanian (1993) argue that the antinuclear movement, by advocating a single piece of legislation, was unsuccessful. In contrast, the environmental movement, especially antitoxic groups, attempted to become a legitimate participant in the regulatory process. By gaining access, the movement has been able to have a substantial long-term impact on policy (also see Costain 1981; Sabatier 1975). In this vein, Mario Diani argues that "social movement outcomes may be assessed in terms of the movement's capacity to achieve more central positions in networks of social and political influence" (1997, 133; see also Laumann and Knoke 1987). In contrast to this negotiation model, movement organizations may achieve positions that are merely symbolic, and movements can generate leverage without directly bargaining with state actors or other authorities (Burstein, Einwohner, and Hollander 1995; Schwartz 1976).

The negotiation model has fewer proponents than the disruption and persuasion models among the sociologists who study social movements. However, the notion that "routine" tactics are most efficacious is consistent with pluralist theories of democracy that view the political system as relatively open to citizen influence. This argument would find greater support among the political scientists who study interest groups, political parties, and the policy process. From this perspective, organization building (especially professionalization, bureaucratization, and centralization) provides movements with the necessary tools to operate in the interest group system, where bargaining is the key mechanism of influence.

Comparing the Models

The movement infrastructure model that I have proposed builds on the insights of the prior three models. First, it assumes, like the disruption and persuasion models, that there are key moments when movements can be especially efficacious. Further, it assumes that disruptive tactics are important for movements to have an impact, especially when they are creatively injected into routine political processes. The movement infrastructure model differs from the others because it emphasizes the building and sustaining of movement infrastructures as an important determinant of the long-term impacts of social movements (in contrast to short-term impacts, like agenda setting). Furthermore, unlike the access-influence model, movements have the greatest impact when they maintain their ability to use both "outsider" and "insider" tactics. Litigation, lobbying, and electoral politics can be effectively employed by social movements. However, movements lose key opportunities for leverage in the political process when they quickly adopt the strategies and tactics of "interest groups" and abandon "insurgent" forms.

Although much of the debate turns on the question of the types of organizational forms that are most efficacious, organization as a concept gets used loosely in arguments and criticisms. For example, Piven and Cloward's (1977) argument is cast as a broad critique of organizations, but their real target is national membership organizations. If we distinguish forms of organizations, we can see that there is variation, with some playing a more direct role in facilitating disruption. In his analysis of the 1963 Birmingham campaign, Morris (1993) illustrates the importance of organizing for large dramatic campaigns. Forman (1972) argues persuasively that SCLC's campaign at Selma (and Albany) depended on the organizing of SNCC field-workers in Selma and nearby Lowndes County. In many cases, especially the most repressive settings, building organizations is disruptive and can be a necessary step before other forms of collective action are possible. SNCC's own measure of success was "the extent to which the people they helped bring into political activity became leaders themselves" (Payne 1995, 318). As a result, building organizational structures was itself a strategic vehicle of the movement.[10] In this study, I pursue these questions about the efficacy of different organizational forms.

I argue that movements are most influential when they can create leverage through multiple mechanisms. The prior three models focus on a single mechanism as the primary means by which movements create change—disruption, persuasion, or negotiation. The movement infrastructure model accounts for the ability of movements to impact political change through multiple mechanisms, and this change can occur when a movement's leadership and organization allow for strategic flexibility and innovation.

The pattern of outcomes for a movement may depend on processes described by each of these models. For example, the negotiation and persuasion models focus on agenda setting as the primary outcome that movements can influence. In contrast, access-influence and movement infrastructure models examine later stages in the policy-making process. Ultimately, researchers should use these models to compare across different types of social movements and political contexts. However, the main patterns identified in this study demonstrate the utility of the movement infrastructure model as applied to the Mississippi civil rights movement and for understanding movement impact more broadly.

Opposition: Countermobilization and Repression

The trajectories and consequences of social movements can only be understood by examining the structure that the movement is attempting to change and the opposition or resistance that it faces. Movements and their opponents attempt to mobilize support and face a set of constraints and opportunities. Within that context, the presence of a movement challenges other groups directly and indirectly, and if the movement is successful, even greater alterations to existing power relations can result. Because of these threats, insurgent movements are accompanied by countermobilization that must be analyzed to assess the movement's impact (or lack of impact).

What groups are social movements likely to encounter as they take shape? States act as the primary agent of repression or facilitation, altering the costs of insurgency by the way in which they respond to movements (Goldstone and Tilly 2001; Tilly 1978).[11] Although scholars often treat states as unitary actors, states are often divided in ways that influence the intensity and form of response to insurgents. In the relatively fragmented U.S. case, cleavages between national and local actors are often critical. Even within the same level of political authority, there can be sharply conflicting strategies in response to social movements—for example, the Department of Justice was often viewed as a key ally while the FBI was unsupportive at best. Beyond the political authorities, movements face challenges from well-organized movements and threats in the form of economic reprisals, violent assaults, and intimidation from these movements as well as individuals and informal groups. These challenges from non-state actors can be as consequential for the future of the movement as the interactions between movements and states. In sum, an expansive focus is required that examines the array of actors that interact with and respond to social movements.

Resistance to a movement includes the tactics employed by individuals, small groups, and large organizations (such as governments and corporations) to undermine a movement and its goals.[12] Most often, repression is thought of as violence, but there are many other forms of action that present obstacles to social movements in general and specifically to civil rights organizers in the South (Earl 2003; Irons 2002). In addition to mapping the array of actors, we need to assess the many different forms of action that can undermine movements and their objectives.

With the use of violence, state-sponsored and private violence often differ because states can mobilize public legitimacy but are also vulnerable to critique concerning their legitimacy. However, this distinction is difficult to draw in the Mississippi case. The individuals directly responsible for the murders of James Chaney, Michael Schwerner, and Andrew Goodman included members of local Klan organizations and the local police (Cagin and Dray 1988). In SNCC's first voter registration project, Herbert Lee, a local NAACP leader, was murdered by a member of the state legislature in public during the day (Dittmer 1985). The Sovereignty Commission, a state organization that monitored, infiltrated, and disrupted the movement, worked closely with and provided state funds to the Citizens' Council (McMillen 1971). These three examples underscore the way in which state-sponsored resistance and private repression were intertwined. This linkage is not unique to Mississippi or the civil rights movement; for example, analyses of Latin American and South African social movements have found similar patterns of coordination (Marx 1992).

Resistance does not only take the form of violence by groups like the Ku Klux Klan. Most important, resistance can take public and institutional forms. In a study of the Mississippi legislature's response to the Voting Rights Act, Frank Parker describes institutional strategies in the form of legal tactics used to dilute the newly enfranchised black electorate—what he calls the "massive resistance" legislation. Parker argues that "black people in Mississippi in 1967 were not writing on a clean slate. . . . In large part, the white supremacy politics of the white majority have shaped post–1965 black politics" (1990, 67). Various municipal ordinances and state laws were employed to harass movement participants, such as local laws against boycotts and picketing (Chevigny 1965). The mayor of Drew in Sunflower County issued a proclamation at the beginning of Freedom Summer stating "that all civil rights workers . . . at the close of the normal working day . . . be taken into protective custody and held in the City Jail until the beginning of the next normal working day" (Wilson 1965). These legal impediments consumed scarce time and resources of movement activists.

Violence attracts high levels of attention even when used anonymously by small groups and individuals. Similarly, the institutional mechanisms described above can be examined because they typically involve formal institutions and the law. However, resistance includes intimidation and harassment, which is more difficult to document systematically, but, like violence, these forms of resistance are dispersed and carried out by individuals and small informal groups. James Loewen has described some of the ways in which intimidation was exercised within polling places, including the following example:

> A 55-year-old black woman with four years of education forty years ago hesitantly lines up at a voting machine. . . . The poll watcher asks, "May I help you, Ma'am" and pulls the lever. He is then inside the booth with the voter. Because the ballot is set up alphabetically by candidate's last name, rather than by party, the voter has to recall twenty names for whom she wishes to vote. "Do you want to vote for Evers?" he asks. Surprised by his fairness, she agrees. The poll worker knows that Evers has no chance statewide; what matters are the local races. He then asks, "Do you want X for sheriff?" mentioning the white incumbent. . . . The effectiveness of such intimidating "assistance" is confirmed by quantitative comparisons. (1981, 36–37)[13]

The case Loewen describes took place in 1971, six years after the passage of the Voting Rights Act. He shows that by "skimming" a small percentage of the black vote in majority black voting districts, white poll watchers contributed to disappointing outcomes for black candidates statewide in 1971. Lester Salamon describes a similar pattern in the majority-black town of Shelby. Voting machines administered by whites perceived as hostile to the black community cast votes 5 to 3 against black candidates. A booth administered by a trusted white turned out a 3 to 1 margin in favor of black candidates (Salamon 1972a). Economic reprisals against movement participants were another important category of resistance. These strategies can diminish the efficacy of a movement without leaving clear indicators. Bob Moses characterizes the difference between the obstacles facing community organizers in Mississippi:

> The drives can be separated out in those counties where you encountered physical and economic reprisals and those counties where you encountered fear, psychological fear, and a great, great deal of immobility on the part of the Negroes. . . . [T]he kind of operation there was day-to-day drudgery, going around in the hot sun, talking to people, trying to get them to overcome their fear, trying to convince them that nothing would happen to them if they went down, that their houses wouldn't be bombed, that they would not be shot at, that they would not lose their jobs. In the other counties, we couldn't convince people of these things because it wasn't true. (1970, 15)

Hence, observers often attribute the effect of repression to the apathy of a movement's constituency. These processes are critical for understanding the impact (or non-impact) of social movements. Although these effects of repression and resistance are difficult to measure systematically, we will see numerous examples in the case studies of Mississippi counties.

Countermovements

Where there is coherence and continuity in the resistance faced by a movement, we can conceptualize it as part of a broader countermovement.[14] This concept leads to important questions about the pattern of interaction between the movement and the countermovement. Mayer Zald and Bert Useem note that these interactions can take the form of a "tight spiral" or a "loosely coupled tango" (1987, 257, 247) Tight spirals are characterized by rapid and escalatory mobilization where each side quickly responds to the actions of the others. In a loosely coupled tango, the dynamic may be more difficult to discern, and the relationship may be mediated by political authorities. For example, countermovements often mobilize in response to and against the "success" of their opponents rather than the movement itself. Hence, the tactical interaction between movements and countermovements is often obscured because of the more visible tactical interaction between movements (or countermovements) and political authorities and institutions.

As David Meyer and Suzanne Staggenborg note, the success of movements creates opportunities for countermovements. They go on to hypothesize that there is a curvilinear relationship between success and countermovement mobilization where "movement victories that are truly decisive preclude the possibility of countermovement action in alternative arenas" (1996, 1637). Less decisive victories provide opportunities to countermovements. Zald and Useem add:

> A victory or defeat in one arena or battlefield shifts the locus of attack, the nodal point for the next major battlefield. For instance, once the pro-abortion forces won the Supreme Court to its side, antiabortion forces shifted to the issue of federal funds for abortion. (1987, 251)

Researchers face another challenge because countermobilization is often regarded as the response of individuals—as backlash. Rather than a simple aggregation of individual resistance, we should treat counter-mobilization as a social phenomenon with social and organizational origins.

This type of interaction characterized the dynamic between the civil rights movement and white southern opponents. As Neil McMillen finds in his study of the Citizens' Council, white mobilization consistently peaked in response to indigenous black mobilization or the threat (perceived or real) of federal intervention. He states:

> The story of Council expansion, then, was not one of steady progress. Represented graphically, its growth in Mississippi, and elsewhere in the South, resembled a fever chart with peaks occurring in periods of racial unrest when the white population's perception of the imminence of deseg-regation was greatest. . . . (1971, 28)

McMillen's observation supports the idea that mobilization and counter-mobilization should be analyzed as a unified process of "tactical inter-action" (McAdam 1983; Mottl 1980).

The Paradox of Repression and Protest

The sociological analysis of repression has made significant theoretical and empirical gains in recent years. However, the implications of repression for an analysis of movement outcomes remain largely unexplored. The key question in the repression literature is sorting out the conditions under which repression works to diminish protest and when repression "backfires," generating higher levels of mobilization. Marc Lichbach frames the paradox as "deterrence or escalation?" (1987, 266). In cases as distinct as the anti-apartheid movement in South Africa (Olivier 1991), protest against the shah's policies in Iran (Rasler 1996), the West German antinuclear power movement (Opp and Roehl 1990), and Latin American peasant mobilization (Brockett 1993), scholars have found nonlinear relationships between repression and protest, and notably all of these studies specify contexts in which repression has positive effects. In her analysis of the Iranian Revolution, Karen Rasler demonstrates how repression both deters and escalates protest. Building on Karl-Deiter Opp and Wolfgang Roehl's 1990 analysis of the West German antinuclear power movement, Rasler argues that "in the long run repression helped launch micromobilization processes that rapidly brought large numbers of people into the streets" (1996, 143). Within the micromobilization contexts, the actions of repressive agents are delegitimated. The short-term effect of repression, measured one week later, is a reduction of protest, yet a mere six weeks later repression increases the rate of protest (140). In a study of Latin American peasant mobilization, Charles Brockett finds that the apparent paradox concerning repression—that sometimes it "works" and sometimes it fails to undermine insurgency—can be understood by looking at the issue of timing, or what he calls "the temporal location in the protest cycle" (1993, 474). The relationship is curvilinear, with repression being most effective at the beginning and end of a protest cycle. When mass protest is rising, the effect of repression can be the escalation of protest. In sum, the literature on repression identifies a number of dynamics that account for the positive impact of repression on protest. Key factors are the micromobilization context and the temporal location in the protest cycle.

Repression and the Legacy of Social Movements

How does repression influence the pattern of movement impact? Here, the evidence is sparse. Gamson's *The Strategy of Social Protest* is one of the few studies to take up the question, and he finds that the recipients of violence are less likely to win "new advantages" or "acceptance" (1990). This poses another paradox involving the role of violence against movements. Repression can, and often does, escalate protest, yet repression can also undermine the "success" of movements.

Like movements, countermovements are unlikely to have total success whether in their efforts to subvert the goals of movements or more generally to reverse broader social changes. The challenge outlined here is to account for the dynamic relationship between movements and their opponents and the consequences of that interaction.

Changes in the Social and Political Context

So far, I have focused on the dimensions of movement infrastructures and the interactions between movements and their opponents. The strongest criticism of this explanatory strategy would argue that some set of external factors explains the rise of the movement, countermobilization and repression, and the institutional changes that seem to follow from it. In other words, claims about the causal significance of social movements are spurious. Many different factors could be identified. In past debates, modernization would be a primary contender. In short, this line of argument would claim that there is a broad process of social change that includes urbanization, development of political institutions, improved technology, increasing education levels, and so forth that accounts for the pattern of movement dynamics and the apparent impact of the movement.

Although this type of argument for a holistic change process is rarely debated in contemporary political science and sociology, there are more recent arguments that point to elements of the movement's broader environment that could explain both the movement and its apparent impact. The most influential and useful variant is political process theory and the related concept of political opportunity structure (McAdam 1982; Tarrow 1998). A key distinction in political process theory is between the internal dynamics of social movements and the political opportunity structure—the broader social, economic, and political factors that shape the opportunities and constraints for mobilization. This dual focus has been used most frequently to examine the origins of movements or "protest cycles" (McAdam 1982; Meyer 1990; C. Smith 1996; Tarrow 1998).[15] Specifically, factors internal to social movements (like those emphasized in resource mobilization theory) include leadership skills, organizational form and strength, informal networks of activists, and connections among social movement organizations.

The primary contribution of political process theory is the focus on the interaction between movements and the "structure of political opportunities." Synthesizing various approaches, the four major components of the political opportunity structure are (1) the role of political allies and supporters, "[2] availability of meaningful access points in the political system, [3] the capacity and propensity of the state for repression, [and] [4] elite fragmentation and conflict" (Brockett 1991, 254).[16] These factors have been shown to be influential in explaining the rise and decline of social movements, and they are potentially important for the analysis of outcomes.

The political process approach has important relevance for the analysis of movement consequences because of its dual focus on these internal dynamics of movements and the broader dynamics of political and economic institutions. Both internal and external factors are consequential in shaping the impact of social movements. The major limitations of political process theory for an analysis of movement impact are (1) the restricted explanatory focus on the movement itself, (2) a static view of the state, and (3) a holistic view of the state focusing on national political actors and institutions. I describe these limitations in greater detail and highlight ways to reformulate political process arguments to examine the impacts of movements.

The major limitation facing political process theory, as it currently stands, is that the object of explanation is the social movement itself—its timing, internal development, and decline. Some theorists treat the relationship in a static and deterministic way. Opportunity structures are either open or closed, and the important source of variation is across regimes, not across time. Two recent suggestions point the way toward a more complex formulation of the relationship between political structures and movements. Sidney Tarrow (1996b) has argued for the concept of dynamic statism—which assesses variation across time and regime type (and, I would add, across subunits of nation-states). Doug McAdam (1996) adds that we should treat opportunity structures as dependent variables (in which movements can create opportunities for themselves and other movements) and that we determine which aspects of the opportunity structure are more amenable to change. Both of these points open room for the analysis of outcomes.

Tarrow's notion of dynamic statism incorporates greater attention to temporal processes. If elaborated, the model would include issues of pace, duration, path dependency, and sequencing and would refine our understanding of movement impact (Aminzade 1992). The effects of social movements and the relations among variables change over time. The analysis of movement outcomes must examine a broad time frame after the decline of a movement. In a study of the 1960s riots, James Button (1978) argues that the federal response (and the enduring consequences) to the riots varied historically. The initial responses were to increase funding for federal programs like the Office of Economic Opportunity (OEO), the Department of Housing and Urban Development (HUD), and the Model Cities Program. By 1969 there was a shift to a "law and order" response with increased funding for police control and intelligence gathering through the CIA, FBI, and local agencies (Button 1978;

see also Mueller 1978). Lester Salamon (1979) raises this issue of timing in his analysis of New Deal land-redistribution programs. Initial assessments of the programs were critical and resulted in the dismantling of the programs. As Salamon shows, these assessments were inaccurate because they failed to consider long-term incremental effects such as the creation of independent small landholders.

A final limitation of political process theory is the disproportionate focus on the national state. This focus is appropriate in some cases. However, many movements mobilize at the local level in response to more proximate variations in opportunity or threat. In this study, I shift the focus from the national arena to the small communities in the South that experienced unprecedented levels of social movement mobilization during the 1960s. As David James notes, "Theories that focus on the national state cannot explain the enormous variation in the local implementation of national policies" (1988, 191). Similarly, theories that focus on social movements at the national level cannot account for state or local variations in the level of mobilization or impact. This study demonstrates the analytic payoff from analyzing the impacts of local mobilization on subsequent political transformations.[17]

As we will see, the four dimensions of the political context identified by political process theorists play a central role in the dynamics and consequences of the civil rights movement. When comparing across the different arenas, institutional openings (or access points) become a major factor in accounting for the aggregate level of movement impact on electoral politics, social policies, and school desegregation. As federal actors took initiatives to design and implement changes, those initiatives varied considerably in the opportunities presented to local actors—whether civil rights activists, local white authorities, or other groups. In addition, I find that the form and magnitude of repression is critical for understanding the patterns of institutional change. Political allies and elite fragmentation are less central than institutional opening and repression in this analysis, though each helps to account for selected patterns in the development of the Mississippi movement. These dimensions of the political context do not have uniform effects on movements. Some movements are better able to find and create institutional openings. Similarly, movements vary in how they respond to repression, with some having greater capacity to turn an "obstacle" into an "opportunity." These dimensions of the political system are critical to understanding whether and, if so, how movements mattered, but their influence operates in interaction with social movements.

Conclusion

In this chapter, I have attempted to harness empirical and theoretical insights from prior social movement research around the question of outcomes. Studying the impacts of social movements requires careful consideration of conceptual and methodological issues. I propose guidelines for addressing these challenges. Specifically, scholars should (1) identify broad arenas where movements have made claims and become involved in collective struggles; (2) examine different types of outcomes, providing a more fine-grained assessment of a movement's impacts at different thresholds; (3) select criteria that constitute collective benefits (or collective costs) to a movement's constituency; (4) expand analysis beyond absolute impacts to examine relative impacts; and (5) examine the movement's impacts on outcomes over a long time period to assess the durability of movement impacts and to identify consequences that do not emerge at the peak of movement conflict. This approach is preferable to the more intuitive but less rigorous strategy of defining and studying "success." Causal explanations of movement impacts should follow a two-step process of identifying patterns of covariance between movement characteristics and changes in the broader society and specifying causal mechanisms through which movement influence operates.

Prevailing explanations for the impacts of social movements have focused on one of three primary mechanisms: disruption, persuasion, and negotiation. There are many cases in the historical literature to marshal support for each of these models of movement influence. I develop a movement infrastructure model that refers to the combination of leaders, organizational structures, and resources that shape the strategic and tactical orientation of the movement, and I identify the type of movement infrastructure most likely to have enduring impacts. I contend that movement efficacy is greatest for movements that can create social change through all three mechanisms.

The trajectory and impact of social movements are shaped by their ongoing interaction with countermovements and states. Although I focus on movements, I have not neglected the broader social or political factors that can have a direct impact on the pace and extent of institutional change. I weave these factors into my analysis of the development and impact of the Mississippi civil rights movement.

Repression by countermovements and state actors has been a major area of scholarship, but the questions that have been asked focus narrowly on how repression influences the dynamics of protest, generating escalation or decline (Davenport 2000). This study opens up a new set of questions about the impact of repression on the long-term consequences of movements. Finally, the dominant way of thinking about political institutions remains holistic and static. This leads to a limited understanding of the ways that states shape movements and vice versa. Specifically, the form and magnitude of movement impact depends on how movement organization and strategy interact with the state interventions and institutions. When states attempt to implement political change, they employ a wide range of strategies, some of which are more open to movement influence than others.

CHAPTER THREE

The Contours of Struggle

How DID the Mississippi civil rights movement emerge and develop from the 1950s through the 1970s? In this chapter, I present a chronological overview of the major events and organizational developments of the Mississippi movement and the changing obstacles it faced from the 1960s to the early 1980s.[1] Local movements were embedded in much broader contexts that shaped the possibilities and constraints for local actors. That context includes the development of statewide and national civil rights organizations and campaigns, the shifting strength and activities of opponents and allies, and the intervention of state and federal political actors. Rather than a comprehensive history of the Mississippi civil rights movement, this chapter paints a broad picture of the movement's development to contextualize the local focus of the chapters that follow.

This chapter is organized around three major sections. The first describes the period immediately before the 1960s escalation of the civil rights movement in Mississippi. I focus on the important set of black activists in Mississippi during this period who provided the foundation for a broader movement, and I discuss the organized opposition to the civil rights movement, which expanded dramatically in the 1950s. In the second section of the chapter, I chronicle the major events of the Mississippi movement during the early 1960s, and I focus on the distinctive statewide efforts at community organizing to build local movement infrastructures. In the final section of the chapter, I describe some of the major events in the period following the national legislative gains of the mid-1960s. This section highlights the ongoing efforts to build and expand the civil right movement. This continuity of the movement raises the core question for this book about the impact of the movement during this period.

The NAACP Infrastructure and White Repression, 1954–60

The Jim Crow era saw few moments of direct public challenges to white dominance by black Mississippians.[2] However, following World War II, there were increased efforts by blacks to organize for change in Mississippi. The most consequential developments took place outside the public arena where a cadre of leaders developed an infrastructure for the civil rights movement in Mississippi. From the outside, it may have appeared that nothing was happening, but key changes were underway.

The networks that were forged during the 1950s provided a preliminary infrastructure for the mass-based movement that took shape in the early 1960s. Medgar Evers began building a statewide NAACP organization in Mississippi through the 1950s. After attempting to enroll at the University of Mississippi in 1954, Evers was offered and accepted the job of field secretary for the Mississippi branch of the NAACP, the first field secretary in the state. His appointment coincided with a flurry of activity (Payne 1995). This period of organizational growth in Mississippi during the mid-1950s paralleled the more assertive movement activity taking place in other parts of the South. Mississippi civil rights leaders had their eye on the mass mobilization across the South and responded to major civil rights victories like the Montgomery bus boycott and the 1954 *Brown* decision.

This early group of leaders included Amzie Moore, Aaron Henry, C. C. Bryant, and many others. As a group, several characteristics stand out. Many had some economic autonomy, such as owning small businesses that catered to the black community or employment by northern-owned companies. There was a large proportion of veterans, and overall these leaders were well educated and had high levels of civic and social involvement. Amzie Moore, for example, had served in the army during World War II, where he experienced the contradictions of segregation and fighting for democracy. The conflict was unavoidable:

> The Japanese were using radio broadcasts to remind Black soldiers that there was going to be no freedom for them, even after the war was over. It became Corporal Moore's job to counter this propaganda by giving lectures to Negro troops on their stake in the war. (Payne 1995, 30)

In 1946 Moore returned to Cleveland in the center of the Mississippi Delta, and he began to establish himself as a small businessman, operating a gas station and purchasing property in Cleveland. In an interview with Howell Raines, Moore suggested that he was elected as president of the NAACP in 1955 at a meeting he did not attend because the prior leadership was "just passing the buck, getting rid of it as a hot potato" (Raines 1977, 234). However, Moore had already established himself in community and political organizations, working with the Regional Council of Negro Leadership in the early 1950s. He was also very effective in his new leadership role with the NAACP—quickly building "the chapter up to 439 members, making it the second largest branch in the state, and he became the vice-president of the state conference of NAACP branches" (Payne 1995, 33).

The NAACP is most often associated with the strategy and leadership of the national organization, and the orientation of these local leaders should be differentiated from the national organization. The local level had much more variation, and leaders were often critical of the national organization's reliance on litigation, centralized decision making, and limited tactical repertoire. This helps to explain the cooperation between NAACP and SNCC leaders in the early 1960s. Amzie Moore observed:

> Mr. Wilkins [the NAACP executive director], he's a fine man. He'd fly down and hold our conferences and hold our annual "days" and raise our freedom money and be advised by different people outa New York office. And that was it. But when an individual stood at a courthouse like the courthouse in Greenwood and in Greenville and watched tiny figures [of the SNCC workers] standing against a huge column . . . [against white] triggermen and drivers and lookout men riding in automobiles with automatic guns . . . *how they stood* . . . how gladly they got in front of that line, those leaders, and went to jail! (Quoted in Raines 1977, 237)

In 1955 local NAACP chapters pursued school desegregation and voter registration campaigns. Some of the strongest NAACP chapters circulated petitions demanding school desegregation. The newly formed Citizens' Council responded swiftly. Some leaders were run out of the state while others were murdered for their challenges to the "closed society." Local repression combined with federal inaction made these efforts of the NAACP "doomed from the outset" (Dittmer 1994, 51). During the summer of 1955, two local leaders in Belzoni, Reverend George Lee and Gus Courts, were murdered. Lee and Courts had led a voter registration drive with some early success. Shortly after, Emmett Till was lynched while visiting relatives in Money, Mississippi (Dittmer 1994). These are only the most well-known murders during a period of massive counterattack by white Mississippians. The violence seems to have dampened the most visible efforts to bring about change in the latter half of the decade, but this did not end efforts to build NAACP organizations in Mississippi.

We should place these early efforts in the context of the broader civil rights movement. During this same period, black communities in nearby states were launching ambitious protest campaigns and winning preliminary victories in the civil rights movement. In the mid-1950s, bus boycotts were launched in Baton Rouge, Tallahassee, and Montgomery. Schools were desegregated under federal authority in nearby Little Rock, Arkansas. In the spring of 1960, there were sit-ins in every southern state except Mississippi. These are compelling indicators of the limited movement infrastructure and the massive repression faced by civil rights activists in the state of Mississippi.

Blacks were not the only group mobilizing in Mississippi during this period. The Citizens' Council was founded in Indianola, Mississippi on July 11, 1954, almost one month after the Supreme Court handed down the pivotal *Brown v. Board of Education* decision. By June 1956, two years after the *Brown* decision, the Citizens' Council could boast organizations in sixty-seven of Mississippi's eighty-two counties (*The Citizen* 1956). The Citizens' Council was associated with the less violent resistance to local black insurgency and federal efforts for change. Intimidation was a key tactic in the Citizens' Council repertoire. In 1957 the organization's influence was described by a Mississippi registrar:

> The Council obtains names of Negroes registered from the circuit court clerks. If those who are working for someone sympathetic to the Councils' views are found objectionable, their employer tells them to take a vacation. Then if the names are purged from the registration books they are told that the vacation is over and they can return to work. (Quoted in Lawson 1976, 135)

Throughout its history, the Citizens' Council included powerful economic and political leaders at the local and state level in Mississippi.

At key historical junctures, Mississippi whites have paved the way for the rest of the South in institutionalizing barriers to black progress. C. Vann Woodward, commenting on the formation of the Citizens' Council, observed that "Mississippi came forward in her historic role as leader of reaction in race policy, just as she had in 1875 to overthrow reconstruction and in 1890 to disfranchise the Negro" (1955, 152). The Citizens' Council played a key role in promoting a new law that required voter registrants "be able to interpret any clause in the state constitution to the satisfaction of the registrar" (Payne 1995, 35).

The State Sovereignty Commission was another organizational innovation that emerged during this period. In 1956 the Mississippi legislature created a new agency that was designed to collect information on civil rights activity in the state (see Irons 2002). The agency compiled documentation on "racial agitators"—individuals and organizations that posed a political threat—and it claimed to have a "network of Negro informers blanketing Mississippi." The organization was also responsible for projecting the "Mississippi Story" outside the South, and it sent representatives to speak to civic organizations about states' rights. In addition, the Sovereignty Commission provided financial assistance to the Citizens' Council by subsidizing their radio and television series. During Ross Barnett's term as governor (1960–64), the Sovereignty Commission made even more substantial grants to the Citizens' Council (McMillen 1971; Irons 2002).

The Sovereignty Commission was created as a specialized arm of state government to resist challenges to racial inequality. This effort was joined by other state agencies to achieve the same goal. Local and state police were notorious for harassing, intimidating, and beating civil rights activists. Welfare and school officials also used reprisals to discourage movement participation. In sum, an elaborate set of state actors within Mississippi worked hard to challenge the threats posed by an emerging civil rights movement and the prospect of federal intervention to promote racial equality.

State actors and civic groups played complementary and often coordinated roles in a struggle with the civil rights movement. The Citizens' Council was the civic organizational arm of a highly unified resistance to the civil rights movement. In addition, Ku Klux Klan organizations and less formal groups played critical roles. By 1960 extensive mobilization had occurred by state actors and white voluntary associations to address potential threats to the political and social order. At this point, the fate of civil rights in Mississippi may have appeared worse than it had ten years earlier. However, changes in the broader civil rights movement would have important consequences in Mississippi.

SNCC and the Escalation of the Mississippi Movement, 1961–65

Despite widespread and violent resistance to change, blacks in Mississippi communities organized strong local movements aimed at achieving political power in the early 1960s. Historian Steven Lawson notes that "in the early 1960s Mississippi . . . served as a laboratory in which the civil rights movement displayed its most creative energies" (1976, 93). The intensity of these organizing efforts was unprecedented in Mississippi history. Other than a brief period during Reconstruction, blacks had been systematically disenfranchised from electoral politics at the municipal, county, and state level in Mississippi (McMillen 1989). How did this transformation within the Mississippi civil rights movement occur?

SNCC, CORE, and COFO: Early Organizing Campaigns

The catalyst for the escalation of the civil rights movement in Mississippi was the community organizing of the Student Nonviolent Coordinating Committee (SNCC). In the early 1960s, SNCC attempted to organize the most dangerous parts of the South with a strategy of building organizational capacity among the most powerless segments of the black community.

SNCC emerged from the 1960 sit-in campaigns of black college students. The first sit-in took place in Greensboro, North Carolina, when a group of four college students from North Carolina Agricultural and Technical College began a demonstration at the local Woolworth. Sit-ins spread rapidly throughout the Southeast through networks of black college students (Morris 1981). The sit-ins successfully mobilized thousands of participants in cities throughout the South. Although arrests of demonstrators and violence were common, the sit-ins achieved many concessions from cities and chain stores in a relatively short period of time. The key question in the spring of 1960 was how the new student activism would be incorporated into the broader civil rights movement. Ella Baker, a longtime activist with the NAACP and the Southern Christian Leadership Conference (SCLC), had the credibility and foresight to organize a conference of student activists at her alma mater, Shaw University, in Raleigh, North Carolina. Although there were some efforts to incorporate the student leaders into the dominant civil rights organizations, SNCC emerged under the guidance of Baker as an independent organization (Carson 1981; Grant 1998; Payne 1995).

SNCC never established the large professional staff of the other major civil rights organizations. Yet SNCC rivaled the more established groups through the 1960s as it developed innovative tactics and expanded the scope of the civil rights struggle. During SNCC's first two years, it acquired a reputation as the "shock troops" of the movement by pursuing strategies that were deemed too dangerous by the NAACP and SCLC.

During these formative years, SNCC pioneered two strategies of social change that would make it the vanguard of the civil rights struggle—high-risk direct action and grassroots community organizing in the rural South. Building on the sit-in campaigns, some early SNCC leaders pressed forward in the implementation of high-risk, direct-action tactics to desegregate public facilities. During this same period, a handful of SNCC activists began to develop community-organizing campaigns in the most recalcitrant parts of the Deep South. At an early SNCC conference, this strategic division almost split the group. However, Ella Baker prevailed on the group to maintain a dual focus by creating two wings of the organization. In practice, the two strategies became intertwined because organizing the Deep South was as disruptive, confrontational, and threatening as desegregating lunch counters and movie theaters (Carson 1981).

In southwest Georgia, a group of SNCC organizers led by Charles Sherrod pioneered the community-organizing approach that became very influential within SNCC and later within CORE and Students for a Democratic Society (SDS). In an influential booklet titled "Non-Violence," Sherrod outlines the basic model. He begins by noting the "predicament" of black southerners:

> We are short-sighted because of our own situation in life. We can see no further than our own personal box. So that in communities across the country, boxed in, they wait for the "Freedom Riders," or the "Snick Boys" or "Dr. King," or the "NAACP." . . . We know that they can do it themselves but they can see no further than the sides of their dimly-lit box. From here we can all see what must be done—*break away the box and let the man see himself as he really is and then as he can be.* This is how I understand mobilization—minus the problems. With the problems—that is, with the box—mobilization must be dealt with in detail, for the nature of the atmosphere inside the box must be known.

Sherrod's analysis echoes Ella Baker's assertion that "strong people don't need strong leaders" and SNCC's criticism of "top-down" strategies that rely on charismatic authority (Payne 1989, 893). Sherrod's document begins with the characteristically lofty, almost philosophical tone of SNCC activists, but he goes on to specify a very pragmatic orientation toward community organizing.[3]

In the remainder of the document, Sherrod provides a fine-grained overview of the details—specific tasks that must be addressed by a community organizer. For example, Sherrod argues that community organizers must take a detailed inventory of existing organizations and leaders, prior events, and the "social values" of the community. Activists must embed themselves in the day-to-day life of a community. Beyond traditional community leaders, one should seek out and forge relations with "young boys in 'gangs,'" and with adults one should "promote the adoption of each of us as their children" and "relate to our professional peers by preaching for ministers; playing chess; discussing medicine, politics, insurance, education, business, etc." Sherrod addresses the cynicism that many organizers would have held toward traditional religious leaders: "The point where the church stops must be *our* point of entry. Do not be fooled here; do not let resentment of the church's failures . . . prejudice you." Much has been written about the facilitative role played by black churches in the civil rights movement. However, this should be seen as a major social accomplishment of the movement—that activists within and outside the church brought these institutions into the struggle. Sherrod showed organizers how to connect with religious leaders and congregations so that churches could be transformed into centers of movement activity.[4]

Sherrod goes on to outline additional issues that the community organizer must face in small towns throughout the South. For example, he argues that financially projects "must be self-sustaining," contending that "it is best from a tactical point of view that we are penniless." Here, strategy and necessity intersected, given the limited budget of SNCC. However, the limited resources demonstrated the sacrifice made by SNCC field-workers, and it made organizers dependent on their communities rather than allowing communities to depend on well-paid organizers.[5]

Sherrod articulated the key elements of SNCC's strategy and tactics that were employed in Mississippi as well. Charles Payne has provided an excellent historical account of this "community-organizing tradition" that has competed with other strategic models within African American social movements. Ella Baker, a lifelong activist who guided SNCC in its early development, distinguished between mobilizing and organizing.

> Organizing . . . involves creating ongoing groups that are mass-based in the sense that the people a group purports to represent have real impact on the group's direction. Mobilizing is more sporadic, involving large numbers of people for relatively short periods of time and probably for relatively dramatic activities. (Payne 1989, 897)

This organizing approach characterized the civil rights movement in Mississippi. During the civil rights movement, the community-organizing tradition was influenced by veteran activists like Ella Baker, Septima Clark, and Myles Horton. Although this approach has many antecedents and was employed elsewhere, it was implemented most thoroughly and successfully in Mississippi.

At the same time Charles Sherrod was organizing in Albany, Georgia, Bob Moses was establishing contacts in Mississippi to initiate voter registration projects in the state. Moses was a high school math teacher from New York City who had been inspired by the sit-in demonstrations. He recalled:

> The sit-ins hit me powerfully in the soul. I was mesmerized by the pictures I saw almost every day on the front pages of the *New York Times*—young committed Black faces seated at lunch counters or picketing, directly and with great dignity, challenging white supremacy in the South. They looked like I felt. (2001, 3)

In 1960 Moses traveled to Atlanta to work for the Southern Christian Leadership Conference. Moses had completed an undergraduate degree at Hamilton College and a master's degree at Harvard University, so he was older than many of the SNCC activists. Nevertheless, he quickly developed relationships with SNCC activists who were using a small desk in SCLC's Atlanta office (Carson 1981; Payne 1995).

In August 1960 Moses went on a trip to recruit people for an upcoming SNCC conference in October. As part of the trip, Moses met with Amzie Moore in Cleveland, Mississippi. The meeting turned out to be very consequential, as the two discussed plans for a voter registration drive in the state. The plans were put on hold for a year while Moses returned to New York to honor his contract at the Horace Mann School. Nevertheless, Moore connected Moses to the network of NAACP leaders throughout the state. As a result, Moses accepted an invitation from C. C. Bryant to work on voter registration in Pike County, in the southwest part of the state (Carson 1981).

In July 1961 SNCC began a voter registration campaign in McComb. Moses and a handful of SNCC workers began holding citizenship classes, trying to avoid the direct-action tactics that were seen as too risky for Mississippi. However, the movement did initiate a sit-in campaign involving local high school students that included marches and a "walkout" at the high school (Carson 1981; Moses 1970).

Violence was extreme in Pike and nearby Amite and Walthall counties. SNCC workers and local activists were harassed, beaten, and arrested. Herbert Lee, another NAACP activist from nearby Amite County, was murdered on September 25 by a member of the state legislature. According to historian John Dittmer (1994), there was support from adults in McComb for the voter registration campaign, but the sit-ins involving high school students (many of whom were expelled) and the murder of Lee undermined the viability of SNCC's program in McComb. SNCC organizers left the area in the fall of 1961, with Moses relocating to the state capital of Jackson. The McComb movement had a lasting impact on the Mississippi movement, with SNCC activists seeing the severe repression and limited federal involvement that lay ahead.

From McComb, SNCC spread to a handful of Mississippi cities and small towns including Hattiesburg, Jackson, and Greenwood, in the Mississippi Delta. From Greenwood the movement spread outward to nearby counties. Historically, the Delta, in the northwest part of the state, has had the highest proportion of blacks because of its plantation economy initially supported by slavery and later tenancy and sharecropping. With the proportion of blacks far exceeding whites in most counties, this area posed a potentially strong base for voter registration campaigns, challenging Mississippi's economic and political elites. Moses envisioned this as an area where blacks could ultimately achieve significant political power and elect a black person to Congress, "which would have tremendous symbolic and political value" (Carson 1981, 78; Dittmer 1994).

During this period the state of Mississippi had become the target of the Freedom Rides, the direct-action protest sponsored by the Congress of Racial Equality (CORE) that challenged the segregation of interstate bus travel. CORE, along with the NAACP, SCLC, and SNCC, was one of the "big four" civil rights organizations that dominated during the early 1960s. CORE was a relatively small, northern organization with a strong pacifist orientation that was attempting to become more involved in the southern civil rights movement. Originally, CORE had planned to send an integrated group from Washington, D.C., to its national convention in New Orleans. In May 1961 the Freedom Rides met massive violence through Alabama and stalled in Montgomery as Attorney General Robert Kennedy attempted to negotiate an end to the protest. CORE agreed to end the Freedom Rides in Alabama, but SNCC activists from Nashville resumed the protest, pushing toward Mississippi. On May 24, 1961, the Mississippi Highway Patrol met the Freedom Riders at the state line and escorted the Trailways bus into Jackson, where the protesters were quickly arrested (Meier and Rudwick 1973). Many other busloads of Freedom Riders came south, and the same pattern was repeated over and over. In Mississippi there was limited public violence, immediate arrests, and jail terms served at Parchman Penitentiary. There was little direct effect from the Freedom Rides on the Mississippi movement outside Jackson. However, the campaign did bring greater attention to the state and gave some activists such as Stokely Carmichael an initial contact with the Mississippi movement. Interestingly, as the Mississippi legislature prepared for Freedom Summer during the spring of 1964, they passed a series of laws designed to meet the same type of protest campaign of direct action. The legislature, possibly because of the Freedom Ride experience, miscalculated the nature of the Mississippi movement and expected large-scale public efforts at desegregation (Chevigny 1965; Dittmer 1994).

In 1962 the Council of Federated Organizations (COFO) was reorganized as an umbrella organization through which various civil rights organizations could coordinate their efforts and avoid conflict with each other's programs in Mississippi. SNCC and CORE made up the vast majority of the staff, with a rough division of labor between these two organizations. CORE worked primarily in the Fourth Congressional District, which included its two major projects in Meridian and Canton. SNCC operated throughout the rest of the state. This division gave CORE a distinct presence in the state, which the national organization could profile in newsletters and fund-raising efforts. In practice, there were few differences between CORE and SNCC, with each pursuing the same strategy of grassroots movement building. The NAACP was the other major organization, and it had considerable influence within COFO because of key adult leaders from Mississippi like Medgar Evers, Aaron Henry, and Amzie Moore. Funding for COFO came from a variety of sources, including grants from the Voter Education Project, a program of the Southern Regional Council. Through 1964 COFO was the organizational vehicle of the Mississippi movement coordinating campaigns, defining the major goals, and channeling resources and staff, and the strategic orientation developed out of the collaboration between the younger SNCC and CORE activists from outside the state and the older NAACP leaders from Mississippi.

By this point, SNCC was developing an overarching strategy of organizing communities for a long-term struggle by facilitating the development of local leadership. Stokely Carmichael summed up the strategy: "It's not radical if SNCC people get political offices, or if M. L. King becomes President. . . . If decisions are still made from the top down, if decisions get made from the bottom up, then that's radical" (quoted in Carson 1981, 154). This vision informed the types of indigenous leaders that SNCC attempted to cultivate in Mississippi.

Between 1961 and 1963, COFO and SNCC initiated projects in a handful of communities. SNCC field-workers combined the broader goal of developing grassroots leadership with the more immediate goal of voter registration—a goal that often led to others such as literacy and poverty alleviation. In addition to Greenwood and Jackson, movements were initiated in Clarksdale, Meridian, Hattiesburg, Canton, and Sunflower and Holmes counties. These efforts brought a new cadre of indigenous leaders into the Mississippi movement that differed from the established NAACP leaders, who tended to be more middle class.

High school and college students such as Hollis Watkins, Sam Block, and Anne Moody were drawn into the movement as full-time organizers. The movement also tapped into new sources of community leadership by recruiting women, small farmers and farm laborers, small merchants and business owners serving the black community, and poor blacks more generally. While these individuals started out modestly by taking citizenship classes and attempting to register to vote, many like Annie Devine, Fannie Lou Hamer, and Hartman Turnbow rose to state-level leadership.

The 1963 Freedom Vote: Community Organizing and Political Leverage

In 1963 COFO organized Freedom Vote, a mock election to symbolically demonstrate the desire of black Mississippians to participate in electoral politics (Sinsheimer 1989). The Freedom Vote was an early effort to bring national attention to Mississippi and leverage some federal intervention to protect the community organizers working in the state. Moreover, the campaign brought together for the first time the various local organizing efforts dispersed throughout the state to coordinate a broader statewide effort. The campaign featured Aaron Henry as the candidate for governor and Reverend Ed King, the chaplain at Tougaloo College, as the candidate for lieutenant governor. The candidates campaigned throughout the state, speaking at rallies designed to energize local movements in the state. The election itself revealed the character of the early movement as ballots were cast in local black institutions, like barbershops and small black-owned stores that provided a foundation for the movement. Overall, the Freedom Vote's success depended on SNCC having "penetrated the state's Black communities" (Payne 1995, 424).

During the 1963 Freedom Vote, Allard Lowenstein recruited college students primarily from Yale and Stanford to assist during the election. Students spent several days in the state working to support the election. This linkage provided a preliminary model for the 1964 Freedom Summer, officially called the Mississippi Summer Project. Through the winter, proposals were put forward to dramatically escalate the pace of mobilization in 1964. The plan included recruiting college students, primarily white and middle class, to work in community projects throughout the state.[6]

The Freedom Vote was combined with a broader strategy of developing an independent registration process using "freedom registration forms." This allowed COFO workers to canvass black communities making initial contacts with potential movement participants. Filling out a freedom registration form was a relatively low-risk way of becoming involved in the civil rights movement that could pave the way to greater involvement in the future.

In addition, this strategy allowed the movement to engage the electoral process despite the enormous obstacles to actual voter registration. The Freedom Vote and freedom registration process were also part of the movement's effort to challenge the claim that low black participation was based on apathy rather than discrimination or threat. The barriers to black political participation during this period have been well documented. Registrars, using various mechanisms dating back to the Mississippi Constitution of 1890, held back the increasing numbers of black registrants. In 1954 a new law required that registrants be able to interpret any section of the Mississippi Constitution, allowing local registrars to determine the section of the constitution and whether the applicant provided a "reasonable" interpretation (Dittmer 1994, 52–53). Not surprisingly, this and other rules were administered in systematic ways to discriminate against black Mississippians. Additional techniques that facilitated disfranchisement included literacy tests, poll taxes, and property requirements. Looming behind the mechanisms of registrars was the potential for economic reprisal and finally violence against individuals and families. Given these obstacles to electoral politics, the Freedom Vote and accompanying freedom registration forms were savvy techniques for generating commitment and building organizational capacity in the movement.

In 1964 COFO recruited college students from around the country to work in Mississippi civil rights projects. The event was a defining moment in the movement's history. The decision to sponsor Freedom Summer was hotly debated within SNCC and COFO. A primary fear of some veteran organizers was the effect this escalation would have on the local emergent leadership in Mississippi.[7] However, many also believed that repression would continue unabated unless national attention could be directed on the state. In addition, they argued that only violence against whites would generate a meaningful response from federal authorities and the broader public. Hollis Watkins summarized the dilemma:

> The summer project to bring students down to Mississippi was a tough issue. Some felt it would bring out more publicity to get more whites involved, that it would serve as a deterrent to keep the whites in Mississippi from doing things. There were others of us, from Mississippi especially, that was looking at this effort in terms of a long-range project. We felt that even though it would do this, that ultimately it would destroy the grass-roots organizations that we had built and were in the process of building. For the first time, we had local people who had begun to take the initiative themselves and do things. For the first time, we had local Mississippians who were making the decisions about what moves to make next. And where the organization should be going and how the organization politically and economically would work and where it would end up.
> (Quoted in Hampton and Fayer 1990, 182–83)

According to Charles Payne (1995), the persistent repression faced at the local level and the unwillingness and inability of the federal government to intervene tipped the balance in favor of the Freedom Summer project.

The national response to the murders of James Chaney, Andrew Goodman, and Michael Schwerner in Philadelphia, Mississippi, revealed the accuracy of this analysis. On June 21, 1964, as Freedom Summer was just getting under way, the three civil rights workers were murdered after investigating the burning of a movement-affiliated church in Longdale outside of Philadelphia, Mississippi. Chaney was a black Mississippian who had been working with the COFO project in Meridian. Schwerner was one of the few whites who had been working in the state prior to Freedom Summer, and Goodman was a Freedom Summer volunteer who had recently arrived for his summer assignment in Meridian. The murders took place at the very beginning of Freedom Summer while many of the volunteers were still at a training session in Oxford, Ohio. With national press coverage, the FBI began a massive investigation, discovering the hidden bodies and identifying the murderers of Chaney, Goodman, and Schwerner by the end of the summer. In short, the response confirmed the analysis of SNCC leaders that public outrage and federal intervention were reserved for white victims.

During the summer, the increased staff allowed many local movements to expand their programs, initiating Freedom Schools and staffing community centers. The Freedom Schools were extensions of the citizenship classes that had been used all along. However, these programs were expanded to include classes for children ranging from the traditional academic curriculum to black history and literature (McAdam 1988).

The voter registration work was now harnessed around the newly formed Mississippi Freedom Democratic Party (MFDP). The MFDP was founded in April at a convention in Jackson, and the party was designed as a parallel institution that challenged the traditional Democratic Party, following the pattern established with the Freedom Vote. If the traditional Democratic Party would not accept black citizens, the movement would create a new party that could wield power at a later date. During the summer, local movements organized for the upcoming Democratic National Convention by holding precinct meetings where candidates were elected to the statewide MFDP convention (Dittmer 1994).

Directly following Freedom Summer, the MFDP led an effort to unseat the all-white Mississippi delegation to the Democratic Party's National Convention in Atlantic City. The details of this challenge are well documented. The MFDP appealed to the Credentials Committee of the Democratic Party to unseat the traditional all-white delegation from Mississippi and confirm the MFDP as the legitimate representative from the state. Initially, the MFDP was heartened by support from state delegations outside the South and members of the Credentials Committee. However, Lyndon Johnson feared alienating white southern voters as well as powerful Democratic members of Congress. As a result, Johnson brought pressure to bear on the Democratic Party, resulting in a compromise offer of two at-large seats for Aaron Henry and Ed King. Within COFO the decision to accept or reject the offer was contested, and influential liberals and civil rights leaders urged the MFDP to accept the compromise. Ultimately, the COFO delegation refused to accept the compromise. The conflict crystallized a rift within the Mississippi movement between a moderate NAACP-led wing and a more radical MFDP/SNCC-led wing of the movement.[8]

By 1965 and 1966, SNCC's direct involvement in Mississippi was declining. In 1966 only one-third of SNCC's field-workers were in the rural South. The remaining staff members were concentrated around the national office in Atlanta or had moved on to start SNCC projects in northern urban areas (Carson 1981, 231). Nevertheless, SNCC's organizing efforts remained an important part of the continuing struggle in Mississippi. SNCC's strategy focused on community mobilizing for long-term struggles by fostering the formation of local infrastructures. In many communities, SNCC left an organizational infrastructure behind with a network of grassroots leaders, community centers, and independent organizations. SNCC's legacy is reflected most strongly in the work of the MFDP, "which assumed much of the style and orientation of SNCC . . . putting a premium on developing participatory democracy among the poor . . ." (Lawson 1985, 94).

Following the challenge at the Democratic National Convention, civil rights groups attempted to regroup and sustain momentum from the summer. The MFDP sponsored another Freedom Vote campaign to coincide with the congressional election in the fall of 1964. The ballot included local activists like Annie Devine, Victoria Gray, and Fannie Lou Hamer, who challenged Senator James Eastland from her own Sunflower County. The 1964 Freedom Vote was part of the evidentiary basis in a challenge to the seating of the Mississippi congressional delegation. The hearings allowed Mississippi activists to collect affidavits and testify to a congressional committee regarding the violence, intimidation, and fraud that accompanied electoral politics in the state. Delaying the ultimate seating of the white Mississippians in Congress, the challenge brought additional national scrutiny to the state, and it probably influenced Congress to adopt significant legislation protecting voting rights in the next summer (Dittmer 1994).

Despite unprecedented levels of political mobilization during the early 1960s, very few blacks became registered voters during this period. Between 1962 and 1964, the percentage of blacks registered in Mississippi rose from 5.3 to 6.7; both the initial percentage and the amount of change are well below that of other southern states.[9] The Voter Education Project (an organization coordinating and funding voter registration drives throughout the South) spent $12.13 per registered voter in Mississippi during this period from 1962 and 1964. This was far greater than the amount spent per voter in any other state. The next most expensive state was Louisiana at \$4.84 per voter, followed by Alabama at \$2.40 (Lawson 1976). Consistent with the pattern in the 1950s, Mississippi was leaving other states far behind in effectively resisting the efforts of the civil rights movement.

The MFDP played a pivotal role in attempting to maintain the momentum and protect the gains from the organizing of the early 1960s. Major activities of the MFDP included voter registration, supporting campaigns, and bringing legal challenges against the backlash legislation at the state, county, and municipal level. In addition to the MFDP, the other major state-level black political organization in Mississippi was the NAACP. SNCC's initial work in Mississippi was dependent on the involvement and cooperation of a network of NAACP leaders. By the time of the MFDP challenge at the Democratic Convention in 1964, relations had become strained between the MFDP/SNCC/CORE wing of the movement and the NAACP wing. These tensions were multifaceted, including generational, regional, and class differences between the leaders of these organizations, and they were articulated around different strategies that the movement should take in the aftermath of Freedom Summer. The MFDP advocated continuity with the early movement objective of building an independent base. In contrast, the NAACP began developing a coalition with liberal or more moderate Democrats (Dittmer 1985, 86–90; Lawson 1985, 93–99). Each of these organizations, the NAACP and the MFDP, shaped the avenues for civil rights and black mobilization in the post-1965 period.

For example, at the 1968 Democratic National Convention, the NAACP joined the AFL-CIO and a group of liberal whites to form the Loyalist Democrats to once again challenge the "regular" Mississippi Democrats at the convention. The Loyalist Democrats were firmly in the hands of the NAACP wing of the movement, but the MFDP still had a presence in the state and by name recognition alone commanded some authority at the national level. As a result, the Loyalists sought out the MFDP's participation in the coalition. With significant discontent at the local level, the MFDP joined the Loyalists, with little power over the platform or leadership of the party.[10]

Continuities and Transformations of the Civil Rights Struggle

Given the national legislative gains of the mid-1960s, the Voting Rights Act is often seen as the final chapter in the southern civil rights movement. In the late 1960s, national attention shifted to the Black Power movement and the urban rebellions in the North. This transition in the black protest movement is an interesting subject in itself, but the historical shift in attention has left questions unanswered about the civil rights struggle in the post-1965 period. Some assume that the effect of the 1964 Civil Rights Act and the 1965 Voting Rights Act established basic legal guarantees within which even the most avid southern racist would be constrained. In other words, black gains were successfully institutionalized. In the electoral arena, for example, this view could be buttressed by the increases in black voters in the South following the passage of the legislation. However, the story for electoral politics, schools, and social policies is more complex, with protracted struggles and substantial countermobilization by white southerners. In the following sections, I summarize the main developments in each of these arenas, including the interactions between civil rights groups and state and federal political authorities.

Gains in Black Voter Registration after 1965

Although the Mississippi civil rights movement had focused primarily on voter registration in the early 1960s, the mechanisms of Jim Crow disenfranchisement held back any gains for blacks. This changed following the 1965 Voting Rights Act. These legal changes facilitated voter registration. In addition to dismantling various regulations, the Voting Rights Act sent federal registrars into many Mississippi counties to oversee the registration process. Registration efforts soared with dramatically increasing numbers of black voters (and white voters as well).

Mississippi blacks moved from well below the regional average to slightly above the regional average over the course of five years, from 1964 to 1969. Between 1976 and 1982, the percentage of black registered voters in Mississippi increased while it declined across the region. The enormous mobilization represented by this change combined with the fact that Mississippi had the highest proportion of blacks in any

TABLE 3.1: Estimated Percentage of Adult Black Voter Registrants

	1964	1966	1969	1976	1982
Mississippi	6.7	32.9	66.5	67.4	75.8
Total (southern states)	31.4	46.8	64.8	59.3	57.7

Source: Steven Lawson, *In Pursuit of Power* (1985) and *Black Ballots* (1976).

state presented a potential threat to white electoral dominance in many Mississippi communities.

The Mississippi civil rights movement spent the first half of the 1960s mobilizing blacks for electoral politics. Given the barriers to voter registration, this became the most immediate goal to be achieved. Yet voter registration was only meaningful if blacks could cast their votes for the candidates of their choice. In 1966 the Mississippi legislature convened in a special session to ensure that newly registered black voters would have little impact on politics. The Mississippi legislature led the way for the South in 1966 during a special session by creating a new set of institutional mechanisms to limit black political power. Frank Parker notes that "the focus of voting discrimination shifted from preventing blacks from registering to vote to preventing them from winning elections" (1990, 3). When compared to the open-defiance strategy of earlier Mississippi governors, this response was unique in its subtlety and willingness to operate within the confines of federal authority. Strategies of legal resistance meant that litigation would become a central tactic during the period after the Voting Rights Act.

In Mississippi, there were three major strategies embedded in the new legislation. First, congressional districts were redrawn to dilute the voting power of blacks that was concentrated in what has historically been the Second Congressional District in the Delta. Second, there were changes in state-level and municipal districts, that is, the move to at-large elections and multimember districts (combining majority-white with majority-black districts). Third, new polices governing the qualifications for candidates were created. This had the greatest impact on independent candidates, including members of the MFDP. A series of court cases was launched by blacks in Mississippi against the "massive resistance" legislation (Parker 1990).

The new legal barriers were buttressed by the continued use of violence and intimidation at the ballot box. Black electoral politics shortly after the Voting Rights Act resembled the earlier period of voter registration work. In short, the struggle for black political power did not end with the Voting Rights Act.

The War on Poverty: Struggles over Economic Development and Local Policy Implementation

In 1964 the Johnson administration sponsored a series of programs nominally directed at poverty and administratively coordinated through the Office of Economic Opportunity. The new initiative had an array of specific programs, including job training, health care, and Head Start. Poverty programs were typically funneled through a community action program (CAP), which was directed by a board of directors. The poverty programs presented a double bind for the Mississippi movement. On the one hand, there was substantial suspicion of the federal government and the Democratic Party. This underlying skepticism made many activists fear that poverty programs were designed to co-opt an independent movement. At the same time, the poverty programs presented opportunities that were often difficult to resist. First, the resources themselves were immediately attractive to poor communities. Second, with the language of "maximum feasible participation" of the poor, the programs and CAP boards were points of potential leverage.

Through the 1960s the movement, especially at the local level, gave increasing attention to the economic needs of black Mississippians. Arguably, movement activists had economic goals in mind when they pursued the vote. In the fall of 1964, for example, local movements attempted to elect candidates to county boards (Agricultural Stabilization and Conservation [ASC] committees) of the Department of Agriculture. The attempts to win representation through these elections were explicit efforts to address the economic problems of black farmers. The ASC boards controlled the allotment of federally regulated crops such as cotton. Hence, representation could allow black farmers to eliminate the systematic discrimination in the process.

From its earliest days, some movement energy focused in an ameliorative fashion on poverty and immediate economic crises. When the Leflore County Board of Supervisors shut off the emergency food distribution programs in Greenwood in 1962, SNCC mobilized resources from around the country. In the spring of 1964, food and clothing programs were components of COFO's organization. At various points, ambivalence was expressed about the programs, and COFO recognized that the "food and clothing program cannot cope with poverty this serious." At the same time, COFO had begun initial strategizing about various federal programs in the areas of housing, job training, agriculture, public welfare, health, and child care. Prompted by local needs and concerns, movements began taking a more creative, long-term approach to the economic problems facing black Mississippians.[11]

Head Start was the first major experience with the War on Poverty in Mississippi. In 1965 an innovative program was initiated throughout the state, the Child Development Group of Mississippi (CDGM). Any understanding of the relationship between the War on Poverty and the

Mississippi movement must begin with the history of CDGM, its rise and fall. CDGM was one of the earliest and most successful Head Start programs in the United States. Initially, the program met with skepticism, if not hostility, from SNCC veterans who had already developed a thoroughgoing suspicion of the Democratic Party during the 1964 National Convention. However, the program met with greater enthusiasm from local activists. CDGM, which assembled a program rapidly in 1965 under the directorship of Tom Levin, had little choice but to build on the "local movement centers" throughout the state. Once in place, the program was, in many ways, consistent with the prior goals of Freedom Schools and other movement-sponsored programs. In addition, CDGM had the financial backing to offer some employment for program directors, teachers, aides, and bus drivers.[12]

In its three years, CDGM became the target of opposition from white Mississippi politicians. The complex history will be examined more fully, so I will present a brief outline here. The recurring charge against CDGM was that it was funding the civil rights movement. Hence, the political participation of Head Start employees was a major source of controversy. Within Mississippi, an alternative agency, Mississippi Action for Progress (MAP), was formed that combined the more conservative wing of the movement with moderate and liberal whites. This coalition, which included prominent figures like Aaron Henry and Hodding Carter, allowed MAP to establish a parallel set of Head Start centers for a short period. The conflict between CDGM and MAP paralleled the conflicts over black electoral politics in Mississippi at the state level. Ultimately, the fate of CDGM shifted to the national political arena, where it was under constant scrutiny. The struggle over CDGM was similar to the conflicts at the local level over community action programs (Dittmer 1994). The trajectory of many local movements became connected to CDGM, community action programs, and the broader War on Poverty.

The Struggle over Schools: Litigation and Countermobilization

School desegregation ranked as a secondary goal for most organizations and activists in the Mississippi movement during the 1960s. However, desegregation did rank high for federal policy makers and maintaining segregation was centrally important for white Mississippians. Hence, schools did become the locus of political struggle. As was the case for electoral politics, the courts influenced the pace and timing of local conflicts.

The first phase of conflict over schools followed the *Brown* decision in 1954. Some local NAACP chapters in Mississippi attempted to initiate school desegregation in their communities. However, there was massive local resistance and no federal support. In fact, the Citizens' Council emerged during this period, pursuing legalistic strategies and mobilizing at the local level to resist desegregation and the civil rights movement (McMillen 1971).

There was little change in the educational arena until 1964, when courts began issuing "freedom of choice" plans. These early plans allowed for "voluntary" desegregation. In short, parents could apply to have their children reassigned to different schools within a district. The result between 1964 and 1969 was minimal transfers of black students to formerly all-white schools. The pace of change shifted following the *Alexander v. Holmes* decision in 1969, which enforced immediate desegregation to eliminate racially identifiable schools in thirty Mississippi school districts (Parker 1987). School desegregation followed quickly. Simultaneously, a system of "white-flight" academies was established throughout the state that served approximately 20 percent of white students. The conflicts around schools reveal the tactical interaction between white and black mobilization. Specifically, white countermovements mobilized in response to the threat of local civil rights movements and federal intervention.

Conclusion

This analytic overview of the Mississippi civil rights movement has identified key points that frame the local focus of subsequent chapters. In the late 1950s, Mississippi experienced a growth in the strength of whites opposed to the civil rights movement and racial equality. This included the emergence and growth of Citizens' Council organizations in most communities, the establishment of a state-level Sovereignty Commission, the election of Ross Barnett as governor, and an overall strengthening of resistance. During the early 1960s, indigenous NAACP leaders worked with student activists from SNCC and CORE to build a statewide movement that developed innovative community-organizing programs to dramatically broaden participation in the civil rights movement. These efforts created new leaders and allowed the movement to build organizations in many rural communities and small towns throughout the state. This chapter has also identified some of the broader forces that shaped the ongoing dynamics of the Mississippi movement. These forces include major legislative policies, court decisions, and the dynamics of the major civil rights organizations. Finally, this chapter has highlighted the key question of this study about the impact of the movement's community-organizing efforts on local institutions in Mississippi.

By tracing the major developments of the Mississippi movement, we can see the context within which local activists worked. In the early 1960s, local movements developed through the organizing efforts of civil rights activists from SNCC, CORE, and local NAACP leaders. At the state level, the major organizational vehicle of the movement, COFO, collapsed following Freedom Summer. However, many movement organizations continued to operate throughout the state. The changing political context presented new opportunities and obstacles to local movements. In the next chapter, I take a closer look at the mobilization process in Mississippi by charting the development and trajectory of movement building in three communities.

CHAPTER FOUR

The Formation of Local Movement
Trajectories in Mississippi

IN THIS chapter, I shift from the statewide organizations and campaigns to the development and transformation of local movements in Mississippi. In the early 1960s, local movements emerged amidst widespread repression, built movement infrastructures, and developed new tactics. In the latter part of the 1960s, local movements built on these organizational forms and strategies and responded to a changing political context. The most important changes were the Voting Rights Act, the War on Poverty, and the resulting programs that became available to local movements. In addition, the local context was altered as the national civil rights organizations declined and white Mississippians employed new strategies to undermine civil rights mobilization and black political gains. This analysis unfolds through a comparison of all Mississippi counties followed by detailed chronologies of the emergence of movements in Holmes, Madison, and Bolivar counties from the early 1960s to the early 1970s.

The fundamental process examined in this chapter is movement building, the efforts to establish independent organizational bases from which to launch social change campaigns. In later chapters, I will focus explicitly on the impacts of these movements. Movement infrastructures turn out to be consequential for the long-term impacts of social movements. As a result, we need a clear picture of how these structures take shape and are transformed over time.

A key finding from research on social movements is the central role of established organizations in facilitating the emergence of the civil rights movement (McAdam 1982; A. Morris 1984). Hence, it is not entirely surprising that the Mississippi movement developed relatively late. Black colleges, local NAACP chapters, and churches all played key roles in Mississippi. However, those institutions were smaller and, often, less autonomous than they were in the more urban areas of the South. The overarching goal of "community organizing" in the Mississippi movement reflected a realistic appraisal that the movement would have to generate a local infrastructure to sustain campaigns or boycotts. Social movements are often built on prior organizational forms, but they also generate new organizations. In fact, this is often one of the most important legacies of a sustained period of insurgency.

The forms of racial inequality that characterized the U.S. South and Mississippi have been well documented by historians (McMillen 1989). Sociologist Aldon Morris (1984) insightfully characterized the premovement South as a "tri-partite system of domination" in which economic, political, and personal forms of domination overlapped and circumscribed the lives of black southerners. Mississippi is often seen as the state where this system was most thoroughly institutionalized. This pervasiveness is reflected in James Silver's famous characterization of Mississippi as a "closed society" (1964). As the Mississippi movement got under way, blacks were excluded from all political office holding in Mississippi except for municipal offices in Mound Bayou, an all-black town in Bolivar County. Formal and informal mechanisms excluded blacks from participation in electoral politics, facilitating a political system that was dominated by whites and in many cases white planters. Similarly, public resources and institutions (such as schools) reflected and reinforced the overarching patterns of racial domination.[1] The effects of the system could be found in all spheres of southern life, extending into the minutiae of interracial interactions and the distribution of material resources, legal rights, and social status.

Local Variation: Dimensions of Community Context that Shaped the Movement

As we have seen, the civil rights movement was very uneven in its strength throughout Mississippi. Why did the movement involve some communities more deeply than others? This question is significant because we need to know how the communities where the movement emerged differed from those with little or no civil rights activity. These differences could have important analytic significance in any effort to attribute political change to the civil rights movement. For example, if the movement only worked in counties where blacks had greater political or economic resources prior to the movement's emergence, then these factors could be the "real" cause of the movement's apparent success.

We can begin by considering the factors that movement leaders identified as important. Prior to Freedom Summer, COFO produced a report that profiled the various communities where organizers had worked during the early 1960s. According to COFO organizers, the most "open" areas of the state included the counties on the coast with industrial employment and without agricultural dominance. Greenville, in the Delta, was considered relatively liberal. Some have pointed to the white leadership in the city, including Hodding Carter, a local newspaper editor. Overall, the Delta was viewed as a difficult place to organize because of the grinding poverty and the plantation economy and its residues.[2] However, except for Leflore County (Greenwood), violence in the Delta seems to have been less frequent and extreme during the 1960s than elsewhere in Mississippi. This is somewhat surprising because the pattern was quite different during the Jim Crow era, with the highest levels of lynching from 1889 to 1945 concentrated in the black-belt counties of the Delta (McMillen 1989, 231). During the 1960s, the southwest corner of the state including Pike (McComb) and Adams (Natchez) counties were some of the most violent and the center of Klan activity in Mississippi. In addition to these locales, there were several counties running through the middle of the state, including Madison (Canton) and Neshoba (Philadelphia), which had similar levels of violence. The level of violent repression against the civil rights movement can be seen in the map of Mississippi counties (figure 4.1).

COFO distributed a report that outlined the project areas throughout the state to incoming volunteers. After presenting the fine-grained variations for each of the projects, the report reminded volunteers that "actually, Mississippi is oppressive everywhere, and when we speak of moderate or liberal areas (as in Greenville) we are talking about a lesser degree of oppressiveness. Any one of these areas is liable to tighten up and become a terror hole at any given time." The movement operated within this context of repression, and activists constructed savvy techniques to avoid violence, including complex and changing travel routes.[3]

In the early days of the movement, groups with some form of economic independence seem to have participated in greater numbers than those who were vulnerable to economic reprisal. This included black farmers, business owners who catered to the black community, persons employed by the federal government or companies located outside the state (e.g., railroads), and, in some cases, ministers. Organizationally, the black church in Mississippi was less autonomous than was the case in other states with larger cities. As a result, ministers played a more limited role in movement leadership. In rural areas, ministers often had a full-time job outside the

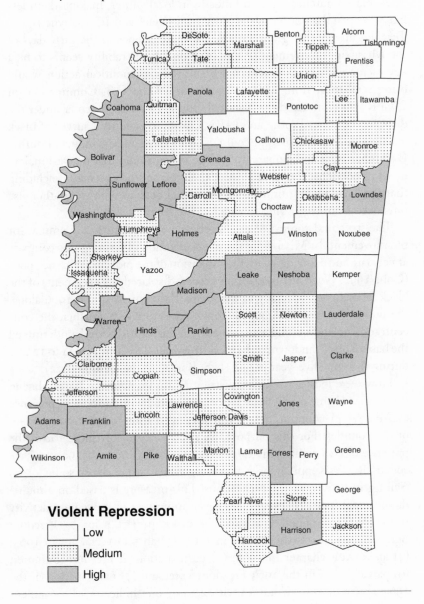

Violent Repression

- Low
- Medium
- High

church and ministered to one or more churches on the side. In other cases, black churches received funds from local whites, making them less likely to open their doors to the movement (MacLeod 1991; Payne 1995). Teachers are another group notable for their absence in the early days of the Mississippi movement. Again, economic vulnerability seems to be a key factor with black teachers, who feared that political action would bring retaliation from white school boards. The U.S. Commission on Civil Rights contracted the National Opinion Research Center under the direction of James Protho and Lewis Lipsitz to conduct a survey of black teachers in four Mississippi counties. Interviews were conducted during December 1964 and January 1965. The survey found that the vast majority of respondents feared the loss of their job and/or violence, concluding that the "shadow of intimidation" prevented persons who were otherwise interested from registering to vote.[4]

The structural context of mobilization presented further dilemmas for the movement. In Mississippi the mechanization of farming was comparatively late and coincided with the expansion of the movement in the 1960s (Cobb 1992; Woodruff 1994). This process displaced large segments of the black labor force, especially in the Delta. Between 1964 and 1969 alone, the number of tenants dropped from 18,580 to 2,657. Further, the concentration of landholding, which increased during this period, undermined the base of black landowners. Black farm owners fell from 14,434 to 12,222 during the same five-year period (U.S. Bureau of the Census 1972).

How were local movements distributed throughout the state? Having summarized some of the basic factors associated with movement presence in Mississippi communities, I will present a more refined comparison of the counties. For this purpose, we need a reasonable indicator of the presence of civil rights activity in a county during the early 1960s. I have coded all Mississippi counties as having either sustained, episodic, or no civil rights activity in the early 1960s. This measure is based on a multi-dimensional index that combines seven indicators of movement activity from 1961 to 1966: (1) a SNCC or CORE project prior to Freedom Summer; (2) an NAACP chapter in 1963; (3) an MFDP chapter in 1965; (4) an NAACP chapter in 1966; (5) participation in Freedom Summer; (6) participation in the 1963 Freedom Vote; and (7) participation in the 1964 Freedom Vote. Counties with zero or one indicator of movement activity are considered non-movement counties. Counties with two to four indicators of movement activity are labeled episodic movement counties, and counties that had five to seven indicators of movement activity are considered sustained movement counties.

	Movement Counties		Non-Movement Counties	State
	Sustained	Episodic		
Population Characteristics				
Urban, 1960 (%)	40.6	18.7	12.8	21.3
Total population, 1960	47,265	20,522	15,399	24,581
Black population, 1960	21,116	9,396	5,317	10,383
Black population, 1960 (%)	49.46	49.12	33.78	42.57
Black voting-age population, 1960	9,811	4,289	2,398	4,767
Black voting-age population, 1960 (%)	43.9	43.1	28.4	36.9
Registered black voters, 1960	788	128	71	258
Registered black voters, 1960 (%)	6.9	3.0	3.8	4.3
Income Characteristics				
Households with income below $3,000, 1960 (%)	53.3	60.9	60.0	58.8
Median income for nonwhite individuals, 1960 ($)	694	551	641	623
Median income for nonwhite families, 1960 ($)	1,615	1,268	1,319	1,373
Class Structure				
Nonwhite farm laborers, 1960 (%)	18.8	22.2	11.9	17.1
Nonwhite domestics, 1960 (%)	17.5	15.7	18.0	17.1
Nonwhite professionals, 1960 (%)	4.0	3.6	3.8	3.8
Nonwhite managers, 1960 (%)	1.3	7.2	7.8	8.9
Most vulnerable occupations, 1960 (%)	15.5	16.3	15.0	15.5
Least vulnerable occupations, 1960 (%)	19.3	20.2	25.6	22.3
Black farm owners (as % of black labor force), 1964	4.9	9.2	9.2	8.2

Continued on next page

	Movement Counties		Non-Movement Counties	State
	Sustained	Episodic		
Landowner concentration, 1964 (%)	52.0	46.0	34.0	42.0
Farms operated by tenants, 1964 (%)	28.7	24.8	17.7	22.6
Repression				
Lynchings (1889–1945)	8.1	5.0	3.6	5.1
Klan organization (% of counties with organization, 1964)	74	48	34	48
Citizens' Council organization (% of counties with organization, 1956)	68	81	60	69
Number of counties	19	27	35	81

Note: This table reports mean values for counties. Hinds County is excluded from this and other tables. See appendix A for further detail.

After sorting Mississippi counties into these three categories, we can compare them to determine whether there are systematic differences between the counties. Table 4.1 compares counties across several background characteristics. The first pattern that stands out is the fact that movement counties had much greater population size than non-movement counties. One can also see that movement counties were more urban than non-movement counties. To avoid misinterpretation, note that the percentage urban measure is based on a U.S. Census threshold of a municipality with 2,500 or more persons. So, it is better to picture the movement operating in southern towns and spreading outward into the more rural parts of a county. For example, local movements emerged in most of the larger Mississippi towns, including Clarksdale (21,105), Greenville (41,502), Greenwood (20,436), Cleveland (10,172), Meridian (49,374), and Hattiesburg (34,989).

At the aggregate level, table 4.1 shows that in counties with sustained movement activity nonwhites had higher levels of personal and household income. In addition, there was less poverty—53 percent in sustained movement counties compared to 60 percent in non-movement counties. These differences show that there were slightly greater economic resources in movement counties that could have been used to support movement efforts. However, this difference should be placed in context. As the case studies will show, direct financial contributions were not the most important contributions that rank-and-file activists made to local movements. Grassroots movements tend to rely more heavily on the time and labor of participants as the key resources rather than financial contributions of supporters.

Movement counties had higher levels of black farm laborers, tenants, and land concentration—all indicators of the traditional plantation economy. These counties often had a county seat that was the hub for social, political, and economic institutions. So, many of these Delta counties were more urban than the "hill" counties in the eastern part of the state where there was less movement activity.

In measuring the composition of the black class structure, I follow an influential study by Lester Salamon and Stephen Van Evera (1973) that examined voter registration and turnout in the Mississippi black-majority counties, finding that class relations constrained black participation. Where a greater proportion of the voting-age population was employed in "vulnerable occupations" (e.g., domestics, tenants), black political participation was lower. The proportion employed in the "least vulnerable occupations" was associated with higher levels of political participation. Nevertheless, the findings are limited by the small sample of twenty-nine counties, and relationships were not as strong when the analysis was applied to the entire state of Mississippi (Kernell 1973).

I have replicated Salamon and Van Evera's measures of black economic vulnerability to determine whether these factors are associated with development of a robust local civil rights movement. The first indicator, black occupational vulnerability, measures the proportion of the black voting-age population especially vulnerable to economic coercion. The second variable, black occupational autonomy, measures the proportion of the black voting-age population that has the greatest independence from white employers. The measure of occupational vulnerability includes the unemployed, tenants, black farm laborers, household workers, and local government employees (which includes teachers). As Salamon and Van Evera observe, each of these groups is noted for their limited participation by movement activists and in the historical scholarship on the civil rights movement. The measure of occupational autonomy includes farm owners, federal government employees, small business owners (nonagricultural self-employed), and manufacturing. In various historical accounts of the movements, these groups have been noted for their "overrepresentation" among movement participants. The analysis here cannot determine whether individuals in these groups were more or less likely to participate. However, these measures reflect characteristics of the black class structure with an expected relationship to the overall level of movement activity and black political participation in a community. As table 4.1 shows, there is not a strong relationship between these characteristics of the black class structure and movement activity in Mississippi counties. For the least vulnerable occupations, the relationship is in the counterintuitive direction. Movement counties had a smaller proportion of blacks in occupations that would provide some insulation from the reprisals of whites. As such, there is no reason to think that these counties had a selective advantage making them somehow "easier" to mobilize because of the composition of the black class structure.

There is some evidence suggesting that movement counties had higher levels of political participation as measured by the number and percentage of blacks registered to vote in 1960. As a percentage of the voting-age population, counties that developed sustained movements had almost twice the level of voter registration as non-movement counties, 6.9 percent and 3.8 percent, respectively. These estimates should be placed in context. Compared to the South as a whole in 1960, voter registration was very low throughout Mississippi, including those counties that developed sustained movements. The U.S. Commission on Civil Rights estimated that 26.5 percent of blacks of voting age were registered in the eleven core southern states (USCCR 1961).

Finally, consider the relationship between prior repression and white racist organizations and the distribution of local Mississippi movements. Here, we see that the movement went to communities that had high levels of lynching in the period before World War II. Perhaps more relevant for the civil rights movement was the presence of Citizens' Council and Ku Klux Klan organizations that were more common in movement than non-movement communities. These indicators suggest that organized opposition was even greater in movement than non-movement counties.

This initial snapshot comparing counties with varying levels of movement activity shows that movement counties had greater population, were more urban, and had higher levels of income and less poverty. These characteristics could be thought of as facilitating conditions. However, along other dimensions, movement counties deviate from common expectations. For example, at the community level, the black class structure does not seem to be associated with movement emergence in ways that many observers have argued or would expect. In addition, local movements emerged in counties that had had greater levels of violent repression in the past, and they were more likely to have Ku Klux Klan and Citizens' Council organizations. This snapshot does not capture what was a more dynamic process whereby prior repression was responsive to earlier organizing efforts by civil rights activists such as the NAACP's voter registration drives and demands for school desegregation. However, this analysis does provide a helpful starting point for building a more complex picture of the context in which local movements emerged.

Statewide Patterns of Mobilization and Repression

Holmes County along with Madison and Bolivar counties were successful at generating local movements in the early 1960s when compared to other communities in Mississippi. Before turning to these cases, it is important to take another look at the broader patterns across the state. During the early 1960s, were COFO projects successful at enlisting local support for movement initiatives? Did the counties that had substantial movement activities in the early 1960s have comparable levels at the end of the decade? There are few moments at which we have a common metric for gauging the early organizing efforts of the movement. As we will see in Holmes, Madison, and Bolivar counties, each community engaged in various independent efforts to bring about local change such as boycotts and establishing economic cooperatives. However, there were several coordinated statewide efforts across all Mississippi counties. In the early 1960s, the Freedom Vote elections were key examples, and I have included the votes cast in 1964.[5] In 1968 there were two major statewide efforts—a demonstration in support of the Poor People's March held in Jackson and a nominating process to elect Loyalist Democrats for the Democratic National Convention. For each of these events, I have measured whether there was participation by civil rights activists from each Mississippi county.

I have also included data on the amount and forms of repression in Mississippi counties. As we will see in the case studies, local movements were shaped by the intense violence faced at the local level. The first indicator of repression refers to incidents where civil rights workers were physically attacked during Freedom Summer, and the remaining indicators refer to different forms of violent repression that occurred between 1960 and 1969.

	Freedom Summer		Movement Counties		Non-Movement Counties	State
	Yes	No	Sustained	Episodic		
Movement						
Freedom Vote, 1964	2,269.2	240.3	—	—	—	716.2
Freedom Vote, 1964 (%)	29.0	6.8	—	—	—	12.0
Poor People's March participation, 1968 (%)	42.0	15.0	42.0	22.0	8.6	21.0
Loyalist Democrats, county nominating convention, 1968 (%)	68.4	24.2	68.4	33.3	17.1	34.6
Repression						
Attacks during Freedom Summer, 1964	2.7	0.1	2.7	0.3	0	0.7
Violence against property, 1960–69	14.0	1.6	14.2	2.4	0.8	4.5
Violence against persons, 1960–69	17.6	3.3	18.1	4.6	2.1	6.7
Murders of civil rights workers, 1960–69	0.5	0.4	0.7	0.4	0.2	0.4
All violence, 1960–69	32.1	5.2	33.0	7.4	3.1	11.5
Number of counties	19	62	19	27	35	81

Note: This table reports mean values for counties.

Table 4.2 compares the number of Freedom Votes cast based on whether or not a county had a COFO-sponsored project during Freedom Summer. Not surprisingly, counties with Freedom Summer projects turned out higher numbers of Freedom Votes. More interesting, the indicators from 1968 show that there was substantial continuity in civil rights mobilization.

Repression has paradoxical effects on social movements. Rather than diminishing the efforts of civil rights activists, some forms of resistance appear to have escalated the confrontation and broadened the level of mobilization in the early 1960s. In other words, repression seems to backfire under certain conditions. Many scholars have argued that the key dynamic of the civil rights movement was the exploitation of white violence by the movement to generate sympathy from and leverage with national actors (McAdam 1982, 1983).

In Madison County, this positive relationship occurred during the boycott and voter registration campaign of late 1963 and early 1964. Although violence was intense, repression did not shut down the mass meetings or freedom days, and it is unlikely that violence undermined support for the boycott. In his study of the Greenwood movement, Charles Payne provides insight into how this escalation of black mobilization and white violence interacted at the local level:

> In the Spring of 1963, those whites desperately opposed to the movement were slow to understand that the calculus of repression had changed. They had now entered a situation in which a significant number of Greenwood blacks, no longer feeling so alone and in some cases no longer fearing that there was much that could be done to them anyway, reacted to each additional act of intimidation by becoming more aggressive themselves. (1995, 201–2)

Payne's discussion of the Greenwood movement supports the argument that the movement infrastructure is an intervening mechanism that explains how repression can lead to a subsequent escalation of protest. We can see a similar positive relationship between repression and movement activity by looking at the 1964 Freedom Vote. There is a strong correlation between violence during Freedom Summer and votes cast during the Freedom Vote. Even when we compare counties with comparable levels of movement activity, higher levels of violence are associated with higher Freedom Vote participation.[6]

The period from June, when Freedom Summer began, to November, when freedom ballots were cast, was a highly exceptional period in the civil rights movement; it combined high levels of national media attention and the most extensive mass mobilization for civil rights in the history of Mississippi. However, timing is critical. Violence visited upon the movement during high points of mobilization only increased collective action in the short term. Over a longer time frame, I find a different pattern, as we will see in later chapters.

These comparisons across all Mississippi counties are revealing. Yet there are other processes of movement building that cannot be measured in this manner. For example, community organizations shaped the patterning of movement activity, including black churches, colleges, and fraternal organizations that provided important pieces of the movement infrastructure. These institutions might help to explain why the movement was located in counties with greater population size and higher urbanization and why some activists had greater success in some communities than others in building organizations and developing leadership. The case studies illustrate these complex forces in the formation of local movements. With this context in place, I turn to each of the case studies.

The Civil Rights Movement in Holmes, Madison, and Bolivar Counties

In the remaining sections of this chapter, I introduce Holmes, Madison, and Bolivar counties, the central cases in this study.[7] For each case, I examine the temporal progression of movement emergence and transformation. I begin with Holmes, a model of a sustained indigenous movement. After presenting the Holmes case, I turn to Madison then Bolivar. Because these counties did not sustain the same type or level of activism as the Holmes movement, they allow for intriguing sets of comparisons.

By 1984 blacks in Holmes County held three of the five positions on the powerful County Board of Supervisors, providing a controlling vote. In fact, the chair, Howard Taft Bailey, was one of the early movement leaders in Holmes County. In Madison County, a combination of repression and structural barriers effectively undermined much of the movement base. By the early 1980s, there were no black members on the Board of Supervisors. Through the 1970s in Madison County, the NAACP did mount a series of aggressive challenges using litigation. However, mass-based tactics and organizations were few. In Bolivar County, one black candidate was elected to the Board of Supervisors in 1967. However, most movement activity took place at the municipal level and little countywide organization developed in Bolivar County around electoral politics. On the other hand, there was substantial mobilization around poverty and economic development. Local activists in Bolivar County were heavily involved in the War on Poverty. While all three counties had black majorities and were well positioned structurally to elect candidates to office, there were eleven blacks elected to county-level positions in Holmes County in contrast to five in Madison and two in Bolivar in the early 1980s. Ultimately, these differences were reflected in the assessments of movement activists. For example, Jerome Smith, one of the early movement organizers who worked in the Madison County area, made the following assessment: "The last time I was there I was disappointed knowing where they had come from and knowing the kind of dues they had paid. . . ."[8] In sharp contrast, Reverend Russell, a local Holmes County activist stated:

> It does something to me when I hear tell of somebody elected in our state or county, and 'specially when we go to Washington—like our senators and

congressmen. We didn't have deputies, and now our sheriff is black. And we didn't have the black superintendent. And we put the state representative, Robert Clark. Had to stay up late, but we did it.[9]

Each view was forged in the long political struggles of divergent movement histories. This chapter elaborates the origins and development of the local movements in Holmes, Madison, and Bolivar counties.

I have presented a summary profile of the counties in table 4.3 that includes the same basic social and demographic information as table 4.1. I have also included specific indicators of movement activity. The counties are very similar along most dimensions. All had high levels of mobilization in the early 1960s. They all have one major town that accounts for the urban population in the county and several smaller towns dispersed throughout the county. Each county has a relatively large black population. Bolivar County in the Mississippi Delta has a larger proportion of farm laborers and tenants, and landownership is more concentrated among large farm owners.

Throughout the chapter, I highlight major organizational developments and tactical dilemmas faced by local movements in their struggles at the local level. I follow the movements over time and raise analytic points, especially where the three cases diverge in their development and impact. I also introduce broad changes that affected all local civil rights movements, such as major court decisions or policy initiatives. While there are interesting patterns of variation among the cases, it is equally important to see where local histories followed similar patterns.

Building local movements based on indigenous resources is important, but there is nothing automatic about this process. Rather, there is a complex process that Doug McAdam (1999) refers to as "social appropriation" through which movement organizers attempt to translate networks, ideologies, and organization into a viable base for a social movement. In some cases, indigenous resources can even block or dampen the emergence of a movement. Aldon Morris (1984) observes that the white repression of the Alabama NAACP in the 1950s, which virtually drove the organization underground, created the space in which the more progressive SCLC could emerge. Similarly, the lack of strong indigenous movement organizations in Mississippi allowed SNCC and CORE to have a much greater influence than they could have had in other areas of the South. There was latitude to pursue new organizational forms and strategies. These case studies show how creative and consequential this period was in Mississippi.

TABLE 4.3 : Profile of Community Studies for Selected Variables

	Holmes	Madison	Bolivar
Movement			
Freedom Votes, 1963	1,000	500	1,000
Freedom Summer Volunteers and Staff	33	52	17
Freedom Votes, 1964	2,598	1,401	1,216
NAACP membership, 1966	353	377	—
MFDP leadership, 1965	5	2	2
Population Characteristics			
Urban, 1960 (%)	20.1	29.5	18.7
Total population, 1960	27,096	32,904	54,464
Black population, 1960	19,488	23,630	36,663
Black population, 1960 (%)	71.9	71.8	67.3
Black voting-age population, 1960	8,757	10,366	15,939
Black voting-age population, 1960 (%)	65.0	65.0	61.4
Registered black voters, 1960	41	607	612
Registered black voters, 1960 (%)	0.5	6.3	4.1
Income Characteristics			
Households with income below $3,000, 1959 (%)	72.0	64.3	69.0
Median income for nonwhite individuals, 1959 ($)	407	552	430
Median income for nonwhite families, 1959 ($)	895	1,106	1,198
Class Structure			
Nonwhite farm laborers, 1960 (%)	30.8	22.0	46.2
Nonwhite domestics, 1960 (%)	13.2	12.9	11.6
Nonwhite professionals, 1960 (%)	3.5	3.3	3.9
Nonwhite managers, 1960 (%)	1.0	1.0	1.7
Most vulnerable occupations, 1960 (%)	15.1	13.5	20.6
Least vulnerable occupations, 1960 (%)	15.6	24.8	13.4
Black farm owners (as % of black labor force), 1964	5.4	5.1	1.2
Landowner concentration, 1964 (%)	60.1	57.1	79.0
Farms operated by tenants, 1964 (%)	30.8	38.7	49.0
Repression			
Lynchings, 1889–1945	8	4	13
Klan organization, 1964	yes	yes	yes
Citizens' Council organization, 1956	yes	yes	yes

Grassroots Organizing and Efficacy in Holmes County

In the early 1960s, Holmes County developed one of the most successful local movements in Mississippi. Organizing began in 1963 when several local farmers went to nearby Greenwood in Leflore County to solicit help from SNCC workers. This initial group lived in or near Mileston, a small community in the Delta, with a very large proportion of black landowners. SNCC workers Sam Block and John Ball began holding citizenship classes in Mileston, and the movement expanded progressively throughout the county over the next few years. Holmes County and Mileston, in particular, have received considerable attention because of the strong local movement that developed in the county.

The high concentration of black farm owners in Mileston can be traced back to a New Deal land-redistribution program. Southern Democrats successfully blocked the extension of many New Deal programs to African Americans (Lieberman 1995; Quadagno 1994). However, in a small number of locales throughout the South, the Farm Security Administration (FSA) purchased land that it resold to black farmers. In Mileston the FSA "purchased five failing plantations . . . and sold the 9,580 acres of fertile land to 107 sharecropping families on long-term, low-interest mortgages" (MacLeod 1991; see also Salamon 1979). Given this history, the community was ideally situated to be the center of a county movement. Even limited landownership could provide insulation from white intimidation and harassment. The base of independent farmers was, according to Jay MacLeod, the "critical resource" for the genesis of the Holmes movement.[10] This was undoubtedly true. However, the transformation of resources into mobilization is a complex process, and a significant resource advantage does not lead necessarily to greater mobilization. If we calculate the number of black farm owners in 1964 as a proportion of the adult population (eighteen and over), Holmes County ranks thirtieth (with 5.5 percent) among Mississippi counties. In other words, landownership was not exceptionally high. Landownership, then, cannot by itself explain the presence or strength of a local movement. Nevertheless, black farm owners achieved almost mythic status in Holmes County. One Freedom Summer volunteer who was assigned to Holmes County wrote to his parents that 74 percent of the land in Holmes County was owned by blacks. If we assume that the average-sized farm was the same for blacks and whites (which they were not), then blacks would have owned almost 25 percent of the farmland in the county.[11] Why did farm owners play such a central role in Holmes County? Although the proportion of black farm ownership was not especially high in Holmes County, the social organization of landownership was unusual and important. The spatial concentration facilitated the growth of independent community institutions. This pattern stands in contrast to other counties where black farm owners would have been more widely dispersed and socially isolated. There is a broader lesson here that individual level resources are often less important than the social organization of resources as a basis for social movements.

The remarkable accomplishment in Holmes County was the diffusion of the movement beyond Mileston and the building of a broader county-wide movement. How, then, was this potential transformed into a viable movement in Holmes County?

Indigenous Organizing

Early organizing in Holmes County centered on voter registration. As in other movement counties, activists conducted citizenship classes and coordinated trips to the county courthouse in Lexington. A small group of fourteen registrants from the Mileston area went to the Lexington courthouse in April 1963. Nine days later one of those registrants, Reverend Nelson Trent, fled Holmes County after receiving death threats. According to T. C. Johnson, this "stopped a lot of the preachers." Following this first trip to the registrar, whites fired into the home of a local movement leader, Hartman Turnbow, in the middle of the night. Turnbow returned fire, and it was rumored that he injured one of his attackers. On the next day, civil rights workers investigating the scene, including Bob Moses, were arrested for arson—establishing this as one of the legendary events of the Mississippi movement. According to local police, movement activists orchestrated the harassment themselves.[12] So the movement in Holmes County faced considerable repression from its origin.

A key challenge for the early movement in Holmes County was generating an organizational presence throughout the county. Bernice Montgomery Johnson was one of the first activists from the eastern part of the county and remembers the diffusion process working as follows:

> Well, they were constantly trying to get new members. I remember when I first started going to Mileston, I encouraged the people in the community where I lived (which was Sunny Mount) to start having a meeting. . . .
> We were constantly going from community to community, from church to

church, asking people to allow us to come into your church. . . . "Set up a community meeting. Elect you some officers—a president, a secretary, a treasurer or what have you—designate a certain time for your community meeting."

By 1964 most of the small communities in the county held monthly meetings sponsored by the MFDP. Susan Lorenzi described a three-stage process used by the Holmes County movement in the early 1960s: "(1) opening up communities, (2) developing strong community organizations and leaders, and (3) developing strong ties between communities into a strong county Movement organization." Even the large statewide campaigns were used to build the local infrastructure of the movement. Mary Hightower described this process of organization building in Holmes County: "[Freedom Vote] did more than just demonstrate that people would vote; it like set up a permanent community activity or community contact; we didn't just use that to say . . . like in a lot of areas— take for instance Humphreys and other places—where people went out to demonstrate this and once that was over that was the end of that . . . and people organized from that."[13]

A community center in Mileston provided a key resource in the efforts to build an independent organization in Holmes County. The Holmes County Community Center, built by local volunteer labor and with financial backing from movement supporters in California, was opened in October 1964. The center served as a model for movements in nearby counties. Richard Jewett, a CORE activist in Madison County, wrote that the Mileston center was an "impressive physical structure" and that "inside one forgets that one is in rural Mississippi: it's that good." Through Freedom Summer, a temporary center was located in an empty building in Mileston, which operated a library and various meetings, classes, and programs. The support for the center led one Freedom Summer volunteer to complain that "we've had so many willing workers that I've been hard pressed to keep them busy." By the fall of 1966, the center boasted of its centrality in the local movement. Daisy Lewis, director of the center, reported:

> The building has been used for polling places for the FDP Freedom elections, check-in points for ASCS Cotton allotment [described below] for these and others. We have had candidates running for county offices, for U.S. representative and for Senator. To get more votes for them, meetings, workshops, voter education programs, etc. were held. In December 1964, we started a kindergarten school with about 50 enrolled.

The center went on to be used for Head Start programs, but the fact that there were movement-sponsored programs that predated the federally funded projects is important. Hence, when Head Start programs were initiated, movement veterans had experience and a movement-centered approach, which informed their efforts to shape the direction of Head Start and other poverty programs. At various points, the center also operated a health clinic that offered physical exams. Lewis commented that "the building has been used for meetings of every kind, sometimes every night of the week," as well as "recreation [such as] dancing, parties, etc., programs [such] as recitals, singing, etc."[14]

One noteworthy characteristic of this early period in the Holmes movement is the absence of public protest. There was little, if any, activity that would be considered protest, such as demonstrations, marches, or even boycotts. The groups applying for voter registration went in small groups, and most effort was placed on building movement organizations that operated as parallel institutions and provided a basis for later public challenges.

Countermobilization and Movement Response

Activists in Holmes County faced intimidation, harassment, arrests, and violent attacks during this early period. The threats and violence directed at the first group of voter registrants is the best known incident of a broader pattern. During Freedom Summer, Eugene Nelson, a volunteer, wrote to his parents that there was "no problem with the law here. . . . The most clear and present danger is, it seems, snakebites." However, two weeks later, recent events included "the bombed car, the pistol packing Whites at the local store, and the bombing attempt in the next town." These events did not seem to undermine the organizing work of the local movement. Nelson observed: "Particularly the bombing in Tchula [a town near Mileston] can only help: the man they did it to was not in the Movement, and it showed everyone that cowardice was no escape either."[15] This relationship between mobilization and violent repression is examined systematically below. Here, it is worth noting that in other settings scholars have found that repression directed toward nonparticipants is more likely to strengthen movement activity than violence toward movement participants (Brockett 1993).

Less violent forms of repression were used as well. In 1964 federal courts enforced a "freedom of choice" desegregation plan where parents could enroll their children in any school in the county. A very small number of parents acted on the new policy, and they were typically persons already involved in the movement. In Durant, a small town in the western part of the county, flyers were posted all over the town listing the names of thirty-two black parents enrolling their children in formally all-white schools. The farmers in the Mileston area who had engaged in economic transactions with the banks, cotton gins, and equipment suppliers in Holmes County were now forced to go outside the county to purchase and sell goods. Similar to other areas in the state, early organizing efforts were met with substantial harassment and violence.[16]

Repression in Holmes County was met fairly early with highly organized responses. For example, Mary Hightower, a local MFDP leader, remembered the following incident:

> [The Klan] attempted to burn a church that we were using as a community center. It's called Second Pilgrim's Rest Church. They threw firebombs in it, in the church, and we managed to put it out, you know, keep it from burning and we had to station something like five or six men there every night; they would stay every night; they would stay all night with guns to protect the church, and we did this for about five or six months . . . near the end of '64 and early '65.[17]

The organizational structure supported programmatic goals like citizenship classes, and it also allowed for a more effective response to repression.

Despite the movement's success in building organization in the midst of repression, there were no major inroads in the electoral arena. In 1964 civil rights activists attempted to gain access to the county nominating conventions of the Democratic Party. There were also frequent trips to the courthouse that added very few registered voters. The Justice Department filed a case against the county registrar in 1964. Even this added pressure did not facilitate gains in voter registration.

Consolidating the Grassroots Movement

Following the Voting Rights Act, voter registration was still a priority, but in the electoral arena more attention was given to mounting political campaigns and confronting new barriers to political participation. Organizing political campaigns and persuading black voters to support black candidates was a challenge foreshadowed by the Freedom Vote campaigns. However, local movements diversified their goals and strategies. Two major factors shaped this diversification: (1) statewide movement organizations became less influential in coordinating the efforts of local movements, leaving local activists in greater control; and

(2) changing features of the political context presented new strategic dilemmas to local movements such as the new forms of white resistance and federal poverty programs. Reflecting this shift, economic goals became increasingly important. Assessing future prospects for the Holmes County movement in May 1967, Henry Lorenzi claimed "that if the movement leaders do not figure out how to solve the economic problems of the poor on a long-range basis, then there is not much hope of our Movement continuing." Whether or not Lorenzi's prediction is entirely accurate, it reflects the growing urgency given to fundamental economic objectives.[18]

By 1967 Holmes County had a network of local movements that held monthly meetings in the small towns throughout the county. A county-wide MFDP organization held monthly meetings and was directed by an executive committee. Resources play a key role in facilitating the emergence of a movement; but as many scholars have pointed out, resources in and of themselves cannot explain the development and persistence of movements. In Holmes County, the central movement organization quickly became the Mississippi Freedom Democratic Party, and it began generating an independent set of resources. There were no significant alternative civil rights organizations to challenge the MFDP in Holmes County until 1966 when an NAACP chapter was formed followed by a Voter's League in 1967. By the time these organizations came on the scene, the MFDP dominated the county. The organizational dominance of the MFDP meant that there was no singular charismatic leader who carried the burden of the movement as was the case in some counties. This organizational coherence reduced factionalism in Holmes County, another problem that destroyed the effectiveness of some local movements. In other counties, movements revolved around a single charismatic leader. However, this left leaders vulnerable to fatigue or charges of self-serving objectives (such as personal fame or financial gain). In addition, movements built around a charismatic leader were more vulnerable because individual leaders could be isolated more easily and goals could shift based on personal and arbitrary decisions. Finally, the strong organizational infrastructure in Holmes County facilitated the coordination of collective action and, in the face of repression, provided a basis for effectively managing fear (Salamon and Van Evera 1973).

The Holmes County movement combined regular meetings and organized campaigns. Thus, the movement was able to minimize the effects of repression and, in some cases, use repression to the movement's advantage. Reverend Russell, one of the movement leaders, described the process: "We drilled our people before we came up to Lexington. Y'see, Holmes County was a bull with long horns goin' in the movement. The way they was keeping us from going to the Courthouse to redishter [register]. Most folks was afraid. We marched and we dehorned that bull. . . . After you dehorned him, he can't do nothing. Following that march we got more people to participate that was afraid. . . . So the march was a success." Mrs. Bee Jenkins, another local activist, recalled that one of the strategies for dealing with intimidation by the crowds of armed whites that gathered to watch the marches was stationing men along the edge of the march with guns who were "ready to shoot lead!"[19]

The Legacy of Small Successes

Over time, the movement developed an additional advantage—a legacy of past successes. The set of organizations and campaigns also developed organizational and tactical skills within the community. Mobilization is, in some cases, possible in the face of continued failure. However, a movement is unlikely to continue indefinitely without some evidence of its efficacy. By 1967 the Holmes County movement could point to a legitimate record of symbolic and substantive "successes." In terms of electoral politics, there had been a massive increase in voter registration jumping from twenty black registered voters in 1964 (up from six in 1963) to over sixty-three hundred in 1967 (over 70 percent of the black voting-age population). In addition, Holmes County had been extremely active in the 1965 Congressional Challenge, sending a hundred people to Washington to lobby in support of the MFDP. Although the MFDP's challenge failed, these statewide efforts allowed local activists to see their movement relative to other counties and to develop stronger lateral ties. Importantly, movement activists began running for office in the county's Agricultural Stabilization and Conservation (ASC) committee—an advisory board to the Department of Agriculture that controlled the system of crop allotments. Across the state, local movements attempted to mobilize for the ASC elections in the early 1960s. Their significance was clear: "The ASC board in each county decides how many acres of, say, cotton each farmer gets. When a white farmer applies for 500 acres and gets it and a Negro farmer applies for 30 acres and gets 10, the county ASC board did it." The ASC board also penalized farmers who planted above the imposed limits. In 1964 nine movement candidates ran for office and only one was elected. In 1965 a larger slate of thirty-seven candidates ran, with ten gaining positions on the ASC countywide committee.[20]

In other areas, the Holmes County movement could point to nine community centers that had been operating for several years and provided a place, in addition to the small number of supportive churches, for meetings, Head Start programs, literacy classes, and so on. There were also three poverty programs operating in Holmes County—two of which were under movement control and a third that had significant movement representation. Most counties had a single CAP board (a body that administered poverty programs) that was under white control, sometimes moderate and sometimes conservative.

Another important characteristic of the movement infrastructure was that it created multiple venues for leadership development. Lester Salamon (1972b) conducted field research in Holmes County in 1969. In the process, he estimated that there were approximately eight hundred formal positions of organizational leadership in the county held by six hundred different individuals.[21] These positions were not limited to political organizations, including economic cooperatives, health clinics, and education programs. Through the late 1960s, organizations proliferated to address more specialized social and economic objectives.

The movement achieved another "small victory" when MFDP lawyers complained to the school superintendent about the harassment of black students on the school bus by white students. The superintendent responded by firing the bus driver. In the fall of 1967, the movement launched a selective buying campaign. By early October, the chamber of commerce recommended to the mayor of Lexington that the city meet some of the demands of the boycott. This is certainly one of the first boycotts to win *any* concessions in Mississippi. In sum, between 1963 and 1967, the movement in Holmes County parlayed a series of incremental gains into a growing and dynamic organization. Ed Brown, one of the early SNCC/COFO workers in Holmes, remembered: "People weren't as afraid [in Holmes County]; people got reinforcement from each other as a result of having been part of an organizational effort . . . and didn't feel that they were kind of out there taking all the risks by themselves." Brown went on to explain part of the reason for the limited harassment in Holmes County: "It was a situation where as opposed to placing the emphasis on confrontational politics we had placed the emphasis on organizing so that in the instances where there were confrontations there was sufficient organizational strength behind it to make the whites think, you know, twice before doing anything."[22]

The structure of the county movement was a loosely coordinated confederation of community movements. This structure tapped into and expanded the repertoire of skills at the local level, and brought local activists into contact with state and national politics. The financial resources reflected this local structure. Some of the fund-raising strategies were collections at the monthly community meetings, plate dinners, and calling on churches to make set donations of, for example, $100 a year. There were also special events sometimes connected to political campaigns. In December 1967 the Holmes County Community Center held its annual meeting that included a "Big Raffle" in which the main prizes were a "Big Quilt" and a cow. The MFDP office was sustained by local collections; in 1966 "over $500 was raised . . . for its phone, rent, lights, some supplies." Local voluntary labor and leadership was the most crucial resource of the Holmes County movement, although there were also contributions from legal organizations and national civil rights organizations. For example, Jay MacLeod identifies "124 movement-related lawsuits" in Holmes County during the 1960s (1991, 16). Short-term donations came from around the country. In February 1965 an article appeared in the *San Francisco Chronicle* on the movement in Holmes County, and in the following two months $1,600 was donated by individuals in the Bay area. As Aldon Morris and others have found for the national movement, these types of external resources were the result rather than the cause of the movement's strength in Holmes County.[23]

These organizational developments and early achievements cannot be explained in any simple way by a more open political environment in Holmes County. In other words, the idea that lower repression in Holmes County allowed the movement to flourish is inaccurate. For example, police harassment and brutality was a very substantial problem for the Holmes movement. And violence against prominent movement activists occurred throughout the 1960s, starting with the initial attack on Hartman Turnbow's home. Throughout the 1960s, homes and churches were bombed, shot at, and had crosses burned in front of them to threaten local activists. As we will see, Holmes was less repressive than some counties, but the strong movement in the county helped to undermine the efficacy of white repression.[24]

By the 1967 elections, the MFDP in Holmes County referred to itself as a political machine (though one without a political boss). To this end, the MFDP had organized a system of block captains responsible for approximately fifteen voters each. Block captains were coordinated by a set of precinct captains. The county as a whole elected a fifteen-member executive committee. The MFDP used the fund-raising strategies noted above for the 1967 elections. At a special meeting in March 1967 to plan for the upcoming elections, the MFDP raised over $1,000. For the movement in Holmes County, the 1967 elections produced disappointment, much as it did throughout the state. With two exceptions, the slate of MFDP candidates lost in 1967. Robert Clark, one of the black candidates, was elected to the Mississippi legislature as the first black member since Reconstruction. Clark's victory was national news and helped consolidate the reputation of Holmes County as one of the strongest movement counties in Mississippi. As was the case with earlier battles in Holmes County, the partial victory in 1967 helped to minimize any internal doubts about the efficacy of the civil rights movement.[25]

Like all local movements in Mississippi, there was a growing concern about the economic problems facing the black community. A decisive question for the movement was whether to pursue economic goals through poverty programs or independent, movement-controlled programs. Lorenzi, a local organizer, concluded his 1967 assessment of the Holmes movement with a "warning about how important it is to consider who we decide to get help from. We must realize that *whoever gives us what we need*—money or technical assistance—*will probably determine how we grow and how independent we will be able to remain*" (emphasis in original). Within the poverty programs, local movements faced the problem of potential co-optation. Activists from the early days of the movement were concerned about the strings that might be attached to federal programs. A statement by the Holmes County Community Center Association suggests this dilemma:

> We believe that the Community Action Program should be organized to use local resources as much as possible. We should try to do everything we can here in Holmes County without the assistance of Washington. But in the event that we cannot by ourselves eliminate poverty in Holmes County, we should use every bit of help from Washington.

In the fall of 1966, Daisy Lewis, director of the community center, expressed a critical stance toward the developing CAP organization:

> CAP came into Holmes County unexpected before the poor Negro or poor white had the chance to take part in it or decide if it would help our county or not. . . . We still cant see how CAP is going to help the poor people at all, as long as its being run by the white power structure, right now a CDGM committee is in the process of trying to write up a proposal to try to get money to run our Headstart centers as a delegate agency through CAP.

Lewis had been chair of the county CAP advisory committee since March 1966. Particular concerns of local activists included the control of CAP boards by local whites, whether criteria (often educational) for hiring employees would disqualify many longtime movement activists from employment, and the regulation of political participation for program employees. For Holmes, there was the additional problem that a community action agency, Central Mississippi, Inc. (CMI), had been set in place for a six-county area including Holmes. While Holmes County could elect movement activists to its seats on the board of directors, the other counties serviced by the agency did not have strong local movements, if any.[26] Thus, the capacity of the Holmes County movement was diluted in CMI's administrative structure.

By the late 1960s, the Holmes County movement had made gains in the electoral and policy-making arena. These inroads did not lead to the rapid dissolution of the broad-based movement nor did Holmes County activists abandon the politics of protest. Boycotts and demonstrations were used in two major campaigns in the 1970s. The first, in 1973, focused primarily on employment discrimination by merchants in downtown Lexington, and a boycott in 1978 was prompted by a police brutality case and quickly expanded to encompass other demands.[27] These patterns will be even more striking when contrasted to the Madison and Bolivar cases.

Early Mobilization and the Consequences of Extended Repression: Madison County

Like Holmes County, the organizing groundwork for the civil rights movement in Madison County was laid in 1963. The project was directed by George Raymond, a young activist from the New Orleans chapter of CORE, and it was based in Canton, the largest town in the county. The movement in Madison County experienced a great deal of success (relative to other communities) and a great deal of repression in its early days. During the first summer, CORE workers focused primarily on voter registration through canvassing and meetings. The project in Canton benefited from the support of key local leaders and a relatively large, experienced, and committed staff. In August 1963 the four other staff members were Anne Moody, Jean Thompson, Barbara McNair, and Hezekiah Watkins. The size of the Canton project made it comparatively well staffed, and a significant amount of mobilization took place during this early period.[28]

Early Mobilization: Local Support and Voter Registration

In August 1963 Dave Dennis, the state director of CORE, wrote a letter to the national office reviewing the projects in Mississippi. Regarding Canton, Dennis wrote:

> We have a very unique program all to ourselves. We are working on several things in the community. The main project is voter registration where we have had much success. Along with that we are attempting to set up educational centers in the city where we can teach students and adults about local governments, how they can receive aid from the Federal Government on farm projects, trying to find means by which more aid can be given to people by the Welfare Department, set up a library where people can read and learn different things, have educational movies, and, of course, educate them in the importance of the movement. . . . We hope to make this county a "model" county.[29]

The Canton project was clearly the centerpiece of CORE's early work in Mississippi. The early success that Dennis refers to in voter registration was even noted by the *Madison County Herald*, in a front-page article titled "Steady Stream of Negroes Take Tests for Voter Qualification in County" on June 20, 1963. The article reported that "a group of about 25 Negroes walked into the Madison County Courthouse to register to vote Monday afternoon." Local whites were put on notice and reminded that "seven Negroes are among this week's additions to vote that is published weekly in this paper, as required by law."[30] During the first three weeks of the project, "75 people went to register and 25 of them passed the test."[31] The level of activity escalated in August, when, as Dennis reported, "we had 30 people to attempt to vote by affidavit because they felt they had been discriminated against. . . . In the next primary election, we held a 'Freedom Vote' election in which 2,274 Negroes in Madison County cast their ballots for their favorite candidates."[32] In addition to printing stories about increased black registrants, the local newspaper listed the names of new registrants, a mechanism that clearly facilitated various forms of intimidation and repression.

Along with these successes, the movement faced harassment and violence from the police and local whites. Madison County had a handful of local grassroots leaders who formed the backbone of the local movement, providing essential resources and insight into the workings of small-town Mississippi.[33] These leaders, like C. O. Chinn, experienced a barrage of harassment from local police. Annie Devine remembered: "They would put us in jail, they would pass by the freedom house and throw molotov cocktails on the porch, they would burn the churches, they did some of everything."[34] A standard tactic involved local police positioned outside meetings recording license plates and, at times, turning people away from meetings. White resistance from law enforcement officials and private citizens in Madison County was especially violent.[35] For example, a local gas station owner fired at a group of five young people leaving a voter registration meeting in June 1963.[36] Following this incident, there was a sharp drop in participation by teenagers, who had been doing the bulk of voter canvassing and were the largest group attending meetings (Moody 1968, 292–97).

Movement Tactics: Community Organizing and Local Boycotts

Community organizing was a tactical device and primary goal of the Mississippi civil rights movement. Voter canvassing, citizenship classes, freedom schools, and mass meetings were all strategies employed to mobilize people by creating new avenues for political participation. Community organizing included a wide range of specific campaigns—events or clusters of events; these campaigns were designed to heighten conflict, demonstrate solidarity and injustices, or force concessions from power holders, whether local, regional, or national. In this area, the Madison movement resembled the work of SNCC and CORE projects throughout Mississippi. The Freedom Vote elections represented this dual strategic focus on building capacity and creating political leverage.[37]

While the Freedom Vote was important, its effects on local movements were probably less enduring than the effects of the campaigns that developed out of the local civil rights movement. In his pivotal analysis of the civil rights movement, Aldon Morris (1984) makes a compelling argument that to understand the movement we must take an indigenous perspective by looking at "local movement centers." The civil rights movement is best known and received enormous attention for the innovation of new protest tactics—sit-ins and Freedom Rides being classic examples. However, the tactical workhorse of black protest before and during the civil rights movement was the boycott elevated to the level of a broader campaign that included an extensive set of demands, mass meetings, marches, and demonstrations. Within local movements, direct-action tactics were employed most often in the context of a broader campaign built on the foundation of a boycott.

Through the summer and fall of 1963, the project workers in Madison County focused on mobilizing the local community by building solid movement support. This organizing formed the basis for a boycott that was initiated in December 1963 and gained momentum in the early part of 1964. The boycott is an important moment in Madison County's history, and it reveals the tactical and organizational form of the local movement and the organized white resistance during the early period of the Mississippi movement. During this phase, "heavily attended mass meetings" generated the organizational mechanism for sustaining the challenge.[38] Demonstrations took place beginning in February 1964, when the Madison County movement launched a major campaign, including a set of three "Freedom Days," which combined a rally, a march, and mass voter registration. The campaigns grew directly out of the prior organizing of the Madison County movement. The first Freedom Day produced a large turnout, an estimated crowd of 350 attempting to register, as well as a large contingent of police. However, only five were allowed to take the voter registration test by Foote Campbell, the local registrar. This delaying tactic was a standard part of the repertoire of Mississippi registrars. In describing the campaign, Claude Sitton noted in the *New York Times* that Campbell's office had "a red, blue, and gray sticker bearing a Confederate battle flag and the message 'Support Your Citizens' Council.'" Campbell was especially notorious for keeping a pistol on top of the filing cabinet in the registrar's office, demonstrating the deep resistance to the movement in Madison County.[39]

Approaching the first Freedom Day, attendance at mass meetings ranged between two hundred and three hundred.[40] Initially, the movement targeted eighteen white-owned stores, and the *Mississippi Free Press*, a statewide movement newspaper, estimated that the campaign was 75 percent effective.[41] The Monday following the Freedom Day, 2,625 students launched a boycott at the junior and senior high schools, protesting a wide range of conditions. A letter to the superintendent of schools delineated thirteen grievances, including limited resources, curriculum, and overcrowding.[42] On Wednesday morning, local police led by Sheriff Jack Cauthen raided the Freedom House. Twelve leaders were arrested and spent the day being questioned regarding their involvement in the school boycott. Only two individuals were actually charged at the end of the day.[43]

The week following the first Freedom Day was especially intense, as each side carefully scrutinized the actions of the other to determine the most appropriate strategy. The evening of the Freedom Day, a large mass meeting was held at Asbury Methodist Church with over two hundred in attendance. Mass meetings were held throughout the county during the week. On the next day, a smaller group of fifty lined up to take the voter registration test, and only two persons were allowed to take the exam. That night "a police car cruised through the Negro areas . . . announcing over a loudspeaker that Canton Mayor L. Stanley Matthews had called a 10 PM curfew for all citizens and that anyone on the streets after that time would be picked up for questioning."[44]

The Madison movement presented boycott demands in the form of a petition to the mayor and the Board of Aldermen, including the following eleven demands:

1. Improving Negro registration in the county and the treatment afforded Negroes by the registrar;
2. Eliminating police brutality and prosecuting policemen involved in it;
3. Zoning schools to better protect black children;
4. Improving the public sidewalks in the Negro sections;
5. Hiring Negroes in city government on a non-discriminatory basis;
6. Removing all segregation signs from public facilities;
7. Desegregating all public facilities;
8. Improving housing conditions;
9. Hiring Negroes on the Canton Police Force, selected in consultation with the Madison County Movement;
10. Forming a bi-racial committee to discuss improving race relations;
11. Integrating the Chamber of Commerce to represent all the people, not just a minority.[45]

Many of these demands would emerge again during the 1970s and 1980s, as blacks in Madison County continued to struggle for many of these same goals. In many areas throughout the South, whites would have responded to a list of demands like this selectively during this period. For example, a typical response was the formation of a "biracial committee" that would investigate issues of race relations.[46] This type of response was largely symbolic, but even symbolic concessions were thwarted in Mississippi. This response would not occur in Madison County until a boycott in 1978. In the early 1960s, the official and nonofficial response was repression.

Intense Repression during the Early Phase of the Movement

In the report to incoming Freedom Summer volunteers, COFO described Madison County as "an extremely strong Citizens' Council town" where "[harassment] is particularly intense from law enforcement officials seemingly directed at local citizens." COFO added that "there has been consistent use of economic reprisals; very severe." Madison County whites began preparation before any of the Freedom Days took place. The day before the first mass registration drive, the *Madison County Herald* reported that "more than 300 people crowded the county courthouse courtroom on Tuesday night in the third such recent meeting for the reorganization of the Canton White Citizens' Council." In a deposition, SNCC worker Michael Slayer reported that "within days all downtown white-owned stores sported Citizens' Council stickers on their doors and windows." The reorganized council included leaders from all sectors of the community, including the state senator from Madison County, the mayor of Canton, the city attorney, the sheriff, the tax collector, ministers, and executives from several banks and major businesses. Slayer, who wrote a broader report on the Citizens' Council, described the Madison organization as a model of success.[47]

The Citizens' Council or its members employed a number of strategies to counter the threat posed by the Madison County movement. Representing the "legalistic" approach of the council, Edward Henry, state senator from Madison County, introduced legislation outlawing economic boycotts and associated activities like picketing and leafleting. At the local level, an ordinance was passed "prohibiting the distribution of literature without a permit."[48] Police continued the tactic of monitoring movement meetings. In the words of one local activist, "The police are always gathering around the church where the mass meetings are being held. After the meeting we found out that they had placed tickets on all the cars . . . and [they] took pictures to make people afraid for their jobs."[49]

Indirect tactics included pressuring black businessmen. For example, a black owner of a small grocery store reported that "the Packing Companies have told me that under these conditions [the selective buying campaign] they would be unable to deliver goods to my store." The *Mississippi Free Press* also reported that "on January 30, police halted operations of all Negro cabs, claiming that their permits were faulty."[50] George Washington, a local business owner and movement supporter, became the target of similar pressure. After refusing to comply with white demands that he withdraw support from the movement, a local oil supplier removed the pumps at his gasoline station. Distributors also refused to deliver groceries to his store and ultimately his property was bombed. The morning following the bombing, Washington was arrested for "failing to report the bombing." The persistence of the Madison movement in this context is remarkable. However, over the long haul, repression took its toll on the movement.[51]

In the early 1960s, Madison and Holmes counties were sites of major organizing campaigns and voter registration drives well before Freedom Summer. Because of this early strength, both communities had large projects during Freedom Summer—thirty-three volunteers and staff in Holmes and fifty-two in Madison. Both communities faced substantial repression, though Madison's was clearly far more severe. David Colby has compiled an index of violent incidents from movement sources and newspaper accounts; he recorded thirty-two incidents in Madison County where civil rights activists had been assaulted, in contrast to six in nearby Holmes County. During Freedom Summer, a total of nine churches were burned in Madison County.[52] As we will see below, repression was sustained in Madison County, and violence routinely accompanied elections in the post–Voting Rights Act period.

In the Madison case, a full range of repressive mechanisms was deployed. The most blatant and the most noted form of repression was violence directed toward the movement and its participants. White resistance could also be activated by using the leverage built into the system of racial inequality. The threat of losing one's job was a barrier that local organizers always faced, and it was most effective for groups who were economically vulnerable. Those counties with high proportions of the black labor force employed in "vulnerable occupations" were obvious targets for the use of economic intimidation (Salamon and Van Evera 1973). A final set of repressive mechanisms was the institutional rules and procedures that white Mississippians instituted or activated to resist the Mississippi movement and its goals, such as laws to prevent picketing and leafleting.

Factionalism in Madison County

Many of the problems in Madison County derived from the effects of repression, yet there were broader organizational problems that affected the Madison movement. These problems may have been exacerbated by the intensity of repression, but they had other sources as well. One of the major hurdles faced by local movements was managing the organizational expansion that accompanied Freedom Summer.

The Freedom Summer campaign impacted the trajectory of the civil rights movement in important ways. Within the Mississippi movement,

Freedom Summer played a complex role. In some locales, strong movement preceded Freedom Summer and persisted long after. This was the case in Holmes County, where volunteers worked within existing programs. In other communities, the problem of bringing a large number of new workers into the program seems to have overwhelmed local projects, resulting in intense internal conflicts and diminishing effectiveness—exactly the fears that some Mississippi activists had expressed prior to the project. Holmes County had some internal feuds over the appropriate role of white volunteers, especially short-term volunteers, but those conflicts were minimal when compared to the factionalism that took place during and after Freedom Summer in Madison County.[53]

The contradictory and complex effects of Freedom Summer are also connected to the events during the Atlantic City Challenge at the Democratic National Convention. The fallout from Freedom Summer and the defeat of the MFDP in Atlantic City have led many observers to define this period as the endpoint of the Mississippi movement. In all three of my cases, local movements were faced with new challenges and perhaps a different political context following Freedom Summer. However, it would be grossly inaccurate to assume that local movements uniformly collapsed under the pressure of these challenges.[54]

In the fall of 1964, the Madison County movement focused on two major programs—the upcoming ASC elections and the Freedom Schools. One report noted that "every staff person and every source of energy [in Madison] has been channeled to the ASC election." A consistent and successful component of many projects was the Freedom School. In Madison the movement operated a "combination roving and stationary freedom school. Two nights a week, freedom school is held in Canton at the community center, and the other nights are divided up in visiting the other rural areas."[55]

Unlike many of the projects, Madison reported no grievances to COFO concerning resources. This is probably because of the movement's ties to CORE, which had greater financial resources than SNCC. In the fall, six staff members received checks from the national CORE organization plus three more staff members received "subsistence" from Mississippi CORE. In contrast, the Holmes County report began: "SNCC has not been paying much of the time. The budget is insufficient. Survival has come from private resources—friends, family, etc."[56] However, problems with resources were not a useful indicator of the overall organizational problems facing the local movement. Through late 1964 and early 1965, activists in Madison County spent many meetings addressing internal problems.[57]

Factionalism was not limited to questions of white participation in voter registration drives. Poverty programs were also a source of major conflict as "C.O. Chinn and George Raymond, those two staunch allies in the Canton voting struggle, became enemies in the late 1960s over their competition for a Head Start job" (Dent 1997, 350). These battles became much broader. Jewel Williams, a black member of the Canton Board of Aldermen, described the scene: "No one seems to be able to ride over it; you're either in one camp or the other. Our trouble really began . . . way back in the sixties with the competition for Head Start jobs" (quoted in Dent 1997, 350).

New (and Old) Forms of Repression

In Madison County, the history of electoral politics illustrates a wide range of voter intimidation and manipulation. These tactics were employed in the 1964 ASC elections, where election observers were threatened, harassed, and arrested. Groups of whites gathered around one polling place and pelted election observers with rocks. The polling official asked one black voter whether he wanted to go to jail when he approached the polling place. The violence was severe enough that the Justice Department held special hearings in Madison County concerning the elections and the complicity of county and city "law enforcement." The Department of Agriculture required reelections in two of the eight districts. In the second election, the movement faced new strategies of resistance; "the tactics used by the white community demonstrates a second level attack—completely within the rule of the [Department of Agriculture] handbook and yet so organized as to split the Negro vote." New black candidates appeared on the ballots. The movement quickly regrouped, arguing that the new candidates had been handpicked by whites and were being used to divide the black vote. At the last minute, the Madison County movement tried to stage a boycott on the grounds that a low turnout would invalidate the elections. Ultimately, the movement-affiliated candidates lost the 1964 election in Madison County.[58] This pattern is in contrast to the Holmes County movement, which demonstrated extensive if incomplete victories, and in Madison County the pattern was replicated in other venues, including, for example, poverty programs. Here, we see what became a common pattern in Madison County—whites employing a broad range of tactics to undermine movement efforts. Further, this period in Madison saw substantial deterioration in the internal relations among staff members. Conflicts erupted over the status of white civil rights workers in the movement, and leaders began accusing each other of mishandling funds.

In early campaigns, many voters came to the polls only to find themselves not listed in the registration books. The obvious countertactic for the movement was having poll watchers from the movement assigned to each polling station. However, this was resisted, and in some cases poll watchers were denied entry when they arrived for their shifts. For example, during the 1966 elections, poll watchers at the Camden precinct in Madison County were told they would have to stand thirty feet from the polling place. In other polling places in Madison County, poll watchers were forced to leave during the tabulation of ballots, making their presence irrelevant. The range of resistance tactics employed to dilute the black vote was quite broad. For example, in 1971 poll books and ballots were taken to white voters who could not leave their homes; in addition, eight poll watchers were arrested and another beaten over the course of the day. James Loewen's illustration of voter manipulation where white poll watchers "helped" black voters in 1971 (described in chapter 2) took place in Madison County.[59]

These direct efforts to undermine black voting buttressed the institutional mechanisms employed in Madison County. Canton, for example, was one of the first municipalities to switch its city council system from a "ward" to an "at-large" system, making it more difficult for black candidates to win elections. Through the 1970s and into the 1980s, Canton used annexations to increase the white population in the city as another strategy to limit black electoral gains.[60]

"Nothing We Can Brag About": The Enduring Effects of Repression

Over time, initial enthusiasm and high turnout by black voters gave way to greater frustration and declining organizational presence. In this context, Annie Devine described the long-term consequences: "So we forgot about many more things that were vitally important—we forgot it was important to still try to keep registered to vote—we forgot that—so we said you know what's the need of all that . . . we have less people voting now than we had in '68 or '72 on like that. . . ."[61] In short, the extensive repression in Madison meant that the local movement was unable to generate a cumulative pattern of small victories. In contrast to Holmes County, the organizational capacity for broad campaigns declined.

While mass-based strategies declined, litigation is the one strategy that was sustained in Madison County. In fact, litigation was employed in a variety of creative ways through the 1970s. Multiple cases were launched challenging employment discrimination by the city of Canton and discrimination in the distribution of public services. Given the barriers facing black candidates and fiscal and institutional constraints once in office, movements often pursued an alternative "route" to the same goal, using litigation to force white elected officials to use funds for streetlights, fire hydrants, water lines, paved roads, and other services in black communities. The same strategy was used to attack discrimination in public employment at the municipal, county, and state level.[62]

Nevertheless, the end result of repression in Madison County was a largely retrenched movement—the two dominant organizations by the late 1960s and early 1970s were the NAACP and a local organization called Madison County Union for Progress (MCUP). The NAACP's major tactic was litigation to combat problems of redistricting and to force the equitable distribution of municipal and county resources. For example, through the early 1970s, suits were brought against the city of Canton for discrimination in the hiring in the police and fire departments. A broader suit was initiated against the city concerning public services such as street lighting, paving, fire hydrants, and plumbing. The suit documented massive discrimination in the distribution of each of these services. In the mid-1970s, Annie Devine captured the local sense that there were few tangible gains ". . . not for the struggle and effort that's been put into very little gain." She added that "politically we don't have anything going for us . . . nothing we can brag about."[63]

Local Mobilization Targeting Rural Poverty: Bolivar County

Bolivar County is an intriguing case and alongside Holmes County provides a portrait of the dilemmas faced in the Mississippi Delta. Bolivar sits in the center of the Mississippi Delta, and historically the county was a classic example of the "plantation economy."[64] By the 1960s that economy was rapidly changing with the mechanization of farming. These economic changes defined the emerging movement in Bolivar in three important ways. First, addressing the consequences of these economic changes preoccupied movement activists more than was the case in Holmes or Madison. Second, the economic dislocations created a difficult context in which a strong countywide movement never developed; instead, localism predominated with strong but generally more sporadic campaigns in the small towns throughout the county. Third, these factors made violent repression less common in Bolivar; instead, economic reprisals or the fear of those reprisals undermined the overall capacity of the movement.

Limited Organizing in the Early 1960s

Cleveland, the county seat of Bolivar County, was the home of Amzie Moore, an NAACP leader and hero of the early movement. Moore was the initial link between Bob Moses and the network of NAACP leaders throughout the state. Moore's strength was not only at the state level. In the 1950s he had organized a very strong NAACP organization in Cleveland (Payne 1995). Given this base, it is somewhat surprising that Cleveland and Bolivar County did not participate more heavily during the early 1960s.

A number of short-lived campaigns were initiated in Bolivar County. However, in comparison to Holmes and Madison counties, Bolivar is notable for the lack of sustained countywide organization during the early phase of the movement before Freedom Summer. Reverend Owen Brooks, a staff member of the Delta Ministry, worked for several years in Bolivar County. In late 1965 his assessments of the various movement activities in the county suggested disarray in almost all areas. The county MFDP "lacked cohesion and direction," and the NAACP was "non-existent." Churches "have been closed to any movement activity" with few exceptions, and there was a "small and extremely weak Mississippi Student Union"—a statewide organization for high school students. A voter registration drive during the summer "never got underway . . . due to the very poor county leadership," and efforts to distribute food and clothing were "rather unsuccessful." The most positive assessments were reserved for the Mississippi Farm Labor Union (described below); the Bolivar County Improvement Association, which was attempting to organize farm co-ops; and the Head Start projects, which were "considered a success locally."[65]

During Freedom Summer, volunteers were sent to a handful of communities in Bolivar County, including Shaw in the southern part of the county and Rosedale and Mound Bayou in the northern area. The project in Shaw had the most sustained activity during this period. Following Freedom Summer, the project report from the Bolivar projects in Mound Bayou and Winstonville exhibited serious problems. Each project was staffed by one person, John Bradford in Mound Bayou and Larry

Archibald in Winstonville. Bradford's brief report documented little about the program in Mound Bayou. Instead, he expressed extreme frustration with the Jackson office, stating:

> We get little or no cooperation from the Office in Jackson. It has become impossible for us to operate on these bases and we don't intend to try it any more—you have stood us up waiting for you to do things that you said you would do and behold, they never get done. . . . I am afraid the next picket line will be the project directors in front of the Jackson Office.

Few reports were as scathing as Bradford's, though many expressed similar frustrations. Archibald's critique was focused on local staff, namely, Bradford, pointing out that neither information nor finances flowed into his project. Like many project directors, Archibald expressed his hope that "there would be some way to increase the budget so that we don't have to depend on undependable checks from the North."[66]

The Shaw project developed quickly into the strongest local movement in the county. The centerpiece of the project was the community center, which became the base for an active Freedom School and a large library. The greater level of activity in Shaw was demonstrated at the first major protest event in Bolivar, a Freedom Day, which was held on July 16 in Cleveland. A group of thirty-nine people attempted to register (twenty-five were able to take the test) while thirty-five students marched in front of the courthouse. The vast majority of the Freedom Day participants came from Shaw, with a few coming from Mound Bayou and Cleveland. The low number of registrants reflects the local policy of only admitting two people into the registrar's office at one time. Only six persons registered between 10:00 and 12:00, then the office closed for lunch; another nineteen persons registered between 1:00 and 5:00. The movement reported no harassment inside or outside the courthouse. Overall, there was no violence associated with the Freedom Day and none of the blatant intimidation that was common in Madison County.[67]

The major barrier faced by the Shaw movement was the severe economic conditions of the Mississippi Delta. There were occasional threats or incidents of violence as well as police harassment. However, this type of repression was limited in comparison to other parts of the state. In contrast, poverty became an institutional barrier and a point of strategic leverage used by whites. Some volunteers were surprised to find that schools for black children closed during cotton-picking season, from September to November. In this context, local blacks were particularly vulnerable to economic reprisal. Bonnie Guy, a summer volunteer, reported that two local men had "lost their jobs for housing summer volunteers."[68]

With a staff of four, the project in Shaw sustained many of its activities through the fall. The Freedom School continued to run a program for ten to fifteen adults every morning and had informal activities for children after school. At night, citizenship classes were held in three different locations with an estimated total of seventy-four students. This organizing work generated some small steps. For example, a group met with the mayor of Shaw to demand streetlights in the black community. Small groups continued to travel to Cleveland for voter registration, and a small sewing cooperative was formed. However, voter registration efforts suffered in Shaw because of limited transportation.[69] In the spring of 1965, community organizing sustained further projects in Shaw. A new community center in the "Promised Land" section of Shaw was completed, and a group of twenty-five students integrated a local theater. Though voter registration seemed to have dropped off, the Freedom School classes for adults were "ripping along," meeting five times a week even though staff members only attended two or three times a week. During this period, local leaders became increasingly autonomous of the SNCC/COFO organizers and took the initiative in key areas. This independence is indicated by the active participation in Freedom Schools, where early plans for a strike by cotton choppers were formed.[70] Other protests punctuated the Shaw movement in the fall of 1964, including a local school boycott and the statewide Freedom Vote. As the above discussion suggests, Shaw had a very active, ambitious, and creative movement in this period during and after Freedom Summer.

The Pursuit of Economic Justice: Indigenous Organizations and Federal Policies

In April 1965 the Mississippi Freedom Labor Union (MFLU) emerged out of the Shaw movement, becoming one of the first Mississippi organizations to explicitly address economic issues as a primary focus. The MFLU faced an uphill battle from the start by calling a strike during a period in which many Delta farms were switching to mechanized cotton pickers. The MFLU gained national attention when it pursued a strategy of stopping the trucks delivering farm laborers to the fields by blocking the roads. From its original base in Shaw, efforts were made to organize farm laborers in other parts of the state. The event most associated with the MFLU was a strike on the Andrews plantation in Tribett in nearby Washington County. After farm laborers were evicted from their homes, they attempted to take over an empty set of barracks at the Greenville Air Force Base. This led eventually to their eviction following a substantial amount of mobilization and national media attention.[71]

In Bolivar and Holmes counties, the largest town was the most difficult to mobilize. For example, the MFDP held an outdoor meeting in Cleveland in February 1965 because of its difficulty in finding an organization that would allow the movement to meet in its building. According to COFO, "the police chief and other whites have pressured ministers and Masons not to allow use of their buildings for meetings, threatening cancellation of insurance and refusal of a building loan."[72]

While the effort to develop a countywide movement was limited in Bolivar, the opportunities presented by the War on Poverty saw increased activity throughout the county. Given the history of the Child Development Group of Mississippi (CDGM) at the state level, we can better understand the development of two competing CAPS in Bolivar County.[73] The first federally funded Office of Economic Opportunity (OEO) programs in Bolivar County were Head Start centers operated by CDGM. As was the case in Holmes and Madison counties, the local movement was caught off guard when a local community action program was formed in 1965. These initial efforts included the mayor of Mound Bayou, but the agency was primarily directed by local whites, including "several planters" and two members of the County Board of Supervisors. The first grant was for a Neighborhood Youth Corps in December 1965, which was followed by a grant for a Head Start program to be operated year-round throughout the county beginning June 1966. Simultaneously, an all-black organization, the Association of Communities of Bolivar County (ACBC), was formed that had greater movement participation and was built on the organizational infrastructure of CDGM.[74]

Overlapping Arenas of Struggle: Schools, Politics, and Poverty

While litigation and electoral campaigns played increasingly important roles in the Mississippi movement, local insurgent tactics persisted. We can see this continuity by looking at a large-scale boycott in Shelby, a small town in Bolivar County. The Shelby boycott also shows the overlapping nature of movement struggles in which movements advanced a set of demands aimed at the quality and control of schools, access to electoral politics, and meaningful economic opportunities for local blacks.

In the late 1960s, a boycott that began in the all-black schools extended to the town itself and launched the political careers of two black elected officials. Black students in Mississippi employed boycotts on a fairly regular basis through the 1960s and 1970s as a way of drawing attention to systematic inequalities. There was a brief school boycott in the spring of 1967, after Joseph Delaney, a history teacher, was fired by the principal of the black high school. In addition to the reinstatement of Delaney, who was involved in civil rights activity, the student boycott petitioned for the removal of Williams (the principal who was considered an Uncle Tom), a free lunch program, and "a special summer session dealing with both academic and cultural education." Williams did resign in April and was rehired as a curriculum coordinator, and Delaney's contract was renewed. Through the summer and fall of 1967, movement activity continued, including an investigation of school deficiencies and spending of Title I funds. Through the fall, the Shelby movement provided the momentum for Kermit Stanton's campaign in the county supervisor elections. Stanton's victory was one of the most important in the 1967 elections. Supervisor positions were the most powerful county-level offices in Mississippi, and Stanton was one of four candidates to win the position in Mississippi in 1967.

In the spring, local and national events coincided, providing the critical juncture out of which a large-scale boycott emerged in Shelby. On April 4, Eddie Lucas, principal of the elementary school and a local movement leader who had managed Stanton's election, was "informed that [his] contract would not be renewed." In addition, two other teachers did not have their contracts renewed for the upcoming school year. On that same day, Martin Luther King was assassinated in Memphis, a relatively short distance from Shelby. On April 9, students at the high school "requested [a] memorial service for Martin Luther King, Jr." The request was denied, prompting a walkout of approximately three hundred students. In early May the boycott was extended to local merchants, and demands were expanded. The city responded with an 8:30 curfew and a mayor's proclamation prohibiting groups of five or more persons to congregate in Shelby. In early May the *Delta Democrat Times* reported that a thousand of the approximately eleven hundred students at Broad Street elementary and high schools were boycotting. In addition, twenty of the thirty-one teachers at the elementary school were participating in the boycott. The Shelby school boycott was not a purely spontaneous outburst but grew out of long-standing grievances and organization. A parent group, the Shelby Educational Committee (SEC), and a student organization had made efforts to have problems addressed through meetings with administrators and school board members. Local leaders circulated a petition supporting the students and articulating demands for school reform that included signatures by more than five hundred adults. The boycott reflected the prevailing analysis of local power relations— that merchants and planters controlled all community institutions. Students confronted the Mississippi lieutenant governor at a ceremony in Mound Bayou, presenting him with a list of demands. By late May the demands had broadened, including

1. Hire black people at Griffin Lamp Company.
2. Use Courtesy titles for people at places of business.
3. Open and equal service at places that are open for business (Joe's Steak House and Frank's Grill).
4. Paved Streets, Stop Signs, and Sewerage Systems in Williams Additions (Negro).
5. Representation on Board of Alderman and School Board.
6. Contracts for Mr. Joseph Delaney and Mr. Eddie Lucas that will include principalship of the school.
7. More employment in the schools and banks.

In a statement to local merchants, the SEC explained:

> This is to serve notice that the "selective buying campaign" being conducted in Shelby is not directed at you, solely. However, we do solicit your support in our efforts to negotiate with the school board for the renewal of our teacher's contracts. These people were customers of yours. Their salaries constituted a sizable part of your income. You owe them your support.

Local whites were resistant to the overall goals of the boycott and used nonviolent or legalistic strategies to confront the boycott, including the curfew. In federal court, two city ordinances enforcing the curfew and a proclamation allowing the police to break up meetings of five or more persons were struck down by Judge William Keady on May 28, 1968. In a countercomplaint, the city sought an injunction against the boycott. Despite some willingness to negotiate through a biracial committee, the boycott continued into the fall of 1968. Simultaneously, Senator James Eastland from nearby Sunflower County pushed an investigation of boycott leaders who were employed by OEO. In its own investigation, OEO determined that the leaders were not actually OEO employees but worked for local organizations that received some OEO grant support.[75]

Ultimately, a member of the Board of Aldermen decided to resign, leaving a vacancy that would be filled by a black candidate in a special election. The candidate was Robert Gray, a teacher, movement leader, and participant in an economic development project in Mound Bayou. Gray's election in 1968 made him the first black person elected to municipal government in Mississippi since Reconstruction (outside of Mound Bayou), and he went on to be elected mayor in 1976. The Shelby boycott illustrates the complex nature of local movement activity. Local activists pursued an expansive set of goals, initially focusing on the quality of schools and an effort to protect local leaders. The movement used what it viewed to be its most efficacious tactic—the economic boycott—to pursue an even broader agenda of change in local schools, employment, political office holding, and even the racist forms of social interaction in public settings. Beyond the election of Gray and the development of parent and student organizations, the movement linked local activists to national organizations like the Delta Ministry. An overlapping development in Shelby was the formation of the North Bolivar County Farm Cooperative (NBCFC).[76]

Like the Mississippi Farm Labor Union, the NBCFC was another organization emerging out of the Delta's Bolivar County that attempted to deal with the problems of employment and subsistence. The North Bolivar Co-op is worth serious examination because of its connection to the local movement in Bolivar and its relative success as a model of movement-sponsored economic development, surviving until the late 1970s. An advisory report and review of the organization stated that "few co-ops in the country have accomplished as much as this one has in so short a period of time." The report went on to document the accomplishments of the first two years, including a membership base of 956 families, 457 acres of cultivated land (the majority was used for vegetables), production of 450,000 tons of food during its first year and 620,000 tons during its second year, and employment for over 300 persons. OEO grants helped get the NBCFC off the ground in 1966. As federal funds became increasingly sparse, private funds helped keep the organization operating, in particular, groups from Boston, Massachusetts, and Madison, Wisconsin. In its earliest days, the co-op emerged under the sponsorship of the Tufts Delta Health Center (DHC), an OEO project in Mound Bayou.[77] The co-op was located in Shelby, and its organizational apparatus and leadership overlapped with that of the local movement, especially the Shelby Educational Committee. In short, the cooperative indicates the prominence of economic objectives and the role played by movement initiatives in addressing those needs. Moreover, the persistence of this organization through the 1970s illustrates the divergence of national and local movement trajectories.[78]

Comparing Holmes, Madison, and Bolivar Counties

The divergent histories of Holmes, Madison, and Bolivar counties illustrate the processes of movement consolidation in the former case and fragmented or sporadic movements in the latter cases. Across the cases, early movement activity is associated with high levels of repression, which had long-term negative effects on the movement. In Madison County, repression predominates, undermining the organizational capacity of the movement and its ability to generate major indicators of movement efficacy. In Holmes County, organization building predominates, resulting in a sustained organizational presence and significant electoral power. Adding a further contrast, Bolivar County shows that even without violent repression, emerging movements face substantial obstacles in their efforts to coordinate a countywide movement. Holmes provides the clearest model of an efficacious movement. Despite their organizational difficulties, the Madison and Bolivar movements did have enduring impacts at the local level. In Bolivar the local movement was able to exercise some control over local poverty programs that brought much-needed employment and services to the county. In Madison the NAACP became increasingly effective at using litigation against the city of Canton and the county, resulting in the redistribution of some public services and employment.

This chapter has shown how movement infrastructures emerged and developed within Mississippi communities. This process involved the long-term development of organizations, the emergence of local leadership capacity, and the mobilization of new networks and resources in support of movement efforts. The building of movement infrastructures was shaped by the interaction between the movement, countermobilization, local authorities, and the broader social and economic characteristics of a community. These patterns have long-term consequences, reflected in the patterns of change in electoral politics, social policies, and school desegregation, as we will see in the following chapters.

CHAPTER FIVE

The Struggle for Political Power

IN THIS chapter, I examine the efforts of the Mississippi civil rights movement to develop political power from the period of widespread mobilization in the early 1960s through the early 1970s. The centerpiece of early civil rights organizing was electoral empowerment through voter registration, so it is appropriate to begin by investigating the impact of the movement in this domain. To frame this research, I assess debates about the Voting Rights Act and the enfranchisement of black southerners. The dominant view holds that the Voting Rights Act enfranchised black southerners. Critics have pointed to the important role of group mobilization in determining the amount and timing of electoral change. In Mississippi increases in black political participation were shaped by the combined effect of the Voting Rights Act, which determined the timing of change, and local mobilization, which shaped the level of electoral participation across communities.

From these debates, I turn to Holmes County to present a detailed account of the efforts to participate in electoral politics and the obstacles faced by local movements. After the close analysis of Holmes County, I step back to determine the impact of the early civil rights movement on the later forms of participation in electoral politics. I track the Mississippi case chronologically, beginning with the early efforts to register voters before the Voting Rights Act. Following the Voting Rights Act, I examine voter registration, voter turnout, and the early campaigns by black candidates.

From Protest to Politics

The Voting Rights Act is widely considered one of the most successful pieces of legislation in American history and an important indicator of the movement's success. Typically, arguments about the impact of the civil rights movement have focused on the movement's contribution to passage of the Voting Rights Act. This conventional account has three main "moments": (1) black-led mobilization throughout the South in the early 1960s creating the momentum for (2) significant federal initiatives to guarantee black political participation, followed by (3) dramatic increases in black voter registration and (presumably) influence. Studying the Mississippi case, Paul Joubert and Ben Crouch argue that "there can be no doubt that the Voting Rights Act brought about drastic changes in black registration in the state" (1977, 166). They optimistically conclude that these changes have resulted in "[black] political power proportionately comparable to that of the white majority" (161). The increase in black voter registration is a commonly noted indicator of the act's efficacy. Again, Joubert and Crouch state that "the increase . . . testifies to the apparent success of the Voting Rights Act" (161).[1]

David Garrow develops this thesis most systematically in his study *Protest at Selma*. He summarizes the argument as follows:

The political sagacity of Martin Luther King, Jr., and his aides, . . . was demonstrated by their very deft creation in Selma of events that spurred support in Washington and across the country for more stringent voting rights safeguards to be enforced not by the federal courts but by the federal executive branch. . . . From their efforts in those early months of 1965, as well as from the efforts of Johnson, his men at Justice, and certain members of Congress, sprang a legislative enactment that was to stimulate as great a change in American politics as any one law ever has. (1978, 235–36)

This view has been echoed many times over. In an impressive analysis of legal change, Gerald Rosenberg claims that "there can be no doubt that the major increase in the registration of blacks came from the action of Congress and the executive branch through the 1965 Voting Rights Act" (1991, 61; see also Alt 1995). This dominant account is well represented in popular presentations of the civil rights movement, such as documentaries, widely read historical studies, and textbooks.

Two of the widely heralded mechanisms included in the Voting Rights Act are the appointment of federal examiners to oversee registration and section 5 of the Voting Rights Act, which required preclearance for local changes in election rules and registration procedures. In addition, the Voting Rights Act eliminated many of the legal requirements that had disfranchised black voters, such as literacy requirements (Colby 1986). Coinciding with the Voting Rights Act, the passage of the Twenty-fourth

Amendment eliminated poll taxes, another mechanism that discriminated against black voters and simultaneously kept many poor whites from registering to vote.

Several empirical expectations are embedded in this account. First, voter registration increases should follow the 1965 Voting Rights Act rather than precede it. Second, increases in black political participation should follow immediately rather than gradually. Third, black political participation should increase where federal intervention is greatest. This narrative does not directly address the relationship between voter registration and the actual political influence of black voters. However, the argument does imply that political influence should flow from the newly acquired access to the ballot. Richard Timpone (1995) calls this the "government intervention" argument because of the key role attributed to federal legislation. Social movement activity plays an important role, but it is through a momentary impact on the legislative process.

In contrast, some scholars have developed an alternative account that places greater emphasis on the cumulative and incremental impact of "mass mobilization" on black political participation and office holding (Andrews 1997; Rochon and Kabashima 1998; Rosenstone and Hansen 1993; Santoro 1999; Timpone 1995). Lester Salamon and Stephen Van Evera (1973) caution against "euphoric" interpretations of the Voting Rights Act's impact. Timpone (1995) has examined this development most systematically. I have reproduced the data used in his time-series analysis of black voter registration in the South in figure 5.1. As the government intervention argument would suggest, there is an upsurge in black registration in the mid-1960s. However, there is a steady rise in black voter registration over the twenty-five years preceding the Voting Rights Act. In addition, Timpone finds that the upsurge in registration begins between 1962 and 1964. He infers from this that the electoral competition around the 1964 elections and the Voter Education Project (grants administered by the Southern Regional Council for local voter registration campaigns by civil rights groups) spurred an increase in black registration before the passage of the Voting Rights Act. In general, the mass mobilization argument focuses on the increases in black voter registration that preceded passage of the Voting Rights Act in 1965. However, this was not the case in Mississippi, where the significant increase in voter registration occurred after 1965. This pattern could indicate that government intervention is only crucial in places like Mississippi that are most resistant to change.

FIGURE 5.1 : Black Voter Registration in 11 Southern States, 1940–86

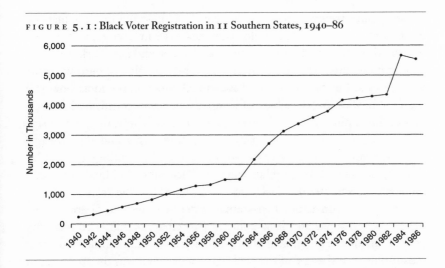

The Voting Rights Act could have been influential because of the implementation and enforcement aspects of the legislation. Specifically, some scholars have pointed to the federal examiners sent by the Justice Department into notoriously recalcitrant counties to supervise voter registration (Garrow 1978). For the entire South, this argument is not very plausible because of the limited number of examiners sent by the Justice Department (Jones 1976; Rosenstone and Hansen 1993). In the most recalcitrant areas of the South like Mississippi, the argument has more plausibility because the increases in black voter registration did come after 1965, and examiners were sent to some Mississippi counties. Even in Mississippi, which received the largest number of examiners, their impact on black political participation is an open question.

Another difficulty in the federal-intervention argument concerns the relationship between black voter registration and measures of electoral influence. Aaron Henry, a major figure in the Mississippi movement, testified before hearings on the extension of the Voting Rights Act that

> reports of tremendous progress in black participation [are] greatly exaggerated. . . . Fair and effective representation of blacks at the most significant levels of government is still far from a reality. Little progress has been made in electing blacks to positions of real power and responsibilities in which we can affect state policy or exercise real political power on the county level. (Quoted in Garrow 1978, 210)

Most scholars have reached a similar conclusion, noting that the increase in black registration was not followed by increases in electoral influence—measured most often by the election of black candidates (Parker 1990).[2] Twenty years after the Voting Rights Act, blacks held 7.3 percent of the County Board of Supervisor positions in Mississippi, the most powerful local political office.[3] As a base of comparison, blacks constituted approximately one-third of the voting-age population. In short, there was a significant lag between the acquisition of voting rights and the effective use of the vote. By 1968 over two-thirds of the black voting-age population was registered to vote, but gains in black office holding were quite modest (Lawson 1976).

Finally, the conventional narrative underestimates the ongoing conflicts and resistance to black political participation that occurred after 1965. Outside the organizing efforts in black communities, the factor that most influenced the fate of the civil rights movement was the strategies of countermobilization used by local whites. Few scholars would disagree with this claim. However, most studies have looked at only certain types of countermobilization. Too often, white mobilization has been analyzed as a response without a corresponding analysis of how white strategies, in turn, impact on black mobilization. One of the most widely noted findings is the increase in white voter registration after the Voting Rights Act. White increases were greatest in the same areas where there were large black increases, and those increases offset black gains in many parts of the South (Alt 1994; Kernell 1973). In the Mississippi case, this question of white countermobilization through increases in white voter registration is examined below.

White voter registration is one of several possible responses to the civil rights movement and black political participation. The political impact of white violence has received far less attention.[4] Perhaps, there is an assumption that violence would have few enduring effects on the political process. Donald Matthews and James Protho found in a 1961 survey that awareness of violence in one's community "is related to relatively low rates of Negro political participation" (1966, 308). This aggregate relationship conceals the interesting finding that respondents who had heard of racial violence connected to movement activity (e.g., voter registration, NAACP membership) participated at higher-than-average levels. Hence, there are two countervailing relationships. When connected to the movement, white violence increases participation. Otherwise, violence diminishes political participation. Matthews and Protho conclude that violence in relation to political participation "can probably be said to encourage participation that would not otherwise occur" (308). The overall negative relationship between violence and participation is largely dismissed because "these incidents tend to occur where Negro participation would be quite low on other grounds" (308). Matthews and Protho present a sophisticated analysis of violence; however, it is consistent with the prevailing view that white violent resistance to the civil rights movement was an anachronistic "last gasp" with few long-term organizational or political consequences. The question here is particularly important in light of the conflicting findings in the social sciences on repression, that repression can escalate or dampen mobilization. There are numerous examples in the case studies, and I will discuss the effect of repression on movement building and impact below.

Opponents can also undermine a movement's ability to achieve its goals by altering the "rules of the game." Southern politicians were able to avoid the Voting Rights Act's preclearance requirement for some changes until civil rights groups brought these violations to the attention of federal courts (see Hester 1982; Parker and Phillips 1981). When civil rights groups were granted relief by federal courts, intervention was rarely retroactive. In other words, courts were reluctant to set aside elections once they had occurred even under discriminatory circumstances. Rosenberg concludes that "delay is built into the judicial system," giving established power holders a distinct advantage (1991, 88). According to some critics, the limited enforcement effort, the burden of bringing challenges to the courts, and the inherent gradualism of the legal process constrained the overall impact of the Voting Rights Act. In this case, white politicians throughout the South enacted a set of legal changes in the period following the Voting Rights Act that limited the influence of black voters. These barriers included new qualifications for political candidates and gerrymandering of electoral districts (Davidson and Grofman 1994; Hester 1982; Parker 1990; Timpone 1997). Both mobilization and countermobilization had longer time horizons than is commonly acknowledged in accounts of the civil rights movement.

The criticisms noted above are not meant to belittle the real impact that the Voting Rights Act did have. In Mississippi this impact was more substantial than in other parts of the South where black enfranchisement began much earlier. For example, the Voting Rights Act set an important precedent, and it figured prominently in the litigation initiated by civil rights groups in later years (Parker 1990). However, the process of political change in the period before and after 1965 was more complex in Mississippi and beyond. The level of political participation increased dramatically in Mississippi, but the political power of blacks did not increase substantially in the immediate period after the Voting Rights Act. Instead, the process of change involved an ongoing interaction between local mobilization and resistance with brief moments of federal intervention. In addition, the patterns of white resistance to black political influence are far more complex and efficacious than widely perceived.

The bulk of quantitative evidence suggests that changing forms of black political participation occurred through a long process of mobilization punctuated by moments of facilitation and repression. However, this body of research has relied on rather limited data on local organization, and it cannot provide much insight into the process of transformation following the civil rights movement (for exceptions, see Button 1989; and Wirt 1970 and 1997). Among those places that had strong civil rights movements, some sustained mobilization through the 1970s and 1980s while other movements collapsed.

This debate about the relationship of the civil rights movement, the Voting Rights Act, and black political participation has significant implications because the civil rights movement has been a model for our understanding of legal, political, and social change more generally. Is the time horizon relatively short, spanning several years, or much longer, spanning several decades? Does change occur through watershed events that have cascading effects on social action or through the longer accumulation of social mobilization? How significant is government action relative to other actors? To what degree and in what ways do social movements shape these changes? These questions form a backdrop for the analysis of the Mississippi movement in the following sections of the chapter.

The Development of Electoral Capacity in Holmes County

How did movement organizations change during this period from the early 1960s to the early 1970s? While few tangible gains were achieved, I show that the consolidation or collapse of organization building during this period had significant consequences for the long-term impact of the movement on electoral politics. Returning to Holmes County illustrates a successful case where the movement infrastructure grew in terms of the number and skills of local leaders and the breadth of movement organizations.

Voter Registration Efforts

In Holmes County, initial efforts focused on voter registration. Leaders were careful not to engage in confrontational protest, although the response from local white authorities and individuals was highly repressive and demonstrated the threat posed by the civil rights movement. Hartman Turnbow, one of the early civil rights leaders in Holmes County, described the initial efforts to register to vote in Lexington in testimony before a 1964 congressional committee. These events from April 1963 are recalled in a lengthy quote that conveys the obstacles faced by local Mississippians.

Oh, the first time [we tried to register] we had lots of trouble. The first time we had heard a citizenship school being taught in Leflore County. Some of the citizens in our area asked them to come down and tell us about it. So they came around and asked us would we meet at the church to hear them. . . . So John Ball, he come, and he talked to us and told us that it was learning us how to register, since we were not familiar with registering in Mississippi—he thought we needed some help to prepare us to go register. So the story sounded reasonable to us, and we told them to come on, we would accept him for our citizenship teacher. . . . So he taught us how to fill the registration forms out for about 2 weeks. So in a 2-week period, 14 of us thought we knowed it well enough to go register. So 14 of us got in our cars. We went to Lexington. We didn't drive our cars up in town. We stopped them outside and we walked uptown. We didn't walk in a big gang. We walked in two's about 10 or 12 feet apart, so they couldn't say we was demonstrating. So we was met by the sheriff. Mr. Andrew P. Smith. He met us at the south door of the courthouse. And he stopped us. So Samuel Block was leading us. And Samuel Block said "march forward." And Mr. Smith put one hand on his blackjack and the other one on his pistol and said, "None of the goddamned forward stuff here." So I stepped out of the line. I said, "Mr. Smith, we only come to register." He said, "Well, Turnbow go around to the northside of the courthouse and stop under that tree and don't go in no big crowd, go in two's." . . . He [the sheriff] came around there under the tree where we were standing and he looked at us, he put one hand on his blackjack and the other on his pistol and raised his voice. He said, "All right, now, who will be first?" And the 14 of us got scared, looked one at the other one. So when the 14 commenced looking one at the other one, I just stepped out the 14. I said, "I will be first, Mr. Smith." Well, no sooner I said I will be first than Mr. Smith calmed his voice. He said, "All right, Turnbow, go down the side, the edge of the curb and go in the courthouse in the first door on the left, and do what you got to do." I told him, "Yes sir." I did that. I got in there. The lady—the Circuit Clerk wasn't in—but the lady was in there. She said, "Well, you have to see Mr. [McLellan] about that, and he is not in here." I said, "May I wait until he comes?" She said, "Yes, you may." . . . So I sat there until 12 o'clock. She said, "Well, I am going to dinner now. He ain't come yet." I said, "Yes, Ma'am, I will be back after dinner." So after dinner, about 2 or 3 o'clock, I went back in and he was in. She had told him about it. He said, "What do you want?" I said, "I want to register to vote." He just handed me the form and I filled it out and signed it and handed it back to him.

In some cases, these early registration efforts were ignored by local newspapers, and in other cases, the events were covered in detail with the possible effect of encouraging repression. Turnbow's efforts received immediate coverage.

So then after that I noticed the next day the *Lexington Herald*, a little local paper they write—they had a write up in the *Lexington Herald* that "Hartman Turnbow was an integration leader," so I noticed that about 2 weeks or a little after that my house was fire bombed and shot in all at the same time. And about 3 o'clock in the morning it took place. My wife and daughter, she is 16, they jumped out of bed screaming and hollering that the house is on fire, it had been bombed. So I woke up—I was kind of hard to wake up—I woke up and my room was full of smoke. . . . I raised the window and took my foot and kicked the screen out so the smoke could get out. Then I had a little old .22 automatic Remington sitting over in the corner. I picked it up and pushed the safety off and got it in shooting position and run out. . . . And no sooner I got out in the open with my rifle in my hand, I saw two white men, and one of them no sooner he saw me he shot at me. So he shot at me the first time. I had my .22 already in position and I just commenced shooting at him right fast. . . . When I started shooting right fast at him, he broke and run. . . . So about 3 or 4 minutes, they all was gone. Then myself and wife and daughter went to pumping water and we put the fire out. And that is what I got for going to register.[5]

Turnbow's account provides great insight into the characteristics of the early civil rights struggle in Mississippi—the heroism and strategic sophistication of local activists, the familiarity and hierarchy of local race relations, and the multiple paths through which local whites resisted challenges. Turnbow's attempt was one of many during the early 1960s. Another black Mississippian described a more common experience during this period as she anticipated participation in the Freedom Vote election:

> I had fear in my heart because as soon as morning came, I had to face a big problem. That was going down town and getting a beating. I know when the police see me they will hit me. I had it all in my mind how it was going to be: one would hit me on the head with a night stick, and the other would hit me in the mouth. Another was going to sic five or six dogs on me. I knew they were going to knock me down and kick me in the face. The moment came for me to go down town. My mind was made up; I looked at the clock—quarter to nine. I was going at nine. If they whipped me for my freedom I would not mind. And all at once Sam Block came in and said the police said they would not arrest anyone. And my heart felt good then; I said "thank God" three times. Then we went downtown and we voted. Nobody bothered any of us. (Quoted in Dorsey 1977, 22)

Although most voter registration attempts did not lead to the intense violence that Hartman Turnbow experienced, all of the local Mississippians that became involved in the movement during this period lived under the pervasive threat of violence.

As I indicated in the last chapter, there were few successful attempts to register to vote, with only twenty black registered voters as late as 1964. In this context, voter registration became an activity around which to organize more than an end in itself. Two important court cases were filed during this period that indicated the threat to white control of the electoral process—the first case was against Sheriff Andrew Smith and another was filed against the registrar, Henry McLellan. In May 1963 a local newspaper reported that "former Holmes County Sheriff Andrew P. Smith admitted . . . in U.S. District Court here that he has not allowed Negroes in the county to pay poll taxes since January, 1956."[6] The Justice Department filed a suit against Henry McLellan, the circuit clerk and registrar in Holmes County, for discrimination against blacks attempting to register. Although the case was initiated in 1963 and ultimately reached a favorable resolution, this result did not occur until 1965, when the Voting Rights Act had significantly undermined the discriminatory mechanisms available to local registrars. In both cases, court action was slow and had little direct effect on the civil rights organizing in the county. Arguably, these cases represented an important symbolic challenge, with highly publicized cases against two of the major figures responsible for thwarting black voter registration efforts.[7]

As I described at the beginning of the chapter, some scholars have attributed significant increases in black electoral participation to the intervention of federal examiners or registrars. However, the experience in Holmes County suggests that these effects have been exaggerated. First, one of the reasons that the federal examiners may appear to be important is because local movements organized around their arrival. For example, the Freedom Information Service published a statewide newsletter to local activists that reported the dates and locations that federal examiners would visit selected cities. Nevertheless, the United States Commission on Civil Rights complained that

> when the Federal Examiner arrived in Holmes County in March, he apparently made no effort to publicize his presence. Commission staff talked to many local black persons—candidates and campaign managers as well as voters—who did not know he was in Lexington until his presence was discovered by accident on his last day there. Predictably, he did not list anyone during his visit to Lexington.

The lackluster efforts of federal examiners raise question about their direct role in the expansion of black voter registration. However, their presence was a basis for movement-initiated registration drives, and they may have undermined continued resistance from hostile local registrars. Overall, the increases in voter registration in Holmes County are more directly attributable to the organized voter registration drives by local civil rights groups than to the sporadic visits of federal officials.[8]

Getting Involved in the Electoral Process

A movement focusing on voter registration faces the inherent challenge that voter registration and elections occur infrequently, but successful political movements require more sustained mobilization. Prior to the Voting Rights Act, COFO and the MFDP used a parallel political process of mock elections, political parties, and nominating conventions to sustain engagement and build organizing skills. This focus on sustained mobilization continued after the Voting Rights Act. Local organizations attempted to participate in any activities of the regular Democratic Party, and there were efforts to win office in the Agricultural Stabilization and Conservation committees of the Department of Agriculture and the boards of community action programs.

The local movement also challenged the nominating process for electing candidates for the Democratic National Convention. Teams were sent to local precinct-level meetings. For example, the following report summarizes the depositions taken from MFDP members about a meeting in Tchula:

> Tchula: Precinct 5. Voters arrived at 9:55 and were not immediately excluded. The meeting started at 10:45. The Negroes were asked what they wanted. They replied that they came to vote for delegates to the County Democratic Convention. They were told that the committee did not have their names, therefore, they would have to be excluded from the meeting unless they could show proof (of registration?) acceptable to the committee. The Negroes then left, returned to their citizenship school, held a meeting and elected a delegate to the county convention.[9]

This sort of parallel organization of political parties continued with the Loyalist Democrats into the early 1970s when the Democratic Party in Mississippi allowed civil rights challengers to participate regularly.

Running for Office

The early campaigns by black candidates were accompanied by many "problems" as blacks attempted to effectively wield the ballot. Many of these problems were generated by subtle forms of discrimination on the part of white election officials. Local campaigns faced an internal problem as well. Movements must effectively coordinate action. In this case, local movements had to overcome fear and intimidation as well as mobilize and educate potential voters.

At the state level, new laws made it more difficult for candidates affiliated with the MFDP to run as independents (Parker 1990). At the local level, less formal mechanisms were used to discourage blacks from running for elected office. For example, the U.S. Commission on Civil Rights reported the harassment faced by one Holmes county candidate:

> Rev. R. L. Whitaker, a Negro Resident of Holmes County, ran in 1966 for a justice of the peace post vacated by the death of the incumbent. . . . In September 1966, Rev. Whitaker was appointed pastor of a Negro rural church with between 50 and 60 members located on one of the big plantations in the county. Two days after his appointment, the elders of the church voted to rescind the appointment. . . . Rev. Whitaker concluded that his appointment was withdrawn because he was running for justice of the peace. The plantation on which the church is located is owned by white persons, and . . . the elders feared that the church might be burned

or other reprisals taken against it or its members if its pastor ran for public office. Only three of the four Negroes on the plantation had registered to vote. . . . (1968, 121)

However, Whitaker's experience may have been atypical for Holmes County. The commission reported on another candidate:

Ralthus Hayes, an official of the Holmes County Freedom Democratic Party and candidate for the U.S. House of Representatives, stated that although there still was some residual fear of harassment and intimidation from local white persons, Negro candidates generally felt free to run and Negro voters felt free to vote in Holmes County because of the large number of Negroes in the county who have their own farms or are economically independent of the white community. Hayes, himself an independent farmer and owner of 114 acres, remarked: "One of the major reasons the movement [in Holmes County] is as strong as it is, is because so many of the people are independent farmers." (130–31)

Nevertheless, this could be a case where Hayes had underestimated the harassment faced by black candidates because of his own economic independence.

The 1966 and 1967 Elections in Holmes County

The 1966 statewide election was the first opportunity for voting in Mississippi following the 1965 Voting Rights Act. In 1966 Clifton Whitley ran for the U.S. Senate, challenging the incumbent, James Eastland. Whitley gained a position on the ballot in the Democratic primary in June and in the general election as an independent candidate. This initial foray was followed in 1967 by the election of county offices, where black candidates ran throughout the state for local office. In both elections, the movement confronted the combination of new and old barriers to black political participation. Daisy Lewis, in the newsletter of the Holmes County Community Center, summarized the successes of voter mobilization during this period. Lewis observed that "some of the plantation people are waking up. They are not afraid of being kicked off the plantation for voting, marching, registering or having anything to do with civil rights people. . . ." However, she went on to note that

We know it is hard for the plantation people because just this Nov. 8 we lost the election in Holmes County, because some people are still afraid of a white man. The minute they saw all those pale officials they got confused and didn't know which way to vote.[10]

In 1966 the Holmes County movement was unable to have black poll watchers appointed by the county election commissioner. In 1967 even though the movement was relatively successful in securing election observers, there were still substantial problems for black voters. To begin, observers were often immobilized by white polling officials. Sometimes this took place officially when black officials and poll watchers were removed from the polling place. Black poll watchers were often kept from helping black voters when whites "preempted it [black assistance] by being more aggressive." Problems extended into the ballot-counting process as well. Outside the polling place, black voters had to contend with white intimidation and violence by groups of whites.[11]

The 1967 election was the first significant test of black electoral strength following the passage of the Voting Rights Act because of the crucial county and state elections. Registration increased dramatically between 1965 and 1967 as formal mechanisms blocking black voter registration were eliminated. For example, the U.S. Commission on Civil Rights reported that 72.7 percent of the black population was registered to vote in Holmes County in 1967. At this point, Holmes County was well above the state average of 50.7 percent. Overall, statewide registration increases led some observers to expect dramatic increases in black elected officials. Throughout the state, expectations were high before the important county elections of 1967. However, gains were minimal—a total of twenty-two new elected officials in Mississippi. One major determinant of black losses in the 1967 elections was a set of newly implemented institutional barriers that diluted the black voting strength, including redistricting and discriminatory qualifications for black candidates. In this context, local movements faced new challenges in their efforts to mobilize support for black candidates. Despite the disappointing losses of the 1967 elections, these early campaigns were turning points at the local level.

In Holmes County, the elections resulted in disappointing losses for nine candidates and a significant electoral victory with Robert Clark's election to the state legislature. In his analysis of Clark's campaign, David Emmons notes that "Clark's election was in a very real sense the achievement of this civil rights movement which over a period of four years secured the preconditions for an effective black politics in a setting where they would seem difficult to secure.... By mid-1967, the movement had spread geographically throughout the county. Regular meetings had been held in most of the county's communities for two years and were linked together in a loose organization by a monthly county-wide meeting and executive committee." Susan Lorenzi reported weekly meetings in fifteen different communities in 1966. A local activist, Shadrach Davis, stated the significance of the electoral gain in 1967: "It took a long time 'fore a black person come able to win an election. Representative Robert Clark won out in 1967. An' that was just amazing 'cause he ran against a real big money man and beat him."[12]

On Election Day, voting proceeded at some polling places without incident. Henry Lorenzi reported:

> In more than half of the . . . precincts there was more than a 50% turnout of Negro voters. . . . In Goodman the Negro turnout was so heavy that the White officials conceded that the Negroes had taken that precinct. Despite high turnout many, many people didn't know how to vote . . . at least 60 people who hadn't registered tried to vote, and some were annoyed when they were turned away. . . . 200 people came to the Lexington FDP office for help on where to vote and how to vote. In Durant the local people handled this themselves from a local café.

At other locations, there were significant conflicts between voters, poll watchers, and local authorities. For example, in Ebeneezer, Robert Clark's town, there was conflict throughout the day. A Harvard law student was arrested in the morning after getting in a conflict with the bailiff about the distance of poll watchers from the registration table and the disqualification of a black woman's ballot. Tension continued through the day with the local clerk reported as saying: "They ought to use these niggers for cannon fodder." After the polls closed, crowds of blacks and whites gathered "because word had spread that Ebeneezer was a trouble spot." During ballot counting, a lawyer from California got into a conflict and was kicked by a local white. The group of blacks pulled out rifles and turned their cars toward the group of whites to blind them, until the county sheriff arrived and diffused the situation by dispersing the crowds. The lawyer was arrested at a local café for assault and battery during the incident. Lawrence Guyot, a state-level MFDP leader, reported that "whiskey had been passed out to Negro voters in Holmes County" by whites to influence black voting. A local MFDP leader reported that the Tchula branch of the NAACP broke ranks and supported the moderate white candidate against Ralthus Hayes, who was running for a congressional seat.[13]

The 1967 elections produced mixed results in Holmes County. With two exceptions, the slate of MFDP candidates lost in 1967. There were significant obstacles as described above, and there was some disappointment at the election results locally and across the state. Despite these problems, Holmes County had higher participation and greater success than many Mississippi counties during the 1967 elections. As we have seen, Robert Clark was elected to the Mississippi legislature as the first black member since Reconstruction. His victory was national news and further enhanced the reputation of the movement in Holmes County.

Further Growth during the 1971 Elections

The 1971 election was shaped more profoundly by the statewide campaign of Charles Evers for governor. Again, Holmes County was noteworthy for the sophistication of its local organization. *The Drummer*, a statewide movement newspaper, declared that "politically, where blacks are concerned, [Holmes County] is one or two steps ahead of most counties."[14] Lester Salamon, reporting on the campaigns, observed the activities in close detail:

> There was confusion and chaos, to be sure, but there was also impressive organizational efficiency. . . . Here, local black leaders trained during seven long years of movement activity and led by Mississippi's only black legislator, Robert Clark, established a campaign steering committee early in the campaign, and proceeded to develop an intricate district and precinct organization reaching deep into the rural countryside. In charge of the fifth district, the plantation region surrounding the tiny town of Tchula, for example, was Saul Sutton, a young black contractor who won his movement spurs during the 1964 Freedom Summer. Sutton quickly designated block captains and recruited local students to canvass every residence in the district to determine how many black voters it contained, which ones needed rides to the polls, baby-sitters, or instructions on how to vote. This information was then scrupulously recorded on a massive detailed map of the district, which Sutton unrolled on long tables in his makeshift campaign headquarters around the corner from the polling place on election day and used to check off black voters as they arrived, and to dispatch block-captains and cars to rally the lagging. The whole operation had the flavor of a sophisticated urban political machine, strangely out of place in the tumbled-down rural setting. And what made it all the more remarkable was the fact that six short years earlier, these skilled political organizers had not even been allowed to vote. (1972a, 44)

Like the 1967 elections, the results in 1971 led to modest increases and general disappointment that the unprecedented levels of mobilization did not generate more successful black campaigns. In his campaign for governor, Charles Evers won 22 percent of the vote. Supporters had expected a number in the low to mid-thirties. Most important, few of the local candidates won elections. After all, Evers's campaign was premised on the formula of creating the coattail necessary to help local candidates in majority-black counties to win elections. Approximately fifty candidates won office, although these "victories were restricted almost exclusively to the less significant posts" (Salamon 1972a, 45). There were continuing accounts of fraud and intimidation: "'They had a hundred ways to cheat us in this election,' Saul Sutton despaired in Tchula, 'and they used 101 of them'" (Salamon 1972a, 45).

> "These guys are scared as the devil about the election," black Election Commission Chairman Howard Taft Bailey of Holmes County noted about his white neighbors. For the election seemed to confirm the worst fears of local whites. "All my land and everything I own is in this county," one white banker explained, "and the same goes for my neighbors. If the blacks take control, we're finished. Now you don't expect us just to stand by and see that happen, do you?" (Salamon 1972a, 45)

Across the state, disappointment was pervasive, but in Holmes County there was continuing evidence of the movement's efficacy as the number of black officials holding state or county positions increased to six.

In the remaining sections of this chapter, I step back to examine the broader patterns of electoral participation across the state of Mississippi. Holmes County was remarkable for its success in building a sustained movement infrastructure. The election of Robert Clark was considered one of the key victories by movement activists across the state, but it was part of a much broader pattern in Holmes. For example, Lester Salamon (1972b) found high levels of organizational involvement in 1969, and Jack Bass describes MFDP meetings in 1974, with the main difference being the presence of black elected officials at the meeting. Given this high degree of success, we should view this case in relationship to other communities in Mississippi.

Local Movements and Electoral Participation in Mississippi

Did counties where the movement was most active have higher levels of electoral participation in the late 1960s and early 1970s than those that did not? We can begin to answer this question by looking at the summary statistics in table 5.1. Here, there are data on three forms of political participation—voter registration, the number of black candidates running for office, and voter turnout—covering the period from 1966 to 1971. In 1967 the number of black registered voters is greater in sustained movement counties than in episodic or non-movement counties. However, the

TABLE 5.1: Voter Participation and the Level of Movement Activity

	Movement Counties		Non-Movement Counties	State
	Sustained	Episodic		
Voter Registration				
Registered black voters, 1967	4,183	1,844	992	2,025
Registered black voters, 1967 (%)	53.1	53.6	47.1	50.7
Registered white voters, 1967	10,166	5,753	5,070	6,493
Registered white voters, 1967 (%)	70.6	71.2	64.6	68.2
Black Candidates for County-level Office				
Black candidates, 1967	3.0	1.5	0.5	1.4
Black candidates, 1971	6.5	3.6	1.5	3.4
Voter Turnout				
Clifton Whitley, 1966	1,661	637	240	705
Clifton Whitley, 1966 (%)	17.8	16.7	9.7	13.9
White voter turnout, 1966 (%)	42.4	48.3	44.2	45.2
Differential (white voter turnout minus black voter turnout) (%)	24.6	31.6	34.6	31.2
Charles Evers, 1971	3,705	1,740	1,057	1,906
Charles Evers, 1971 (%)	40.2	41.4	42.5	41.6
White voter turnout, 1971 (%)	65.9	73.8	76.4	73.1
Differential (white voter turnout minus black voter turnout) (%)	25.7	32.4	33.9	31.5
Number of counties	19	27	35	81

Note: This table reports mean values for counties.

actual number is influenced by the size of the black voting-age population. The percentage measure shows that counties with sustained and episodic movements have very similar levels of voter registration.

The second set of indicators presents the number of black candidates running for county-level office in 1967 and 1971. In the South, counties are the most important local political body, and it is possible to compare the efforts to win elected office. Here, the relationship of black candidates and the level of movement activity is very strong, with movement counties having much higher levels of political mobilization. Although these candidates rarely won elections during this period, their campaigns represented an important development in the longer struggle toward greater black political power.

Finally, I estimate the voter turnout for blacks and whites in two elections by candidates for statewide office—Clifton Whitley in 1966 and Charles Evers in 1971. Both candidates had been involved in civil rights organizing. Whitley, for example, held state-level leadership positions in the Mississippi Freedom Democratic Party and was an MFDP delegate to the 1964 Democratic National Convention. Evers's relationship to the movement was more controversial. His brother, Medgar Evers, had been the NAACP's field secretary in Mississippi and was shot down outside his home by Byron de la Beckwith in 1963. Charles Evers returned to Mississippi shortly thereafter, and he began building a political base in the southwest part of the state. While he was never fully embraced by many civil rights activists, he was a prominent state-level leader by the late 1960s. In the Whitley election, we see a pattern similar to voter registration where movement counties (sustained and episodic) had higher levels of black electoral participation than non-movement counties. In the Evers election, there is very little difference between the counties based on the level of movement activity (a pattern I examine more carefully below). Finally, note the indicators of turnout differential—the gap between white voter turnout and black voter turn out. The pattern here shows that increases in voter turnout in movement counties are not offset by increases in white voter turnout. Surprisingly, this differential is narrowed in movement counties, suggesting that there are relative gains for black turnout in these counties. This evidence contradicts the expectation that local civil rights activity escalated white countermobilization.[15] In the following sections, I examine these patterns of political participation in a more systematic manner to determine whether these relationships hold under more rigorous analyses.

Voter Registration

In much of the South, black voter registration had been increasing since World War II. However, in Mississippi voter registration campaigns produced very minimal increases in the early 1960s. The Justice Department had already filed suits against the registrars in several Mississippi counties, and the Southern Regional Council's Voter Education Project spent $12.13 for each new voter added between 1962 and 1964 (Lawson 1976, 284). Voter registration in Mississippi increased dramatically following the passage of the Voting Rights Act. The period from 1965 to 1971 saw substantial increases in black political participation but minimal increases in black office holding.

In 1968 the U.S. Commission on Civil Rights consolidated data on voter registration in a comprehensive report, *Political Participation*. The report documents the number of newly registered black voters in Mississippi counties, and it also indicates whether a county was assigned federal examiners between 1965 and 1967. Federal examiners were usually sent to counties that were known for their discrimination against black registrants. Deep South counties were the target of the vast majority of federal examiners, with Mississippi receiving examiners in thirty-one counties by 1967 (USCCR 1968, 244–47).[16] These data provide an initial indication of the emerging patterns of black political participation in Mississippi.

We have already seen that movement counties had slightly higher levels of black voter registration, but it is important to use techniques that account for additional factors that may influence registration levels. In table 5.2, I use an OLS (ordinary least squares) regression model to examine the factors that influence black voter registration. In addition to measures of social movement activity, I measure the impact of federal examiners and white violence on black voter registration. The size of the black voting-age population in 1960 is used as a control variable in analyses for the total number of registered blacks in 1967.

The Voter Education Project argued that federal examiners had a more substantial impact on black registration rates than movement organization (Black and Black 1987, 135). The analysis I present in table 5.2 shows a greater effect for local organizing than for examiners.[17] Most significantly, I find that both organizing during Freedom Summer and NAACP membership are better predictors of a county's level of black voter registration than the presence of federal examiners, with Freedom

TABLE 5.2: Coefficients from OLS Regression Predicting Electoral Mobilization: Voters Registered in 1967 and Votes for Two Black Candidates for Statewide Office

	Voter Registration, 1967	Whitley, 1966	Evers, 1971
Freedom Summer volunteers and staff, 1964	.358***	.229*	−.003
	(51.339)	(14.864)	(−.344)
NAACP membership, 1966	.135*	.138*	.191***
	(98.800)	(45.595)	(110.632)
Violent Resistance Index, 1960–69[a]	.100	.115	.022
	(15.914)	(8.235)	(2.825)
Federal examiners, 1965–67	.119*	.246***	.054
	(437.704)	(408.363)	(158.858)
Black voting-age population, 1970	.400***	.423***	.796***
	(.190)	(.091)	(.301)
Percentage urban, 1970	−.066	−.050	.019
	(−5.278)	(−1.785)	(1.228)
Constant	—	—	—
	(500.937)*	(−61.768)	(149.620)
R-squared	.683	.649	.867
Adj. R-squared	.657	.621	.856

* = $p < .05$; ** = $p < .01$; *** = $p < .001$ (one-tailed tests)

Note: The standardized coefficient is presented followed by the unstandardized coefficient in parentheses.

[a] Although the index covers the period 1960–69, only 2 incidents out of 657 occurred after 1966.

Summer being by far the most powerful predictor.[18] These findings suggest that the resources (Freedom Summer staff and volunteers) and results (NAACP organization) of the early period of organizing were primary factors in shaping higher levels of voter registration after the Voting Rights Act.

In the next sections, I examine other forms of black political participation that have received less attention—specifically, voter turnout and the campaigns by black candidates for office. Registration is an intermediate outcome because it does not reflect particular gains for the black community but is preliminary mobilization aimed at achieving other goals.[19]

Electoral Mobilization: Voter Turnout and Black Candidates

Movement activists ran for office in several statewide elections. Often this was a strategy for unifying the local campaigns where black candidates had a much more realistic opportunity to win office. The statewide campaigns provide a way to gauge the turnout of black voters. For electoral mobilization, I have used votes cast for two black candidates, Clifton Whitley in 1966 and Charles Evers in 1971, in their campaigns for statewide office.[20]

Treating the votes cast for black candidates as an indicator of black voter turnout raises some potential questions. For example, could whites have voted for these candidates, or could blacks have voted for white candidates? Extensive research has documented the persistence of "racial bloc voting" or "racially polarized voting" throughout the South and in major cities during this period (see, for example, Loewen 1990; McCrary 1990; and Murray and Velditz 1978).[21] With votes cast for Whitley and Evers, I am assuming that only blacks voted for these candidates. Undoubtedly, some blacks voted for white candidates, as documented by the cases in which white poll watchers or employers have manipulated the black vote for white candidates (Berry 1973; Loewen 1981; Salamon 1972a), but no systematic data on such manipulation of the black vote is available by county. Moreover, votes cast for black candidates for statewide office is a useful indicator of black electoral strength because it suggests the degree to which the votes of black citizens can be coherently and effectively marshaled in support of state-level black candidates.

Like the changes in voter registration, voter turnout is examined in terms of the impact of the movement, federal registrars, and other variables noted above. The results of the analysis are presented in table 5.2. The results for the Clifton Whitley campaign are quite similar to those found for voter registration in 1967. The movement (Freedom Summer and NAACP) and federal examiners have significant positive effects on the number of votes cast for Clifton Whitley. In fact, examiners have a slightly greater effect than Freedom Summer. In 1971 the Evers campaign shows an important difference—the effects of Freedom Summer volunteers and federal examiners are no longer statistically significant. The short-term impact of federal examiners is consistent with James Alt's study of voter registration across the South that found "the absence of a significant effect [for examiners] after 1967 . . . [which] suggests that the relative impact of federal examiners' presence on black registration rates wore off over time" (1994, 371).

The Evers campaign for governor in 1971 appears to be a departure from the Whitley campaign in that the movement base of the early 1960s does not play a significant role; however, the NAACP variable, measuring mid- to late 1960s movement strength, does have a significant positive effect. The pattern of black political mobilization in Mississippi did not follow a linear path through the late 1960s and 1970s, underscoring the need for multiple outcome measures. As mayor of Fayette in Jefferson County, Charles Evers's political strength was concentrated in several majority-black counties in southwest Mississippi (e.g., Claiborne, Wilkinson, Jefferson) that had had little civil rights activity from 1961 to 1965 (Berry 1973).[22] While the electoral successes of these counties have continued at the local level, they represent a different pattern of mobilization than that found in pre-1965 movement counties.

The 1967 county and state elections in Mississippi were widely viewed as the first opportunity for black Mississippians to make significant gains in office holding by building on the massive gains in registered voters. Over a hundred candidates ran for office in twenty-six counties with twenty-two candidates winning office in the November general election. While the victories were important, they were also disappointing, leading Frank Parker to conclude that "the 1967 election results were a substantial victory for Mississippi's massive resistance to black political participation" (1990, 73). As we saw in Holmes County, despite the importance of Robert Clark's election, many local leaders were surprised and disappointed by the results of the 1967 election.

In which counties were blacks most likely to launch campaigns for elected office? Table 5.3 presents the results of an OLS regression analysis predicting the number of black candidates running for office in 1967 and 1971. The same set of independent variables is used from the earlier analyses with two exceptions. The control variable, black voting-age population, is now included as a percentage of the total voting-age population.[23] A measure of voter turnout for Clifton Whitley is used as an indicator of mass participation in electoral politics in the immediate aftermath of the Voting Rights Act.

The most interesting results of the analysis are that federal examiners had no significant impact, Freedom Summer and NAACP had significant positive effects, and that violent resistance had a significant negative effect. The positive effects of Freedom Summer and the NAACP are clear indicators that the movement infrastructure had expanded to support electoral campaigns and leaders.

The statistical nonsignificance of federal examiners is interesting because the presence of examiners should indicate a greater "openness" of the polity. However another dimension of the political opportunity structure is the use of repression by elites and other actors. Here we see that the use of violence by local whites decreases the number of black candidates for office. This probably operated through a variety of avenues. Black candidates would have been more likely to experience harassment

TABLE 5.3: Coefficients from OLS Regression Predicting Number of Black Candidates Running for Office in 1967 and 1971

	Black Candidates, 1967	Black Candidates, 1971
Freedom Summer volunteers and staff, 1964	.369***	.342***
	(.081)	(.161)
NAACP membership, 1966	.159*	.193**
	(.177)	(.461)
Violent Resistance Index, 1960–69	−.192*	−.211**
	(−.047)	(−.110)
Federal examiners, 1965–67	−.091*	−.017
	(−.510)	(−.209)
Percentage vote for Whitley, 1966	.372***	.013
	(9.294)	(.676)
Proportion of the black voting-age population as total, 1970	.371***	.577***
	(6.119)	(20.351)
Percentage urban, 1970	−.061	.012
	(.007)	(.003)
Constant	—	—
	(−2.081)***	(−4.643)***
R-squared	.596	.606
Adj. R-squared	.558	.568

* = p < .05; ** = p < .01; *** = p < .001 (one-tailed tests)
Note: The standardized coefficient is presented followed by the unstandardized coefficient in parentheses.

and violence in highly repressive counties, and some potential candidates may have withdrawn from elections or avoided electoral politics completely. In addition, a broader infrastructure of organizations and leaders was less likely to develop in highly repressive communities. In sum, repression minimizes the development of the movement infrastructure used to launch local campaigns.

Racial Disparities in Voter Turnout

I have already noted the impact of white violence on the number of black candidates running for office. More routine tactics were available to white Mississippians to counter black political power, including voting for segregationist candidates for local, state, and federal office. The analyses of voter registration and turnout reported above indicate absolute levels of black participation. However, electoral power is a matter of relative power, so a key indicator of change is the level of black political participation relative to white participation.

Voting patterns can be used to assess the tactical interaction between black and white mobilization. Given the persistence of racial bloc voting, we can assume that increases in white registration undermined the potential power of black voters. The trend is striking for the 1960s where "three new whites were enrolled in the Deep South for every two blacks." Earl Black and Merle Black note that "it is difficult to say how much of this huge increase . . . can be attributed to racism" (1987, 139). In a multivariate analysis for the entire South, James Alt finds that white registration increases were greatest in counties with high black proportions, "suggesting a continuing fear among whites of the possibility of black electoral dominance" (1994, 354). Data on white voter registration is limited for Mississippi. Instead of using the limited voter registration data, I have analyzed white voter turnout in statewide elections—the same elections reported above: Clifton Whitley's campaign for the Senate in 1966 against the incumbent James Eastland and Charles Evers's campaign for governor in 1971. I estimate white voter turnout as the votes cast for white candidates as a proportion of the white voting-age population.

The relationship between white and black turnout is estimated by taking the difference in these two proportions. In all counties, white turnout exceeds black turnout, so this measure provides an estimate of the overall disparity in black and white electoral mobilization. This measure allows for a refinement in the earlier analysis by assessing black and white mobilization in relation to one another. For example, movement mobilization may increase black turnout and simultaneously increase white turnout at even greater levels. The same is true for federal examiners or any other of the variables analyzed above. Table 5.4 presents the results of the OLS regression models for the 1966 and 1971 elections. The primary independent variables from earlier equations are included in the analysis: early (Freedom Summer) and late (NAACP) movement organization, white violence, presence of federal examiners, and percentage urban. In addition, the proportion black of the voting-age population measures whether turnout disparities were different as the relative size of the black population increased. For the equations, negative coefficients indicate smaller differences in the level of voter turnout; in other words, the gap between black and white turnout is narrowed.

In both elections, the turnout disparity was positively related to the proportion black, which could indicate depressed rates of black turnout in these counties or increased white turnout. The latter is the case in

	1966	1971
Freedom Summer volunteers and staff, 1964	−.332**	−.049
	(−.004)	(−.0004)
NAACP membership, 1966	.134	−.231*
	(.008)	(−.011)
Violent Resistance Index, 1960–69	.022	.019
	(.0002)	(.0002)
Federal examiners, 1965–67	−.222*	−.111
	(−.064)	(−.027)
Proportion black of the voting-age population, 1970	.564***	.421***
	(.478)	(.298)
Percentage urban, 1970	−.163	−.350**
	(−.001)	(−.002)
Constant	—	—
	(.208)***	(−.296)***
R-squared	.392	.359
Adj. R-squared	.343	.308

* = p < .05; ** = p < .01; *** = p < .001 (one-tailed tests)

Note: The standardized coefficient is presented followed by the unstandardized coefficient in parentheses. The racial disparity measures are determined by the proportion white turnout minus the proportion black turnout. Negative coefficients indicate smaller differences in turnout rate.

Mississippi. In fact, black turnout is positively correlated with the proportion black in a county for both elections. For example, during the Whitley campaign, the correlation coefficient is 0.37. White turnout is related to the proportion black at an even greater magnitude; the correlation coefficient between white turnout and proportion black during this same election was 0.70. These results suggest that the electoral threat posed by a larger black electorate generated huge turnouts by whites in 1966 and 1971.

In the Whitley campaign of 1966, the presence of federal examiners and the civil rights movement resulted in smaller disparities between white and black voter turnout. The earlier analysis showed that these two variables predicted higher levels of black voting. Importantly, examiners and movement organization also narrow the gap between black and white voting levels. Here again, the movement has a larger impact than federal examiners on the disparity. For the 1971 elections, NAACP organization and percentage urban predict smaller disparities in turnout. In short, the results reported in table 5.4 confirm that local movement organization resulted in relative gains (by narrowing the gap between black and white turnout) as well as absolute gains (more black voters). Nevertheless, white turnout rose dramatically as the proportion black in a county increased.

Conclusion

Let me conclude by summarizing the main lessons of this chapter. With the case of electoral politics, civil rights mobilization continued to shape electoral outcomes well after the peak of the movement. The significance of these findings will be clearer when I turn to the election of black candidates to office in the late 1970s and early 1980s.

The counties that established strong movement infrastructures in the early 1960s experienced significant success in expanding black political participation in the late 1960s and early 1970s. This included less demanding forms such as voter registration and more demanding forms such as voting and running for elected office. These patterns are especially strong in Holmes County, where an elaborate movement infrastructure surpassed the early organizing efforts sponsored by SNCC and COFO. In an article about this new black leadership, the *New York Times* quoted a national reporter who had been covering Mississippi: "Up until a couple years ago . . . when we came to Mississippi there was always that bright young black or white college kid from the North to interpret Mississippi to the press. Now it's all black, and it's all Mississippi black." This leadership included "many scores of elected officials, farmers, housewives, clergymen, laborers, and professional people who make up the highly diversified Mississippi black activist leadership."[24]

This period of mobilization for electoral empowerment illustrates important dynamics about the nature of repression. Repression does, in certain circumstances, escalate protest, as was the case in the early 1960s. But I have shown that repression quite often has a large negative impact on the ultimate ability of the movement to achieve its goals (Gamson 1990). Although many candidates ran for office during this period, very few were able to win—even in Holmes County. The white massive-resistance legislation was effective to the extent that it prevented the election of a black candidate to the U.S. House of Representatives for over twenty years, as well as candidates to many lower-level offices.

In some cases, a persuasive argument can be made that violent resistance backfired, generating higher levels of movement mobilization—or in Charles Payne's words, the "calculus of repression" changed (1995). Does this mean that repression is ineffective? The qualified conclusion we can draw is that when a movement is strongest (and, perhaps, when media attention is highest), violent repression can be used by movements in ways that broaden mobilization. Over a longer time frame, however, violent resistance severely limited the acquisition of black political power, at least in Mississippi, by lowering the number of black candidates running for office, and it undermined the efforts to consolidate organizational gains of the early 1960s.

CHAPTER SIX

The Politics of Poverty

IN THIS chapter, I examine the role of local movements in the War on Poverty. This ambitious policy initiative created a new set of opportunities and constraints for the civil rights movement. The programs brought substantial resources into impoverished Mississippi communities. In addition, the War on Poverty provided new opportunities for blacks to influence the shape and direction of policy. Regardless of what policy makers intended, the principle of "maximum feasible participation of the poor" signaled an opportunity to many local movements. At first glance, it is surprising to see how thoroughly local movements became involved in the War on Poverty. After all, the publicly stated goal of the movement in the early 1960s was gaining access to electoral politics. However, the underlying goal of the Mississippi movement was building local movements that could define and pursue their own goals. The early movement organizations (SNCC, CORE, and COFO) had little direct involvement in the War on Poverty in Mississippi. However, local movements continued to operate political programs and community centers in the post-1965 period. These were the groups that attempted to shape the local implementation of poverty programs. Many local activists defined economic empowerment as a natural outgrowth of the political empowerment pursued through voter registration. In fact, many believed that political power would be meaningless unless black communities could generate viable economic programs (e.g., Dorsey 1977).

Even with the opportunity implied by "maximum feasible participation," there were substantial obstacles to movement influence in the War on Poverty. Many scholars have noted that funding for the War on Poverty was modest from its beginning in 1964 and declined over time. Moreover, the objectives of federal agencies constrained the ability of local movements to direct the War on Poverty on their own terms. For example, the "professionalization of reform"—the use of educational credentials as a criterion for key leadership positions—could reduce the participation and influence of the poor to a primarily symbolic role (Alford and Friedland 1975; Helfgot 1974). These contradictory forces shaped the relationship between the movement and the War on Poverty. The patterns of local mobilization shaped the distribution and development of antipoverty programs in Mississippi, and the programs themselves shaped the direction of local movements. This chapter examines a small piece of the broader War on Poverty to examine the role of local movements in the implementation of federal programs.

The programs can be treated as an outcome not because the movement explicitly demanded federal antipoverty programs. Rather, once the War on Poverty was initiated, local movements in Mississippi and across the country attempted to secure resources and shape programs (Patterson 1994, 146). The question of the intellectual and political origins of the War on Poverty has dominated the historical scholarship. As Jill Quadagno notes, "The debate about origins . . . matters little. In fact, it obscures the crucial linkage that unquestionably did develop between the civil rights movement and the War on Poverty" (1994, 28). That linkage is explored in close detail throughout this chapter.

With the earliest poverty programs, local movements exercised considerable influence because white political leaders unilaterally opposed the programs, rather than attempting to control them. Hence, the movement possessed the only infrastructure that could administer and operate poverty programs. Once political leaders at the state and local level saw that there would be poverty programs in Mississippi, their strategy changed and the question became who would control local programs. A struggle ensued. In many cases, movements were preempted as local elites set up programs that excluded movement participants. This, in turn, was followed by local efforts to gain access to the local administrative bodies of the War on Poverty. The programs were not monolithic, and movement influence depended on the structure of the particular program and the policies of the Office of Economic Opportunity (OEO), which could constrain or facilitate movement influence. The relationship between local movements and the War on Poverty changed dramatically over time.

Overview of the War on Poverty: The National Context

On August 20, 1964, Lyndon Johnson signed the Economic Opportunity Act, a key component of his Great Society agenda.[1] The initiation of the War on Poverty coincided with a set of national policy initiatives of the early 1960s including the Civil Rights Act of 1964, the Elementary and Secondary Education Act (ESEA) of 1965, and the Voting Rights Act of 1965. The legislation altered the political context of the civil rights movement. The War on Poverty included a cluster of programs administered primarily through the newly formed Office of Economic Opportunity. Lacking a unified approach conceptually and administratively, the War on Poverty was assembled in a patchwork fashion. For example, the 1964 legislation included plans for VISTA, Neighborhood Youth Corps, community action agencies, Head Start, and college work-study programs (Patterson 1994). Through the 1960s, OEO administered the majority of these programs, allowing programs to bypass the old-line agencies like the Department of Labor that were less open to influence by civil rights groups and leaders. Over time, though, the major poverty programs were phased out or shifted over to the more conservative agencies (Quadagno 1994).

In the early 1960s, the Mississippi movement did not anticipate Johnson's War on Poverty. Nevertheless, state policies can shift the goals and tactics of movements. In Mississippi Head Start and community action programs (CAPs) were centers of movement activity through the 1960s and early 1970s. Communities across the state became involved in struggles at the local level and with federal agencies. Head Start established service-intensive centers for preschool children, providing daycare and targeting the nutritional, medical, and educational needs of poor children. In Mississippi there was an affinity between Head Start and the activities of Freedom Schools and the after-school programs administered through movement community centers. Head Start was influenced by local movement activity, and centers were frequently staffed by movement activists (Greenberg 1969).

Among the various poverty programs, the CAPs[2] received the greatest attention and for some became almost synonymous with the War on Poverty. Policy makers pushing "community action hoped to stimulate better coordination among the melange of public and private agencies delivering social services" (Peterson and Greenstone 1977, 241). This objective, however, was abandoned in favor of "citizen participation." OEO and local CAPs had little impact on the established agencies providing services to poor communities. As a result, CAPs administered the new antipoverty programs. The notoriety of CAPS was tied to their unique organizational form designed to bypass local political bodies. CAPS were coordinated at the local level through a CAP board that served as the overarching administrative body. Typically CAP boards included leaders from politics, business, community, and religious groups. CAP boards, by definition, were public bodies that claimed to be a representative forum for the deliberation of community goals. In comparison to programs like the Child Development Group of Mississippi (CDGM), CAPS posed greater challenges for movement influence. Under the mandate of maximum feasible participation of the poor, civil rights groups did have a wedge in to the decision-making process that put them in ongoing interaction with white leaders, so in contrast to other social service programs or political bodies, CAP boards were the exception to the broader pattern of all-white institutions. This opening paved the way for intense conflicts between local groups attempting to influence the flow of OEO funds and the content of poverty programs.

Battling Poverty in Mississippi

From its origins, poverty programs in Mississippi were closely tied to the dynamics of the civil rights movement. One of the earliest and most celebrated programs, CDGM administered Head Start centers across the state, building directly on the movement base of Freedom Schools and community centers. The history of CDGM is an essential point of departure for an analysis of the movement and the War on Poverty in Mississippi, revealing the successes and obstacles faced by movement activists.[3]

CDGM was formulated by a small group of policy makers and psychologists with loose connections to the Mississippi movement. For example, Tom Levin, the first director of the program, had participated in Freedom Summer through the Medical Committee for Human Rights. Despite these ties, when proposals for CDGM were circulated in early 1965, the response from SNCC and the MFDP was a combination of skepticism and opposition (Payne 1995). Following the MFDP challenge at Atlantic City, many movement leaders were suspicious of the federal government and the initiatives of white liberals (Dittmer 1994). From the state-level civil rights organizations, there was little effort to support CDGM. Even without the formal endorsement of the movement's leadership, CDGM quickly diffused through the local movement infrastructure. For the first summer, Payne reports that "on opening day of the eight-week session, eighty-four centers opened across the state, serving fifty-six hundred children" (1995, 329). At the local level, the affinity between CDGM's program and the movement-sponsored Freedom Schools was clear. In addition, CDGM brought considerable resources that could allow local movements to upgrade and expand their existing programs. Moreover, local movements had a point of leverage over the new program. The movement was the only group positioned in 1965 to provide an infrastructure for Head Start centers. For the most part, public school boards were unwilling to provide access to their facilities, staff, and resources. The few proposals submitted by school boards were typically rejected because they did not involve community participation and made minimal efforts to generate white participation. The movement could offer access to the community centers and supportive black churches in Mississippi where the emerging program could develop. This combination of forces favored the expansion of CDGM through local civil rights movements in Mississippi.

Over time, the movement's initial skepticism of CDGM was supplanted by enthusiastic support. The staff and objectives of CDGM became almost indistinguishable from movement organizations. For example, Bernice Johnson, who worked with CDGM in Holmes County, recalled that community centers were used for Head Start in the day and the MFDP at night. The same core groups of activists participated in both activities.[4]

The distribution of CDGM projects (see table 6.1) shows that the majority of counties with sustained movements had a CDGM-sponsored Head Start project. In contrast, only two of the thirty-five non-movement counties developed a CDGM project. This occurred because of the direct involvement of local movements in promoting CDGM at the local level.

TABLE 6.1: The Child Development Group of Mississippi and the Level of Movement Activity

	Movement Counties		Non-Movement Counties	State
	Sustained	Episodic		
% with CDGM project, 1965	79.0	19.0	5.7	27.0
% with CDGM project, 1966	84.0	33.0	5.7	33.0
Number of counties	19	27	35	81

Note: This table reports mean values for counties.

The records of movement groups and the Office of Economic Opportunity demonstrate the diffusion of CDGM through movement networks.

The strong relationship between local movements and CDGM made the Head Start program a target of widespread opposition and violence. In fact, some CDGM projects were threatened and attacked by local whites. The primary threat to CDGM's existence came from Mississippi's powerful Congress members. CDGM's earliest critics were influential Mississippi politicians like Senator James Eastland, who chaired the Judiciary Committee, and Senator John Stennis, who chaired the Appropriations Committee. However, the opposition to CDGM resonated with growing fear from around the country that OEO was funding black insurgency (Quadagno 1994).

As a result of these constraints, OEO began a process of policing itself, investigating charges that funds were channeled into political activity and the organizational affiliations of poverty program employees. Incidentally, OEO's investigations of CDGM show the strength of the relationship between the movement and the new Head Start program in close detail. In July 1965 an investigation into the "impartiality" of CDGM had two major findings: "There is evidence that personnel for this program are being recruited on the basis of their civil rights activities, rather than on merit alone. The FBI believes the Communist Party may have infiltrated the program." While these charges of communist infiltration went undocumented, OEO's investigator did find that staff at the state and local level had affiliations with civil rights groups, including COFO, SNCC, CORE, the NAACP, the Urban League, the Delta Ministry, and the MFDP.[5]

The relationship between the movement and CDGM was especially strong in Holmes County. An inspection during the second year of the program found that 102 of the 108 CDGM staff members in Holmes County were active members of the MFDP. Reflecting the strength of the local movement, the investigation found that "many of the Negroes in the communities around the centers have donated money and time to build buildings for the centers and work with the programs."[6] Local activists were not just passive recipients of federal programs. Instead, they were making substantial contributions to the programs and using Head Start programs to expand the movement's capacity.

From its earliest days, CDGM was the target of various investigations. The 1965 report also recommended a financial audit of CDGM. The actual "irregularities" found in an independent audit were minimal and "never exceeded more than 1 percent of the total cost of the program," according to Jule Sugarman, Head Start's associate director. In early 1966, following the recommendation of the 1965 investigation, OEO had the FBI conduct background checks on CDGM employees, finding very little other than arrests during civil rights demonstrations. However, the accusations reduced CDGM's credibility and diverted the attention of program administrators.[7]

OEO initiated a policy that further undermined the viability of CDGM by stipulating that in counties with a CAP, Head Start must be administered through the local agency. The policy solved a number of problems for OEO. Head Start was the most visible poverty program. By turning Head Start over to CAPs, this gave the local agencies a high-profile presence in the local community. The policy also localized control in the CAP board, giving local whites a direct role in the administration of Head Start programs and lowering the influence of civil rights groups in many communities. This allowed OEO to demonstrate the racial integration of its program, and it depoliticized the program by reducing movement influence.

By 1966 CDGM had expanded into thirty-seven counties. The programs in many of those counties were shifted to local CAPs. CDGM administered programs in only fourteen counties during the following summer when Head Start programs were placed under CAP control. Many of the former CDGM programs were turned over to local CAPs, which, as we will see, meant less influence for civil rights groups (Dittmer 1994).

This opposition to CDGM paved the way for more conservative groups in the state to develop Head Start programs. CDGM's major competitor was Mississippi Action for Progress (MAP), which successfully applied for OEO funds in 1966. MAP included many of the same organizations and individuals who would later form the Loyalist Democrats, a combination of black and white moderates (Dittmer 1994; Simpson 1982). MAP received the largest Head Start grant for 1967 to operate centers in twenty-four counties by moving into non-movement counties and locales without a CAP. This marked a clear shift away from CDGM to a more conservative organization in terms of ideology and structure (Payne 1995).[8]

The Formation and Funding of Community Action Programs

Community action programs became the centerpiece of the War on Poverty. Once again, we can ask the question of movement impact. In this case, how did local movements shape the formation and funding of CAPs in Mississippi? Community action programs were the administrative body through which a wide array of specific projects were administered, and the composition of CAP boards was contentious throughout the history of OEO. Turning to table 6.2, we see that sustained movement counties were more likely to have a community action program, and those counties had greater total funding and funding per household in poverty. In counties with sustained movements, CAP funding per household in poverty was over twice as much as non-movement counties. So, the movement counties had greater absolute levels of funding and greater funding relative to the amount of poverty.

Using OLS regression models, I have analyzed the funding of community action programs during two phases, the initial development from 1965–68 and the latter stage from 1969–71 when the amount of funding declined.[9] These results are presented in table 6.3. The independent variables in table 6.3 include a measure of poverty (number of households with income below $3,000 in 1959) and percentage urban in 1960. The local movement is measured by two variables: MFDP and NAACP organizations.[10] This allows me to distinguish between the effects of the militant and moderate wings of the movements. Some counties had both organizations. However, there was an increasing differentiation at the local level after 1964. The role of white countermobilization is measured by three different variables: the presence of Klan organizations in the county, Citizens' Council organizations, and incidents of violence against the civil rights movement.[11] The formation of a community action program required some support and participation from local whites, typically from the County Board of Supervisors. Hence, the areas that had most

TABLE 6.2: Poverty Programs and the Level of Movement Activity

	Movement Counties		Non-Movement Counties	State
	Sustained	Episodic		
% with CAP, 1965–68	57.9	48.2	34.3	44.4
% with CAP, 1969–71	57.9	48.2	34.3	44.4
CAP expenditures, 1965–68 ($)	1,508,582	279,961	185,913	527,518
CAP expenditures, 1969–71 ($)	850,889	235,907	119,324	329,787
CAP expenditures per household in poverty, 1965–68 ($)	1,159	492	397	607
CAP expenditures per household in poverty, 1969–71 ($)	619	365	253	376
Number of counties	19	27	35	81

Note: This table reports mean values for counties.

	CAP Funds, 1965–68	CAP Funds, 1969–71
Poverty, 1959 (proportion of households earning less than $3,000)	.590*** (474.876)	.551*** (227.540)
Percentage urban, 1960	–.146 (–8,557.097)	–.047 (–1,424.613)
MFDP leaders, 1965	.226* (124,964.510)	.238* (67,440.541)
NAACP membership, 1963	.050 (26,806.864)	.101 (27,716.848)
Citizens' Council organization, 1956	–.006 (–16,555.876)	–.046 (–66,310.699)
Klan organization, 1964	–.175* (–451,598.047)	–.130 (–172,176.118)
Violent resistance during Freedom Summer	–.128 (–14,794.040)	–.142 (–8,401.192)
Constant	— (611,732.072)*	— (–309,269.455)
R-squared	.355	.380
Adj. R-squared	.293	.321

* = p < .05; ** = p < .01; *** = p < .001 (one-tailed tests)
Note: The standardized coefficient is presented followed by the unstandardized coefficient in parentheses.

resisted the civil rights movement would be least likely to seek out federal programs. In some counties, for example, local whites became the target of repression when they met with civil rights groups (Dittmer 1994; Harris 1982).

The pattern reported in table 6.3 indicates, not surprisingly, that the aggregate level of poverty was associated with higher levels of CAP funding. In addition, I find that movement and countermovement variables shaped a county's level of funding. For both panels, all three of the countermovement variables have negative coefficients, and the measure of Klan organization is statistically significant for the 1965–68 period. In addition, the MFDP measure predicts higher levels of funding for both periods.

Most CAPs were initiated in the early years following the 1964 legislation. As budget cuts were initiated through the late 1960s, the funding of new grants was minimal. In addition, OEO's policies for distributing budget cuts were not precisely defined. However, the broad guidelines were to make reductions of "approximately equal percentage" while allowing room for administrative discretion. The results reported in tables 6.2 and 6.3 indicate that within this policy guideline shifts over time in the distribution of funding were minimal in Mississippi.[12]

The key theoretical finding from this analysis is the significant positive relationship between the movement and the funding of CAPs even when controlling for the level of poverty and other community characteristics. However, the relationship does not reveal the *mechanism* through which movements influenced CAP funding. One possibility is that local movements were directly involved in the formation of CAPs. However, another possibility is that local movements posed a threat that mobilized other groups in the county to seek out poverty program funding. Here, the case studies are particularly helpful for refining the relationship.

Refining the Link between Local Movements and Community Action Programs

In *The Strategy of Social Protest* (1990), William Gamson argues that movement impact occurs under two very different circumstances. Success occurs when movements gain access to the policy-making process and generate substantive gains. On the other hand, movements are preempted when substantive gains are achieved without access to the policy-making process. My statistical analysis does not indicate which of the two occurred in Mississippi. The case studies show that initially movements were preempted followed by long struggles of varying degrees of success to achieve access in the policy-making process. Movements that mobilized early and forcefully to gain influence over community action programs were more successful because OEO was more responsive to movement demands at the early stage of its development.

In 1965 and 1966, CAPs were formed without substantial participation from movement activists. Black participation often included traditional leaders not affiliated with the civil rights movements (neither moderate NAACP nor more militant MFDP representatives) such as ministers and teachers. OEO was, in fact, aware of what it called the "Tom" problem. In early 1966, OEO's southeast regional manager of the community action program reported that in Mississippi "the most frequent problem and the one which requires the most time in its solution is representation. Boards on original submission are almost always hand picked and packed in favor of the Governor.[13] Negro representation is always 'Tom.' . . . Protests almost always follow the selection of such initial Boards and resolution generally takes from 3 to 4 months." Even though they were aware of the problem, OEO's grant administrators often did not have detailed information about the local situation and lacked, in their words, "the technical competence necessary to help with Board problems." This problem was particularly acute in the early years. During this period, OEO depended on local movements to act as whistle-blowers.[14]

In the following sections, I present brief histories of Holmes and Bolivar counties. In each case, CAPs were formed with little direct involvement from activists. However, this changed as each movement attempted to influence local CAPs. The cases differ with regard to the specific strategies deployed by local movements and the way that local elites responded to those efforts. In Holmes County, activists were able to secure positions and influence within the CAP administration and staff. In Bolivar County, activists used a variety of tactics to gain an independent poverty program that operated alongside the local CAP.

Holmes County

As we have seen, Holmes County developed one of the most successful local movements in Mississippi (MacLeod 1991; Payne 1995). The Holmes County movement was a loosely coordinated confederation of local centers of movement of activity across the county, which expanded the repertoire of skills at the local level and brought local activists into contact with state and national politics. The movement developed an infrastructure with broad leadership, multiple organizations, indigenous resources, and strategic flexibility that allowed the movement to play a central role in local poverty programs.

Initial efforts to form a CAP in Holmes County bypassed the strong movement infrastructure. In the fall of 1965, a committee appointed by the Board of Supervisors began plans to join Central Mississippi, Inc. (CMI), a multicounty CAP. OEO's Southeast Regional Office was skeptical of CMI's initial proposal. Bob Westgate, an OEO staff member, noted that "although there are three Negroes on each of the [five] seven member county boards, I have my doubts of their real value to their people, whether they were really 'elected' by their people, and suggest that they should be checked by someone from this office. At least eight of the 15 Negro members are dependent upon the white power structure for their jobs or welfare pension payments (five principals or teachers, two on welfare and one maid)." Westgate sought out information through CORE and the NAACP contacts. Neither organization could provide contacts because they did not have organizations in the counties. Originally, CMI had submitted a proposal reporting that 25 percent of the population was black, and OEO required an increase in the number of "minority representatives" when it discovered that the population in the six counties was actually 58 percent black.[15]

OEO was also concerned that "eight of the 20 white board members are 'Johnson colonels'"—men who contributed funds and support during Governor Johnson's campaign. The governor exercised considerable power over CAPs because he had to sign off on grants and the organization's charter. With CMI, Johnson "allegedly held up the signing of the charter until these eight [supporters] were appointed on the board." The president and vice president of the CMI board were Johnson loyalists, and they had strong ties to the local political structure. For example, Rupert Ringold, the president, was the attorney for the Board of Supervisors (the most powerful local political body in Mississippi) in Montgomery County.[16]

The formation of CMI occurred outside the public arena, so it could not be contested by local activists. Daisy Lewis, director of the Holmes County Community Center, observed that "CAP came into Holmes County unexpected before the poor Negro and poor white had the chance to take part in it or decide if it would help our county or not. . . ." A group of approximately forty white leaders held a planning meeting in February 1966 to coordinate efforts. The *Lexington Advertiser* reported that "leaders were told that they have a choice of the county conducting it's own anti-poverty program and 'taking the Negroes along with us' or not acting and have the 'Negroes and civil rights workers' take over." Despite being taken off guard, the movement quickly mobilized to participate in the program. On March 7 a public meeting was held with approximately five hundred blacks and thirty whites in attendance. Activists brought a series of demands, including the dissolution of the existing board. A compromise was reached where six additional members were elected to a temporary advisory committee. Additional changes were made, including the election of a thirty-one-member permanent advisory committee. This committee would elect a six-member board of directors. In addition, each Head Start center would elect a separate advisory committee. The organizational reforms were meaningful because the small communities throughout the county were already organized, so the movement could elect a majority to the advisory committee and influence key decisions of the CAP (Salamon 1972b).[17]

The Holmes County movement had restructured the organization of poverty programs during the course of a single meeting. These policies meant that there would be a high level of participation in future program implementation. By securing access to the administration of CAPs, the movement was able to maintain control of Head Start centers through an independent delegate agency. In addition, CAPs initiated several projects that went beyond job training to address rural poverty in Holmes County. The poverty programs provided services, but they also provided jobs, constituting the single largest employer in the county (Salamon 1972b).

Bolivar County

Compared to Holmes County, the Bolivar County movement was weaker in the mid-1960s. Community organizers had begun campaigns in several towns (e.g., Shaw), but several communities had no movement activity. The movement was held together by a loose network of activists, but it did not have the regular meetings, diverse organizations, or comprehensive presence that Holmes did. Nevertheless, civil rights activists mobilized a successful widespread campaign to secure an independent parallel program. This campaign became a major vehicle for building a movement infrastructure in Bolivar County.

As in Holmes County, the initial plans for a community action program occurred without movement participation. The Bolivar County Community Action Committee was formed in 1965 with key support from local elites including the Board of Supervisors and the chamber of commerce. As editor of the *Bolivar Commercial* and president of the chamber of commerce, Cliff Langford provided considerable support for the program.

From its beginning, local activists criticized the program for excluding movement participation and appointing conservative blacks to the CAP board. As was the case in many CDGM counties, mobilization crystallized in early 1966 when local leaders in Bolivar County learned that Head Start could no longer be administered through CDGM. Consistent with its new policy, OEO recommended that the Head Start program be shifted to the local CAP. The CDGM group formed a local organization called the Association of Communities of Bolivar County (ACBC). A campaign was launched that simultaneously attacked the local CAP for excluding movement activists and demanded the continuation of Head Start through the established CDGM program. A similar strategy was used in Sunflower County (Mills 1993). Black members of the CAP board were singled out as "Tom's" appointed by the "power structure." The CDGM group was especially outraged that one of the black ministers appointed to the CAP board had denied CDGM access to several churches in 1965.[18]

The primary leader of the challenge was Amzie Moore, one of the early NAACP leaders in Mississippi. However, the leadership included a large number of local ministers (from churches where Head Start centers operated) and the staff from Head Start programs throughout the county. These efforts also received support from the Delta Ministry and the MFDP. The challenge could quickly mobilize throughout the organizational infrastructure that had been used to operate Head Start. The local movement, calling itself the Committee of the Poor in Bolivar County, held mass meetings, circulated a petition, and operated the CDGM centers for approximately twelve hundred children on a volunteer basis through the spring of 1966. The volunteer programs demonstrated the commitment of the local movement, and it posed an ongoing challenge to the legitimacy of the funded project in the county. In addition to the local activities, leaders went to Washington, D.C., to lobby OEO for maintaining the CDGM-based program in Bolivar County.[19]

The Bolivar County CAP tried to respond to charges that its board was unrepresentative by holding open meetings at the local level to discuss program objectives and consolidate support. These meetings became an opportunity for representatives of the CDGM-based group to publicly criticize the CAP board and build support for their challenge. These events culminated in a meeting between CAP and the CDGM group in March. At the meeting, the Bolivar County CAP voted down a proposal to transfer funds to the CDGM group and allow them to administer the program. This forced OEO to make a decision regarding the two groups.[20]

OEO was initially opposed to having parallel organizations and favored a reorganization of the existing CAP board. Summarizing an extensive investigation for OEO, Bill Seward emphasized that "it is *crucially* important that the Bolivar County Community Action Committee be given every consideration for funding." Despite his support of the local CAP, Seward concluded that "although representing less than a third of the Negro population, [the CDGM group] is a potent and vocal force that must be recognized and included in any further OEO programs. . . . [F]urther postponement [of funding] will raise the level of emotional discontent of the Negro/poor from one of frustration, channeled into constructive effort, to one of frustration resulting in overt demonstration. In other words, there had better be a Head Start and quick *before* the lid blows." This analysis led Seward to recommend dividing the funds evenly between CDGM and the local CAP. In early April, this was the compromise that OEO reached in Bolivar, funding two separate Head Start programs with separate staff and administration.[21]

Despite its initial opposition, support increased for the movement-based program, which applied for funding as the Association of Communities of Bolivar County (ACBC). A 1967 report noted that "preliminary evaluations indicate that the ACBC programs are probably better than the CA[P]'s." Even though the Bolivar County CAP was making efforts to subsume ACBC within its program, OEO representatives in Mississippi stated that "our position will be to support and maintain ACBC as a separate entity." The Bolivar movement leveraged a response from OEO because of its sustained mobilization using conventional and disruptive tactics. In the 1966 Year-End Report, the southeast regional director singled out the Bolivar County situation because of the "lessening of over-all community tensions."[22]

The Bolivar County movement was able to use sustained protest to secure an autonomous poverty program. Despite initial opposition, OEO officials came to see the duplication of administrative staff and costs as preferable to an ongoing challenge to their legitimacy in Bolivar County. The movement challenge depended on an expansive network of activists that could run Head Start centers, coordinate mass meetings, and negotiate the grant-writing process with OEO.

Movements in Holmes and Bolivar counties were successful at maintaining movement-controlled Head Start centers. In addition, both movements posed a credible threat that compelled local political elites to establish well-funded community action programs. However, the cases diverge in important respects. In Holmes County, activists achieved greater impact on the structure of CAP itself by capitalizing on a strong movement infrastructure. In Bolivar County, activists protected movement-affiliated Head Start programs but ceded control of the broader CAP organization. This outcome resulted from the relatively greater opposition and the less developed movement infrastructure in Bolivar County.

Contrasting the Analyses of CDGM and CAPs

The histories of CDGM and CAPS present seemingly contradictory findings. In the case of CDGM, movement influence was substantial from the beginning. Movement control over Head Start declined as CDGM was undercut by OEO's policy of shifting Head Start program to local community action programs. In contrast, movements had little control over the formation of CAPs and fought hard to gain influence and representation. The difference between these two trajectories can be found in an analysis of OEO's policies and the leverage possessed by the movement.

OEO realized that the undermining of CDGM would shift the attention of movement activists toward the local CAP. In November 1966 OEO's southeast regional director wrote to Sargent Shriver explaining that "CDGM . . . had a large number of local poor people involved or hired. These same people can be expected to become involved in local CA[P] activities as their concern or experience warrants."[23]

With CDGM, the civil rights movement had the capacity to shape the organization through its access to local communities. The movement was in a position structurally to exert influence over the local implementation of OEO's program. However, the civil rights movement was only one of the many groups attempting to determine the fate of poverty programs in Mississippi. CDGM acquired its second grant for the 1966 summer after a massive mobilization. In February 1966 CDGM activists took their program to Washington, D.C., where "forty-eight black children and their teachers turned the hearing room of the House Education and Labor Committee into a kindergarten," after which CDGM was funded at $5.6 million. In response, "Governor Johnson and his allies came to see that by setting up CAP agencies in Mississippi communities, local whites could prevent the flow of federal dollars into programs like CDGM. Under continuing attack from segregationists, OEO was eager to recognize any CAP agency in Mississippi, regardless of its composition" (Dittmer 1994, 375). In Mississippi the War on Poverty was shaped by a "tight spiral" of tactical interaction between the movement and its opponents (Zald and Useem 1987). Both sides were highly mobilized and responded quickly to the tactics of the other in an attempt to exert maximum leverage over local poverty programs.

The Constraints of Federal Agencies and the Limitations of Movement Impact

So far, I have focused on the movement's efforts to influence the War on Poverty. However, these patterns were shaped by the objectives and policies of OEO. Overall, the extent of movement impact on funding and the extent to which movements gained access to poverty program administration is significant and noteworthy. Nevertheless, there are three areas where OEO constrained the extent of movement impact.

First, as the analysis of CDGM showed, OEO was under pressure to distinguish and distance itself from the civil rights movement. The pressure stemmed from OEO's fear that "scandals" would decrease public support for its programs. OEO's institutional position, which was weak from the start, required annual appeals for congressional funding and avoiding the veto of its programs by southern governors.

The pressure exerted by southern politicians placed OEO in the position of monitoring its programs carefully for excessive movement participation. In 1966 OEO overrode the veto of Governor Paul Johnson for the funding of CAPS in the southwest part of the state. However, it maintained its willingness to "promptly investigate" where there was "specific information of a derogatory nature concerning any specific individual elected to a CA[P] Board."[24]

A second factor constraining movement influence was the conflicts between OEO and local movements over integration. OEO was under close scrutiny by the United States Commission on Civil Rights and was publicly committed to integration. Ironically, Sonny Montgomery, a Mississippi congressman, complained that OEO was allowing CDGM to operate all-black programs while applications for Head Start programs by local school boards were denied because they would have been held in black schools.[25]

The pressure for integration meant that OEO needed to point to integrated programs in terms of staff and beneficiaries. In Mississippi this created a tactical dilemma. OEO had to circumvent local white institutions and avoid having its programs administered solely by local governments. One resolution would have been administering programs through liberal white organizations such as churches and labor unions. These institutions were simply too weak to be a viable alternative in Mississippi. Hence, many of OEO's programs were administered through black institutions, which meant there would be minimal white participation in Mississippi. Despite this structural barrier, Mississippi programs were under constant pressure to "integrate."

From the perspective of many local movements, the key problem was not integration. Poverty programs were useful to the extent that they provided services and employment, especially resources that were not controlled primarily by local whites. Employing whites from outside Mississippi was one strategy used to integrate the staff of Head Start programs. However, this fostered internal conflict as local blacks felt that the need for employment was far greater among local Mississippians. Furthermore, critics argued that this solution did not further OEO's goal of integrating the South anyway because it did not change local race relations.

Participation in the War on Poverty generated a further constraint for local movements. OEO's programs had a distinct organizational form that promoted some forms of leadership and undermined others. This final point has led some critics to argue that participation in government programs leads to the co-optation of local movements. For example, the use of formal educational credentials to determine leadership conflicted with SNCC's goal of developing leadership at the grassroots level. In addition, the organizational forms based on a highly stratified system of authority conflicted with the idea of group-centered leadership that Ella Baker had developed and SNCC had cultivated in Mississippi.

Conclusion

The War on Poverty presented a dilemma to local movements by promoting different organizational forms, leadership styles, and authority structures than had been developed within COFO/MFDP projects. Herein, we find the source of many of the conflicts that emerged between the movement and OEO. In particular, the professionalization of poverty programs and the use of formal credentials to make hiring decisions conflicted with the movement's effort to seek out and develop "grassroots leaders." In many cases, this movement strategy had circumvented and undermined the traditional black leadership in many communities and pushed forward other groups. The War on Poverty was one mechanism by which those more traditional leaders could reclaim authority. However, this was not a monolithic trend and the organizational structure of community action programs and the idea of "maximum feasible participation of the poor" gave movements a point of leverage to influence CAPS.

A striking finding reported here is the extent to which movements shaped the implementation of local poverty programs. This influence was certainly less than local activists would have desired, but it was considerable nonetheless. The quantitative analysis shows that the capacity of local movements had a positive impact on the diffusion of CDGM programs and on the amount of CAP funding in Mississippi counties. The case studies support my interpretation of the quantitative evidence, and they show how movements influenced the formation of CAPS by carving out areas of administrative control.

The pattern of local mobilization around the poverty programs and Head Start is reflected in statewide data for Mississippi. In a quantitative analysis of antipoverty expenditures in the United States, Andrew Cowart (1969) found that Mississippi was a "deviant case" because of the unusually high level of expenditures in a statistical model controlling for poverty levels and other demographic characteristics in the states. Remarkably,

Robert E. O'Connor (1998) came to a similar conclusion in a quantitative analysis of the enrollment success in Head Start programs in 1990. The participation levels for Head Start were so exceptionally high (82 percent of eligible black children enrolled) in Mississippi compared to other states that O'Connor reports two sets of models because the inclusion of Mississippi changed the analysis. Remarkably, twenty-five years after CDGM began setting up Head Start programs in Mississippi, the strong institutionalization of this program is reflected in aggregate statewide enrollment statistics. Clearly, this is an important legacy of the Mississippi movement.

The movement infrastructure model shows how movements exert influence through multiple causal mechanisms. The three most crucial mechanisms observed in this chapter are (1) direct implementation of poverty programs, (2) indirect influence by challenging the political authority of local elites, and (3) disruptive and persuasive protest that compelled OEO to act on behalf of the movement. These forms of influence all derive from the organizational capacity of local movements. Direct program implementation required an extensive leadership cadre that could maintain ongoing ties to OEO officials, other programs throughout the state, and community members. In Bolivar County, activists secured independent programs over the initial opposition of OEO administrators and the local CAP. The movement-affiliated centers (formerly CDGM) continued to operate Head Start programs in 1966 without funding, illustrating the underlying strength of the local organization. The second form of influence flowed from the first. Because local movements were capable of operating poverty programs independently, they undermined the authority of local officials who had historically administered social programs. Finally, local movements used protest, including disruptive protest in Bolivar County, to bring additional pressure to bear on OEO and to mobilize national support. OEO officials came to see this as an inevitable part of the implementation process in Mississippi.

CHAPTER SEVEN

Federal Authority, School Desegregation, and Countermobilization

THE MISSISSIPPI movement directed the majority of its resources toward gaining political access and power. In many communities, the movement was opportunistic in using this organizational capacity to address the grinding poverty in Mississippi's black communities. When we examine the efforts of movement groups and activists, schools were less central than political and economic objectives throughout this period. Nevertheless, schools were transformed in the period following the 1964 Civil Rights Act and the 1965 Voting Rights Act. These massive changes and the conflicts around them merit serious consideration. Although it varied considerably from community to community, desegregation generated major changes in the public school system. The pattern of change was complex, as many whites mobilized around a set of parallel educational institutions, segregationist academies, which were designed to maintain white institutional control and protect white privileges. Further, school desegregation was implemented in ways that sustained ongoing racial inequalities, such as the displacement of black schoolteachers, a key segment of the black middle class (Arnez 1978; Cecelski 1994).[1]

The Mississippi Movement and the Politics of Schools

I begin by outlining the contours of the civil rights movement's development in Mississippi as it pertains to schools and desegregation.[2] With education, resistance passed through several phases marked by distinct strategies. The first wave of widespread resistance followed the *Brown v. Board of Education* decision in 1954. The *Brown* decision's major impact in Mississippi was the consolidation of white resistance in the Citizens' Council. Efforts were made in a handful of school districts to act on the implication of *Brown* in the mid-1950s. In Yazoo City, Clarksdale, Natchez, Vicksburg, and Jackson, petitions for desegregation were circulated through some of the most established NAACP chapters in the state. John Dittmer (1994) argues that the Citizens' Council response was two-pronged: (1) public announcements, including full-page advertisements in local newspapers listing the names of petition signers; and (2) economic retaliations, including firing employees and boycotting black business owners. In short, moves toward implementation of the *Brown* decision were met by swift "massive resistance."

In 1956 the Mississippi legislature invoked the legal principle of interposition to claim that the Supreme Court's decisions on school desegregation were "in violation of the Constitution of the United States and the State of Mississippi, and therefore, are considered unconstitutional, invalid and of no lawful effect within the confines of the State of Mississippi." The legislature "directed and required" any state officials to block implementation of the decisions "by any lawful, peaceful and constitutional means." More specifically, the legislature authorized the governor to close any public school when it was in the public's interest, and this authority was granted to local school districts in 1960 (USCCR 1969, 14).

Throughout the late 1950s and early 1960s, the Mississippi legislature passed extensive legislation, often meeting in special sessions to buttress the system of segregated schools. These included general restrictions on civil liberties and expanded the legal support for segregation (Southern Education Reporting Service 1964). Governor Ross Barnett made the maintenance of school segregation a key issue throughout his administration. Most notably, Barnett led a massive effort to block the admission of James Meredith to the University of Mississippi in 1962 (see Dittmer 1994).

Freedom of Choice Plans and Token Desegregation

Beginning in the early 1960s, desegregation suits were being filed in Mississippi by the NAACP Legal Defense Fund and the Justice Department. In addition, following the passage of the 1964 Civil Rights Act, the Department of Health, Education and Welfare (HEW) was authorized to withhold federal funds from school districts that were not desegregating under Title VI provisions. These provisions allowed HEW to withhold funds when schools were not engaged in systematic efforts to reduce segregation. Following the Elementary and Secondary Education Act (ESEA) in 1965, the federal government took on an increasingly important role in subsidizing the funding of local school districts, especially in the impoverished rural areas of the South. This expanded role provided potential leverage to generate compliance from local school districts. Frank Parker points out that this pressure generated a two-stage process. The first stage was court-ordered "freedom of choice" plans that produced token desegregation followed by a second stage of massive desegregation prompted by the Supreme Court's decision in *Alexander v. Holmes County* (1969).[3] The freedom of choice plans allowed parents to "voluntarily" switch schools for their children. Freedom of choice plans were an obvious stalling mechanism generating very little change. Black parents and children who did enroll in formerly all-white schools faced violence and economic reprisals. Prior to the *Alexander* decision, HEW reported that 88 percent of blacks attended all-black schools and 12 percent of whites attended all-white schools (Munford 1973). In other words, there was "token" integration. In most school districts, a handful of black children attended formerly all-white public schools. Parker concludes that the first stage "generally left the black schools all-black, and resulted in very little integration of the white schools" (1987, 691).

In the fall of 1966, there were an estimated 6,407 black students attending desegregated schools in Mississippi. There were more students in counties that had sustained civil rights movements (151.4) than those with either episodic (71.6) or no civil rights activity (31.6).[4] However, these numbers were very modest even in the counties with the most extensive participation in the freedom of choice plans. Throughout this period, civil rights attorneys attempted to monitor the implementation of desegregation. Marian Wright and Henry Aronson wrote to civil rights leaders that even though many school districts were filing desegregation reports,

> a majority of the school boards within the State of Mississippi have submitted a plan to [the] Office of Education of the Department of Health, Education, and Welfare providing for the desegregation of their school districts. These plans have been submitted by local school boards to enable them to receive federal funds. We know that many school districts have not complied with the full conditions of the plans which they have submitted.[5]

The withholding of federal funds was a key source of leverage throughout the desegregation process. The plans were often implemented over multiple years, desegregating several grade levels at a time. In many cases, school districts started at the lower grades and worked up to the higher grades over three or four years. Frederick Wirt notes that "the advantage often lies with the regulated, who have the expertise and strong will to push their views of detailed decisions" (1970, 184). In other words, local school districts were in a position to influence the extent and form of school desegregation if there was a thorough effort to resist.

The small numbers of black students attending predominantly all-white schools elevated fears for black parents and students. In 1965 Stanford University's Oral History Project sent researchers to conduct interviews and tape-record meetings in the South. One researcher recorded the efforts of Susan Lorenzi in Holmes County while she was talking with parents about registering children to attend desegregated schools. The recording provides a fascinating glimpse into the concerns of parents in rural Mississippi about school desegregation. One parent wondered how her students would get to the new school, whether their clothes were in good-enough shape, and whether her welfare benefits would be cut off in retaliation for sending her kids to the all-white school. Lorenzi referred repeatedly to the other parents who were committed to sending their children, and several meetings had been organized in Mileston and throughout the county to provide additional solidarity and information about the registration process.[6]

Reports of harassment by other students, teachers, and administrators were common during this period. For example, Thomas Bartley, who desegregated Shaw High School in Bolivar County, was "subjected to harassment and intimidation from white students," including "being tripped on the stairs, roughed up on the playfield during physical education, thrown down and punched in the showers, having his clothes urinated upon while in the showers, and called 'nigger.'" He was later arrested and charged with using "vulgar and indecent language" for allegedly saying, "I'm gonna beat your ass" to another student on his way home from school.[7] The U.S. Commission on Civil Rights reported that the harassment, threats, and violence toward black students desegregating all-white schools were major reasons for the ineffectiveness of these plans. A small number of families stepped forward to enroll in formerly all-white schools, but even in counties with strong movement infrastructures, the obstacles undermined the possibility of substantial change. In many cases, these were the children of local civil rights leaders, such as C. O. Chinn in Canton and Velma Bartley in Shaw.

What accounts for the widespread failure of freedom of choice plans? It should be obvious by this point that there were significant formal and informal barriers to "choosing" to attend desegregated schools. These included concerns about reprisals, such as job loss and cuts to welfare benefits and concerns for children, including their well-being, educational needs, and exposure to social isolation, harassment, and violence. In his study of Panola County, Wirt (1970) reports that many students faced serious problems keeping up with the curriculum in desegregated schools. This may have resulted from poor preparation and neglect or discrimination from white teachers in the new schools. Civil rights attorneys working in Bolivar County pointed out that this situation was an indictment of the segregated school system because it demonstrated the extreme inferiority of black schools or discrimination against the black students attending historically white schools.[8] In Canton, six seniors who had transferred to Madison Ridgeland High School were told by teachers and the principal that they would have to stay in school an extra year to graduate. The determination required to enter these hostile school environments suggests that discrimination was common.[9] Nevertheless, Wirt notes that news of black academic failure in desegregated schools traveled widely in the black community. Certainly, these barriers and the efforts by white school authorities to implement desegregation at the slowest possible pace went a long way toward undermining freedom of choice plans.

However, another possible factor is that school desegregation was not as highly valued as some of the other goals around which black communities mobilized in Mississippi. In this repressive context, it would be difficult to assess whether black Mississippians would have preferred to send their children to desegregated schools. Moreover, one has to be careful in trying to assess what any group "wants" because of internal heterogeneity within any group and the massive social inequalities that shaped preferences and collective action. With those cautions in mind, the best indicators of collective preferences can be found in the moments where there were collective challenges concerning educational institutions. I have already described the extensive mobilization that took place in Shelby during the late 1960s concerning the quality of the schools and the attempts to fire politically active teachers. In the early 1960s, a similar conflict occurred in Shaw, where a student-initiated protest began in the cafeteria and escalated to a school boycott with a broader set of demands. Following a mass meeting on August 3, 1964, a boycott of McEvans High School began following an incident where students were prohibited from meeting with COFO workers in the school cafeteria. The students' initial list included four demands: "(1) Brand new, up-to-date books for our school, (2) well-equipped workshop and laboratory, (3) a well-stocked library including a section on Negro History, and (4) foreign language courses and other courses which meet the requirements for entrance to accredited colleges." The students sought meetings with the local school board to voice their concerns, and the conflict escalated when a more comprehensive list of demands was issued by the "Parents of Shaw School Students." The parent's list of twenty-eight items stated that "we want all schools in Shaw integrated beginning in September, 1965, and that all grades should be integrated." Nevertheless, all of the other demands referred to specific ways to improve the quality of instruction at McEvans High School, including a qualified principal and teachers, art and music classes, a better playground, a complete library, a better gym, workshop equipment, better and free food, and driver's education. The parents also wanted teachers removed who beat their children and an end to the split session (a school calendar established so that students could pick cotton during the fall) and the establishment of a standard nine-month schedule. Among other things, desegregation allowed a small number of blacks to gain firsthand knowledge of the systematic differences between black and white schools. In Bolivar and Madison counties, students and civil rights activists wrote detailed reports documenting these differences. This new information may have heightened demands for the improvement of all-black schools, where the majority of black students continued to go to school.[10]

These and other educational demands during this period demonstrate that educational quality was very central to black Mississippians. Historical studies of Mississippi and the United States suggest that there was a long tradition of individual and collective struggles for high-quality education in black communities (Lieberson 1980; McMillen 1989). In addition, surveys of black Americans throughout this period show strong preferences for integration (Kinder and Sanders 1996). However, black collective action in Mississippi illustrates a more complex picture of the demand for school desegregation and school reform more generally. These demands are neither an endorsement of integration for its own sake nor a statement of support for black separatism. Rather, the demands suggest a pragmatic orientation built on the desire to gain the highest-quality schools possible. Nevertheless, school desegregation was on the horizon regardless of whether or how strongly it was desired by black or white Mississippians, and I examine this process and how it shaped Mississippi communities in the next section.

The Alexander v. Holmes Case *and Rapid Desegregation*

The second stage in the desegregation of Mississippi schools began in the middle of the 1969–70 school year through the mandate of the Supreme Court's decision in *Alexander v. Holmes County.* The decision combined a set of nine Justice Department suits and sixteen NAACP Legal Defense Fund suits. The outcome of this complex trip through the legal system was an end to freedom of choice plans in thirty-three Mississippi school districts and a court order to desegregate thirty districts in the middle of the 1969-70 school year.[11]

In the summer of 1969, the Fifth Circuit Court of Appeals ordered desegregation for the upcoming school year. At the local level, white Mississippians began mobilizing. For example, in Cleveland the local Farm Bureau sponsored a mass meeting of a thousand local whites to protest the decision. The meeting was attended by local political leaders, who vowed to fight the decision.[12] The desegregation order was followed by an unusual intervention on the part of the Nixon administration, when the secretary of Health Education and Welfare, Robert Finch, requested a delay in the implementation of the decision. While the Fifth Circuit panel of judges granted the delay, the lower court's decision to delay was quickly reversed by the Supreme Court on October 29, 1969 (see Munford 1973). Frank Parker notes that "within ten months [of the Supreme Court decision], 146 of Mississippi's 148 school districts had been forced to abandon ineffective freedom of choice plans and to adopt new desegregation plans that revised attendance boundaries and employed zoning, pairing, busing, and other remedies to achieve fully integrated school systems" (1987, 693).

Table 7.1 summarizes the aggregate pattern of desegregation of Mississippi counties. I have measured the level of segregation using a dissimilarity index. This is a standard indicator in studies of school segregation that can be interpreted as the proportion of black students who would

---

TABLE 7.1: School Desegregation, 1968–79

	1968–69	1970–71	1972–73	1978–79
Index of Dissimilarity (mean of counties)	0.849	0.312	0.311	0.316

Note: This table reports mean values for counties.

---

have to be transferred to achieve a racially balanced distribution of students within a school district. High values indicate higher levels of segregation (James and Taueber 1985). Table 7.1 shows that there was a substantial transformation of the public school system from the late 1960s through the early 1970s. Despite open resistance, a massive institutional change occurred in an amazingly brief period of time.

The National Education Association (NEA) sent a team to observe and collect information on the desegregation process in the spring of 1970 for the counties covered by the *Alexander v. Holmes* decision. The report provides a detailed and immediate assessment of the changes that were taking place in Mississippi. The NEA team identified three major concerns about the unfolding desegregation process: (1) the extent of meaningful integration within desegregated schools, (2) the rise of private segregationist academies, and (3) the displacement of black teachers and administrators. Their findings merit detailed consideration because there is little evidence this close to the ground during this process.

The NEA's findings described ongoing mechanisms to avoid integration within formally desegregated schools. Again, they noted several communities where community groups such as the League of Women Voters or a local Human Relations Council attempted to broker a smooth transition through this period. Nevertheless, there were many indications that the resistance was quite strong:

> Virtually all elementary schools have maintained internal segregation, with white and black classes retaining their former composition and teaching personnel. Black and white students eat lunch at separate hours, have separate recess periods, and in at least one school, use separate libraries. . . . In another school, bells to signal class changes ring at different times for black and white students so that even walking through the halls is segregated.

Segregation in extracurricular activities was pervasive if not stronger. Especially noteworthy is the NEA's observation that there was no in-service training of teachers and other school personnel to facilitate desegregation and that school officials regularly complained about the lack of support and leadership from state authorities.[13]

The NEA's second set of findings pertained to the formation of private segregationist academies. I describe this process in greater detail below, but it is worth highlighting some of the NEA's findings during this peak period of school desegregation. In some communities, white leaders took an active role in moving toward a unified public school system. However, in many school districts, there was a "massive exodus." The report describes the process in one community from local press coverage:

The public school, opened in 1947, was declared surplus by school officials in June 1969 and sold to an individual, using sealed bids for $1,500. Team members learned that the purchaser, in turn, sold it to a private group for $10. The school, a relatively modern and well-built facility, is now privately operated for white students only; former public school buses, also declared surplus and put up for bid, have been obtained and are now being used to transport the students to the school. In another county, a retired district superintendent set up a private school; in still another district, a local judge is responsible for the establishment of the private school.[14]

The NEA team speculated that the support for these academies might be short-lived, but as we will see below, this was not the case in most Mississippi communities.

Finally, the NEA noted the potential threats to black teachers and administrators during the process of desegregation. Department of Health, Education and Welfare data show that there was a decline in the employment of black teachers and administrators during this period. Data are available for sixty-two Mississippi counties for the period from 1968 to 1972, and they show that the absolute decline was relatively small (fifty-two fewer teachers in 1972), but the relative decline was more substantial because the total number of teachers in these counties grew during this period with an increase of 1,177 white teachers.[15] The NEA staff did not find cases of black principals who were fired, but most did have their authority significantly reduced. In the mergers, there were often black and white "co-principals," with the black principal taking on "responsibilities that are either undefined or of a clerical or menial nature, or restricted to black students and teachers." In many cases, black teachers continued to teach all-black classrooms, and they were also vulnerable to having their responsibilities and authority reduced. The limited involvement of teachers in the civil rights movement may have reduced the likelihood of a collective mobilization to address these developments.[16]

The picture that emerges is a major process of systemic reorganization with significant cross-pressures that left black students and school personnel open to new forms of discrimination. In addition to the trends noted by the NEA, another key element of this story is the social organization of program implementation. Like the freedom of choice plans, most of the negotiation occurred between HEW staff and local school administrators, making the process closed to civil rights groups, teachers, parents, and the broader public. Unlike the poverty programs that established formal mechanisms for community input, school desegregation was a process administered by professionals. The lack of clear forms of communication closed off avenues for public input, and it also led to significant confusion and misinformation because there were minimal channels through which the details of school desegregation could be communicated to the broader community.

The Formation of Private Academies

The process of public school desegregation was mirrored by the process of private school formation by whites. Mississippi's State Department of Audit tracked the enrollment decline for the districts covered by *Alexander v. Holmes County*, finding that enrollments declined 15.29 percent from the 1968–69 school year to the beginning of the 1969–70 school year before the implementation of desegregation. Enrollments fell another 15 percent from the beginning of the fall to the beginning of the spring semester.[17]

State and private support were critical in the formation of the academies. State support came through tuition grants, tax exemption, and school materials that were transferred from the public to the private school system. The flow of these resources was eventually challenged by civil rights groups, but this was after an initial "boost" was provided to the new "private" institutions by the state (Graham 1970; Rosenthal 1970). For example, the state legislature provided a tuition stipend of $240 annually to students attending private schools (Wooten 1970b). During these formative years, state support ranged from 17.2 percent to 90 percent of the total tuition costs at private school.[18] Terry Carroll conducted a study of the formation of private academies in Mississippi, and in his interviews with local academy leaders, he found that "some early private school founders have questioned the possibility of operating their organizations without this early state support" (1981, 134).

Court documents reveal the funding for the Cruger-Tchula Academy in Holmes County, one of the first academies in Mississippi. For the 1965–66 school year, the school took $104,685. This included "$94,210 in cash, $9,749 in non-cash contribution of labor and equipment, . . . and $725 in textbooks given by the State of Mississippi." The cash contributions included $38,831 in tuition of which $22,200 came from the state as tuition grants.[19] In Canton 579 desks from the public schools were reportedly sold for fifty cents each, and three buses were sold for $500.[20]

Sociologist James Loewen was on the faculty of Tougaloo College in the late 1960s and 1970s, and he organized a project with the Southern Regional Council where Tougaloo students conducted intensive field research on school desegregation in Mississippi towns. During the 1972–73 year, one of his students conducted research in Lexington in Holmes County. She found that the public schools in Lexington had been abandoned by all but three white students, and black faculty were shocked to find after desegregation that much of the school infrastructure had been removed, including athletic and shop equipment.[21]

In addition to the flow of resources from public to private institutions, the public school system sustained a $12 million budget cut by the state legislature because of the loss of students.[22] State support for public schools was based on the average daily attendance, so the abandonment of public schools undermined the resources of the public school system.

A second type of resource for the emerging academies was the mobilization of private funds into the academy system, which included donations of money, land, materials, and labor. In Canton, for example, parents and students spent part of the Christmas break renovating a former tent factory that would serve as a new private school. One teacher noted that whites in Canton "have decided that the battle with the Federal Government is over and that there is nothing left to do but either let their kids go to school with the coloreds or pay tuition to keep them apart" (Wooten 1970a, 28). Additional resources came from religious institutions like the Baptist Church, which attempted to organize and support academies, and local banks, which provided low-interest loans to the new academies (Reed 1969; 1970)

To what extent were academies linked to the prior organizational foundation of the Citizens' Council? Although the Citizens' Council claimed to sponsor 150 academies throughout the South by 1969, the role of "sponsor" was vague (Bigart 1969). Only a small percentage of the academies were actual "Council Schools," and these were concentrated in Jackson, the state capital and the headquarters of the organization. While the Citizens' Council did not play a direct organizing role in most academies, it did play two pivotal roles. First, the Jackson headquarters "served as 'a clearing house of information,' maintaining a register of private schools and available instructors and administrators, as well as potential physical facilities" (McMillen 1971, 303). By the mid-1960s, much space in the organization's monthly newsletter was reserved for articles such as "How to Start a Private School" and "Private Schools Continue to Increase." The second role played by the Citizens' Council was the residue of informal ties solidified in many Mississippi communities from earlier organizing. As social movement scholars have noted, one of the most important legacies of a movement organization is the networks left behind when the organization collapses (Tarrow 1994). These ties were also mobilized in the Mississippi Private School Association (MPSA), a statewide organization that linked academies and sponsored activities including athletic events. The MPSA held its first statewide meeting in 1968, building upon the earlier foundation of the Citizens' Council and the Council School Foundation.[23]

Figure 7.1 presents yearly totals of the number of students attending private academies and other private schools. There is a substantial increase in the enrollments at private academies for the 1969–70 school year (22,919) over the 1968–69 year (5,393). Enrollments quadrupled followed by further increases in the early 1970s. Some studies of "white flight" find that after the implementation year, substantial numbers of whites reentered the public school system at times, offsetting the initial losses. Private school attendance clearly dropped by the mid-1970s, though the drop is slight. More detailed data would be required to determine whether this drop actually represented white public school reentry.

FIGURE 7.1: Growth of Mississippi Private Academies, 1966–74

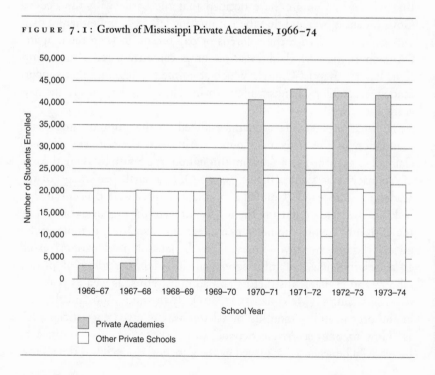

In general, the academies that were established and survived several years were likely to continue beyond the 1970s.

Private academies are distinguished from other private schools such as parochial, military, and all-black private schools. Enrollments at these schools remained relatively constant before and after 1969 and were not the strategy pursued by whites resisting school desegregation in Mississippi. For the most part, this is because parochial schools were concentrated in a different set of counties than those where academies were established in the late 1960s and early 1970s.

By the fall of 1970, the types of desegregation orders that had been implemented in the *Alexander* school districts were being implemented in school districts throughout the state. Hence, the aggregate pattern observed in figure 7.1 shows a substantial lift in the 1969–70 school year followed by a near doubling of that number for the 1970–71 year. This makes the 1970–71 school year the pivotal year for the establishment of academies.

Indicators of School Desegregation and White Resistance

Table 7.2 compares the patterns of desegregation and academy attendance for counties by the level of movement activity. Here, we see that the counties with sustained civil rights activity had much lower levels of desegregation during this period and much higher levels of academy attendance. Ironically, the counties that resisted desegregation most effectively also had the strongest private all-white school systems. It seems likely that in these counties there was a dynamic interaction between the private and public systems. In movement counties, public school administrators may have worked harder to resist desegregation as they attempted to keep white parents from enrolling their children in private academies. To a large degree, the most intense and successful efforts to resist desegregation occurred in communities with highly mobilized civil rights movements.

Black mobilization seemed to be a unifying threat for whites, creating the solidarity necessary for widespread countermobilization. Some scholars have found that a similar phenomenon occurred with voter registration where increases in black voter registration escalated white voter registration (Alt 1994). These findings underscore the importance of examining the interaction between movements and countermovements.

There are several additional factors that played a role in determining the extent of desegregation in Mississippi counties. Counties that were included in the *Alexander v. Holmes* decision had much higher levels of

TABLE 7.2: School Desegregation and the Level of Movement Activity for Mississippi Counties

	Movement Counties		Non-Movement Counties	State
	Sustained	Episodic		
Segregation: Index of Dissimilarity				
1968–69	0.912	0.881	0.777	0.849
1970–71	0.480	0.267	0.255	0.312
1972–73	0.451	0.262	0.267	0.311
1978–79	0.433	0.289	0.269	0.316
Private Academies: Enrollment as percentage of white school-age children (ages 5–17)				
1966–67 (%)	2.8	3.8	0.0	1.9
1967–68 (%)	3.3	4.1	0.2	2.2
1968–69 (%)	4.4	5.8	0.8	3.3
1969–70 (%)	16.8	13.2	7.8	11.7
1970–71 (%)	24.1	21.9	12.4	18.3
1971–72 (%)	25.4	21.9	13.1	18.9
1972–73 (%)	24.9	21.6	13.2	18.7
1973–74 (%)	23.9	20.8	13.8	18.5
1974–75 (%)	23.3	18.6	11.3	16.6
Number of counties	19	27	35	81

Note: This table reports mean values for counties.

support for the academies (37 percent of white school-age children attending academies in 1970–71 as compared to 12 percent in all other counties). Surprisingly, this case had no effect on the level of desegregation as measured by the dissimilarity index. In terms of academy formation, the *Alexander v. Holmes* counties were given a tactical advantage in the establishment of academies. These counties were part of one of the key desegregation decisions to go before the Supreme Court receiving enormous public attention. The "weightiness" of the situation combined with an external actor to mobilize against gave local countermovements an opportune context within which to organize new institutions. In Bolivar County, a thousand whites rallied against the decision before it was even clear that the decision would be implemented. In addition, the final decision called for desegregation to take place at the beginning of the second semester. This disruptiveness may have provided extra incentive to those inclined toward organizing a private academy or sending their children to one, and this may have added to the sense of institutional crisis. In the counties covered by *Alexander v. Holmes*, whites were likely to be busy organizing academies during the first half of 1970, while their counterparts in the noncovered counties were watching to see what happened next.[24]

The academies were also facilitated by the organizational residues of local Citizens' Council organizations. Counties that had Citizens' Councils in the 1950s also had greater levels of support for private academies: 22.7 percent of school-age whites attending academies in Citizens' Council counties versus 8.4 percent in all other counties. This relationship makes sense when combined with the key role played by the state-level Citizens' Council in encouraging the development of academies. However, there is no relationship between the presence of a Citizens' Council organization and the level of desegregation in a county.

Finally, one might expect that the percentage of black students in a county would be related to the support for academies and the level of desegregation. In fact, one might also expect that the relationships described above could be accounted for if the percentage black is taken into consideration. First, it is true that the percentage black in a county is correlated with academy attendance and desegregation. For example, 52.3 percent of white school-age children attended academies in majority-black counties (10.5 percent in all other counties). The mean dissimilarity score for majority-black counties is 0.501 compared to 0.274 for all other counties (note that higher values indicate greater levels of segregation).[25] Although it is true that the percentage black in a county is related to resistance to desegregation, this factor does not undermine any of the other relationships described above in analyses that take all of these factors into account.

Explaining White Countermobilization

An important line of argument suggests that the primary determinant of white resistance to black challenges is the level of contact between blacks and whites that would result from changes in existing institutions. Susan Olzak and her colleagues (1994) make a variant of this argument that they call "competition theory." The theory proposes that conflict emerges within a sequence of processes. In particular, conflict is most likely as intense forms of ethnic boundaries break down (i.e., housing or labor markets) and competition over institutional resources increases. Olzak et al. argue that "both anticipated fears that racial contact will rise and actual shifts in interracial contact foster racial conflict that has been generated by competition processes" (1994, 201). According to competition theorists, labor markets are key sites of interracial competition that can lead to conflict. In venues beyond the labor market, competition theorists have found support for this claim. For example, a recent study on the rate of antibusing protests in U.S. cities was predicted by "(1) increases in white's exposure to African-Americans, (2) decreases in school segregation, and (3) decreases in whites' residential isolation levels" (Olzak, Shanahan, and West 1994, 232).

Research on white flight finds strong support for competition theory, showing that the proportion of the population black plays an important role in "virtually all" of the studies reviewed by Christine Rossell, a leading scholar of school desegregation (1983, 31). Luther Munford, in a study of the thirty school districts affected by the *Alexander* decision, argues that "a demographic factor—the Negro percentage within the school district's boundaries—appears to have an extraordinary influence on white resistance to unitary desegregation" (1973, 23; see also Bullock and Rodgers 1976).[26]

Typically, white flight is considered to be the aggregation of individual calculation. However, in Mississippi, whites faced a situation where the two obvious individual choices of moving to different school districts or attending already established private schools were either not available or not sufficient to accommodate all of the whites resisting integrated education. Certainly, many whites pursued "individualistic" strategies for dealing with the perceived consequences in desegregation. For example, in Natchez, where a system of zoning was implemented, the school superintendent found many whites submitting "change of address" forms to remain in a majority-white school (Reed 1969). Because Mississippi had repealed its compulsory attendance law in 1956, parents also had the option of withdrawing their children from school altogether. At the level of collective action, Mississippi whites engaged in boycotts and protests. Yet, ultimately, the establishment of academies became the dominant countermovement strategy.

The resistance to desegregation was part of a broader countermovement strategy that flowed out of the prior history of organized white resistance to the civil rights movement. In other words, whites were not only responding to the proportion of African Americans in their community, but to the *social movement mobilization* of that community—the history of protests, boycotts, voter canvassing, legal action, and other activism. In addition to movement mobilization, more conventional electoral mobilization, such as black candidates running for office, influenced white resistance to school desegregation.

Countermovements are often distinguished from social movements along a number of key dimensions, including membership, structural position, tactics, and goals (see Lo 1982; Meyer and Staggenborg 1996; Mottl 1980; Zald and Useem 1987). An elite base was especially important for the academies—a strategy requiring the mobilization of substantial resources. This is in contrast to less "costly" strategies like antibusing protests or letter-writing campaigns. This difference in the "cost" of the strategy helps to differentiate the establishment of academies as an elite-sponsored strategy versus antibusing movements, which seem to have a working- and lower-middle-class base (James 1989; Mottl 1980; Olzak, Shanahan, and West 1994).[27] In the case of large metropolitan areas, upper- and middle-class whites were likely to move from school districts experiencing desegregation (Rossell 1983). This strategy was not viable for many white elites (and nonelites) in Mississippi.

As I claimed in chapter 2, movements and countermovements become involved in complex interactions that are shaped by the intervention of the state. Successes for movements can become opportunities for countermovement by crystallizing the threat. This insight is crucial for understanding the "opening" created by the *Alexander* decision for advocates of an all-white private school system.

Not surprisingly, when whites began establishing private academies, this created a new set of tactical dilemmas for the civil rights movement. The most important was stopping the flow of public resources into the private school system. In the case of Mississippi, the *Alexander* decision signaled a major shift in the political opportunity structure. The shift would have impacted groups across the South interested in resisting desegregation. However, the signal would have been loudest and clearest to those within the school districts covered by the *Alexander* decision.

The resistance to school desegregation shows the underlying political nature of educational institutions (James 1989). Christine Rossell notes that "few studies have examined systematically the effect of [white] protest and leadership support for desegregation on white flight, primarily because the costs of collecting such data are quite high" (1983, 35). Studies that examine the political mobilization of blacks are even less common. Munford's study of the school districts affected by the *Alexander* decision showed that the population ratio (proportion black in a district) was the single most important factor explaining white flight (Munford 1973). At the end of his study, Munford begins to reflect on the factors associated with the relative proportions of blacks and whites, and he speculates that the perceived threat of black political power was the motivating force for parents exiting the public school system.

The effort to establish segregationist academies was linked to a broader countermovement aimed at resisting the civil rights movement. This argument contrasts with the idea found in individualistic explanations of white flight as a direct aggregation of white parental preferences (e.g., Conlon and Kimenyi 1991). Movements can present a threat through the development of ongoing local organizations. When movements do emerge, they are likely to engender countermobilization—in this case, white support for a system of private schools.

Conclusion

The research presented in this chapter speaks to several unresolved theoretical debates on the study of social movements and provides further insights into the process of institutional formation and social change. Patterns of racial contention are undoubtedly shaped by racial competition as proposed by ecological theories. However, political processes and movement dynamics have effects independent or beyond these aggregate structural characteristics. The primary questions addressed here concern the relations between social movements, the political and legal context, and institutional outcomes.

The research presented here demonstrates that strategies of white resistance were shaped by broad features of the local social structure—in this case, the relative size of the black population. The salience of this factor may model perceived threat of interracial contact in schools, or it could be related to the indirect factor of white institutional control of schools and an electoral-political threat to white political dominance at the municipal and county level.

Aggregate structural characteristics are central but incomplete explanations of this particular case of countermobilization. The actions of the Supreme Court in the *Alexander v. Holmes* decision had differential effects for Mississippi school districts, which is reflected in the higher levels of support for academies in the covered counties. The decision provided a window of opportunity when a new pathway of institutionalized resistance was open to would-be challengers. Resource mobilization arguments have been faulted for overemphasizing organizational factors (at the expense of ideological and cultural factors) and for limited attention to the factors external to the movement. However, in this case, the organizational capacity of movements and countermovements explains the extent of white resistance to school desegregation. Many scholars have noted that the process of movement mobilization sets in motion the process of countermobilization (Lo 1982; Luker 1984; Meyer and Staggenborg 1996; Schwartz 1976; Zald and Useem 1987). However, there have been few efforts to specify beyond a narrative or descriptive level the interactive dynamics of this process and the outcomes generated by these dynamics. By focusing on the process of institution building and transformation, this analysis challenges prior research that focuses on education and white flight after the institutions had been established. The lower levels of desegregation and higher levels of academy support show that white Mississippians responded to the political threat of the civil rights movement to maintain institutional control of schools.

CHAPTER EIGHT

The Acquisition of Political Power

FROM 1965 to 1971, there was a massive increase in black political participation in Mississippi, with thousands of newly registered voters and hundreds of candidates campaigning for elected office at the municipal, county, and state level. Given that Mississippi had the largest black population of any state and many counties had a majority-black population, there were high hopes that blacks would attain significant political power. Despite some early successes such as Robert Clark's election in Holmes County, blacks had not made substantial gains by the early 1970s. I have pointed to the formal and informal obstacles that undermined black political power. In this chapter, I begin by describing the legal obstacles in greater detail—showing how they worked and how they were dismantled through the courts. Then I turn to the electoral campaigns of the mid-1970s through the early 1980s to show how blacks acquired more substantial political power in Mississippi. Finally, I describe the struggles to wield political power by black politicians once elected to office in Mississippi.

Dismantling Obstacles to Black Political Power

Following the Voting Rights Act, white politicians began instituting "vote dilution" mechanisms—rules governing electoral politics that served to minimize the potential influence of black voters. These mechanisms included gerrymandering of congressional districts and the creation of multimember districts for the state legislature by merging majority-black and majority-white districts. Some counties and cities switched from district to at-large systems for the election of county supervisor boards, school boards, and city councils. In general, at-large districts made it more difficult for black candidates to win elections. Requirements for independent candidates were made more stringent. Some municipalities used annexations to increase the proportion of white voters in the electorate. Finally, some formerly elected offices were switched to appointed offices. As a result of these changes, the potential power of black voters was substantially undermined, and a long series of legal battles began.

State Legislature and Congressional Districts

Connor v. Johnson (1979) was the first major case following the Voting Rights Act, with the MFDP and eight black activists using the one-person, one-vote principle to challenge the restructuring of congressional and legislative districts. Frank Parker, a lawyer involved in many of the cases, notes that "the lawsuit was filed after a statewide mass meeting at the black Masonic Temple in Jackson called by the Mississippi statewide civil rights coalition, COFO. . . . [T]he lawsuit reflected the strategic thinking of the MFDP leadership that a major vehicle of political entry into Mississippi's closed political system was federal court litigation" (1990, 86). MFDP leader Lawrence Guyot saw the case following the "challenge concept" that the MFDP had used at the Democratic National Convention in Atlantic City (Parker 1990, 86). The *Connor v. Johnson* case began in 1965 and was continuously litigated over fourteen years with nine trips to the Supreme Court.

The history of this case illustrates the discriminatory effect of the massive resistance legislation in the battle over the Mississippi legislature. Parker divides the litigation over reapportionment of the state legislature into two phases. The first phase from 1965 to 1976 focused on the discriminatory character of multi-member districts and the move to countywide elections, which diluted black votes that were geographically concentrated within the county. Multi-member districts diminished black voting power by pairing majority-white and majority-black districts together, which forced black candidates to run for office in the consolidated district where there were fewer black voters proportionately. The second phase from 1976 to 1979 focused on discriminatory boundaries or gerrymandering of single-member districts (Parker 1990, 105–6). The MFDP plaintiffs won this part of the *Connor v. Johnson* case in a 1977 Supreme Court decision. The Mississippi legislature was compelled to implement a new single-member district plan in 1979. The new plan was followed by the election of seventeen blacks to the state legislature, indicating the political significance of the decision (Parker 1990, 106).

The *Connor v. Johnson* case also challenged the redistricting of congressional boundaries. For congressional districts, proposed plans attempted to divide congressional districts horizontally across the state to pair the predominantly white counties in the eastern part of Mississippi with the predominantly black counties in the western side of the state. On the case's first trip in 1967, the Supreme Court issued a "nondecision" that the plaintiffs must prove discriminatory intent on the part of those designing the plan rather than proving discriminatory effect (Parker 1990, 91). As a result, it was not until 1981, when "the Justice Department objected under section 5 to a 'least change' plan . . . that a federal district court restored the Delta district as Mississippi's Second Congressional District" (Parker 1990, 91). Another five years passed before Mike Espy was elected to Congress from the district in 1986. Thus, Mississippi's massive resistance efforts limited black political influence in Congress for two decades following the Voting Rights Act.

At-Large Election Systems in Counties and Municipalities

The switch to at-large county supervisor elections was one of the first changes to be overturned by civil rights lawyers in the federal courts. The *Allen v. State Board of Elections* (1969) case was the consolidation of three separate Mississippi cases with a Virginia case that focused on changing methods of administering election and election rules. The Supreme Court's decision was a major victory for blacks in Mississippi because the Court interpreted voting in section 14 of the Voting Rights Act in "the broadest possible scope" to mean "all action necessary to make a vote effective in any primary, special, or general election" (Parker 1990, 97). The Court decision made any changes in electoral process after November 1, 1964, subject to preclearance by the Justice Department under section 5 of the Voting Rights Act. Prior to the decision, only changes in voter registration policy were subject to federal preclearance. The *Allen* decision had an important impact on county supervisors and school board elections, and the structure of city councils was challenged under a parallel set of legal cases.

In Canton the city had switched to the at-large election of city council members for the 1969 elections, and this change was successfully reversed in the *Perkins v. Matthews* case because the change was subject to federal review. However, many city councils had switched to at-large elections prior to the November 1, 1964, deadline. Therefore, plaintiffs used the Fourteenth Amendment, and they had to establish the more difficult standard that the changes were designed or maintained for the purpose of racial discrimination. In 1973 civil rights attorneys challenged a 1962 state law requiring thirty Mississippi cities to switch to at-large election systems. In *Stewart v. Waller*, the plaintiffs used "contemporary newspaper accounts [that] were unanimous about the bill's purpose." William Caraway, sponsor of the bill, stated that the new law would allow Mississippians "to maintain our southern way of life." The *Jackson Daily News* ran a story titled "Bill Would Make It Harder for Negroes to Win Elections," and the *Delta Democrat Times* stated: "The Senate today approved a bill designed to prevent the election of Negroes as city aldermen" (USCCR 1975, 284). In 1975 the Supreme Court ruled that the thirty municipalities would have to return to the district systems in place prior to the 1962 legislation. Because the Supreme Court did not "expand its injunction to all at-large municipal elections in Mississippi," other cities "would have to be litigated on a case-by-case basis" (Parker, Colby, and Morrison 1994, 141). Nevertheless, this litigation had a dramatic impact on the composition of municipal governing boards following 1975.

Through the 1970s and early 1980s, there were continuing legal battles to determine the exact standard for challenging at-large election systems. As part of the 1982 extension of the Voting Rights Act, Congress amended section 2 to eliminate the requirement of discriminatory intent. Following a judicial standard set in *Thornburg v. Gingles* (1986), plaintiffs had to demonstrate that "(1) a single-member district could be created in which minorities have a majority; (2) minority voters bloc vote for certain candidates; and (3) minority-preferred candidates usually are defeated by white bloc voting" to challenge at-large systems (Parker, Colby, and Morrison 1994, 142). This opened the door for a further round of litigation that virtually eliminated at-large election systems in Mississippi.

What is the significance of this long, complex period of legal battles following the Voting Rights Act? First, it shows that the rules governing the electoral process are critically important and that these rules can be used to undermine social movements. Second, this legal structure is not static but modified through the implementation of political strategies. Shifting to the courtroom prolongs the conflict through the slow machinations of the legal system, and it has the potential to demobilize social movement activists. Legal expertise and strategy become more important, and financial resources are required to sustain these struggles.

Aggregate Patterns of Black Office Holding

Before turning to the county-by-county analysis, I describe the statewide aggregate trends in black office holding. This brief sketch provides a backdrop for the analyses that follow. We have seen the trends in voter registration indicating a rapid and enduring increase in black registration. Table 8.1 reports the number of black elected officials in Mississippi for selected years (1968–85).

Increases in black office holding came more slowly and have never matched the overall proportion of the black population or the proportion of blacks among registered voters. The pattern of increase mirrored the successes of civil rights litigation challenging discriminatory electoral arrangements. Parker concludes that "in the post–Voting Rights Act period electoral structures were a key determinant of black electoral success or failure and . . . voting rights litigation to eliminate these barriers remained a critical component of black political progress (1990, 152). For

TABLE 8.1: Number of Black Elected Officials, 1968–85

	State Legislature	County Board of Supervisors	Magistrates, Justices of the Peace, and Constables	Mayors	Municipal Governing Boards	School Boards	Total BEO
1968	1	4	15	2	5	1	28
1969	—	—	—	—	—	—	—
1970	1	4	16	3	32	5	81
1971	—	—	—	—	—	—	—
1972	1	4	17	3	30	20	95
1973	1	8	41	4	39	31	152
1974	1	8	42	7	61	30	191
1975	1	11	39	7	53	37	192
1976	4	16	47	7	58	46	210
1977	4	16	47	14	124	60	295
1978	4	16	48	17	122	56	302
1979	6	17	48	17	141	58	327
1980	17	27	67	17	143	67	387
1981	17	27	69	20	162	80	436
1982	17	27	66	20	161	75	424
1983	—	—	—	—	—	—	—
1984	20	29	69	21	163	82	430
1985	20	38	64	21	162	83	444

black office holding, 1980 was a key turning point after movement lawyers challenged reapportionment plans based on the 1980 census. In the state legislature, gains came prior to this point in the 1979 elections. The victories in 1979 followed the favorable ruling in the *Connor v. Johnson* case that challenged multimember legislative districts.

For municipal elections, a primary challenge was the system of at-large elections. Here, litigation proceeded on a city-by-city basis rather than court rulings that applied across the jurisdiction of the federal courts. Following the disappointing municipal elections of 1969 and 1973, a cluster of suits was filed between the 1973 and 1977 municipal elections contesting the at-large election structures, and we can see the increases in blacks elected to municipal governing boards following this period of litigation. Even when at-large systems were successfully challenged, black chances of electoral success could be thwarted by gerrymandering or discriminatory annexation plans designed to increase the proportion of white voters in districts.

For county office holding, the system of at-large election of county supervisors was successfully challenged in the 1969 Supreme Court case *Allen v. State Board of Elections*. The Court ruled that these changes were subject to the preclearance requirement of the Voting Rights Act. Movement litigation was successful against this component of the massive-resistance legislation much earlier than in other arenas. This success stemmed from the fact that at-large county elections were instituted after the Voting Rights Act, so the discriminatory intent was much clearer than at-large municipal systems that often predated the act. Even with the favorable ruling in the *Allen* decision, black office holding did not increase substantially. Here, we see the effect of carefully gerrymandered boundaries that successfully divided the black electorate among the five districts in a county. As a result, movement lawyers pursued a county-by-county pattern of documenting the effect of these boundaries on black political exclusion. This brief sketch of black office holding illustrates the importance of examining white resistance and electoral structures. We see that the Voting Rights Act did not "automatically" translate into significant black political power. Further, we find that registration was only one intermediate outcome in an effort to secure electoral power. Hence, we must compare these different outcomes to one another. Yet many questions remain. In particular, what accounts for variation in political participation and office holding across Mississippi counties? I turn to this question in the remainder of this chapter.

Getting Elected to Office

Voter registration and voter turnout in statewide elections were mobilization tactics directed toward the obvious goal of electing candidates who would better represent the interests of black Mississippians. The best indicator of success in this arena is the election of black candidates to office. I examine the success in electing black candidates in the 1970s and early 1980s. The 1967 and 1971 elections were held well before the major components of the massive-resistance legislation were dismantled through the courts and by Justice Department intervention (Parker 1990). From the mid-1970s on, significant gains were made in electing black candidates to office. My analysis therefore uses the number of county-level black elected officials at three points (1974, 1979, and 1984) as dependent variables. Statewide, in 1974 there were 49 county-level black elected officials statewide; the figures for 1979 and 1984 are 99 and 132, respectively.

Studies of black politics in the South have found a consistent relationship between the proportion of the population that is black and the number of black elected officials. In electing black candidates to office, the racial distribution of the population plays an overwhelming role. In his study *Black Votes Count*, Parker supports a "65 percent rule": a black population of 65 percent is required to elect black candidates consistently. He notes that "all of the black county supervisors who have won office have been elected from majority-black districts, most of them 65 percent black or more" (1990, 159). A number of counties with a strong organizational base have faced a structural block prohibiting them from translating that organizational base into electoral representation, leaving blacks "in districts with a black population of less than 65 percent . . . dramatically underrepresented" (Parker, Colby, and Morrison 1994, 144).

Table 8.2 presents the relationship between the level of movement activity in the early 1960s and the number of county-level black elected officials—the total of black elected officials and the number of local school board members and county commissioners. As with voter participation and poverty programs, we see that movement activity is correlated with higher levels of black political power. We can also see here that there were significant increases in black office holding in the early 1980s, which followed successful movement litigation, reapportionment based on the 1980 census, and the 1983 county elections. Surprisingly, for several years the number of black elected officials in counties with episodic movements rivaled or exceeded those in counties with sustained movements in the

TABLE 8.2: Black Elected Officials and the Level of Movement Activity for Mississippi Counties

	Movement Counties		Non-Movement Counties	State
	Sustained	Episodic		
Total Black Elected Officials				
1974	1.16	0.85	0.11	0.60
1979	1.79	1.96	0.34	1.22
1984	2.26	2.30	0.54	1.53
Total Black Board of Education Members				
1974	1.11	0.67	0.09	0.52
1979	1.32	0.93	0.23	0.72
1984	2.21	1.26	0.23	1.04
Total Black County Commissioners				
1974	0.21	0.33	0.09	0.20
1979	0.21	0.41	0.09	0.22
1984	0.42	0.52	0.11	0.32
Number of counties	19	27	35	81

Note: This table reports mean values for counties.

1960s. This reflects the successful mobilization in the southwest part of Mississippi, where Charles Evers played an influential role from the late 1960s through the 1970s. Evers was mayor in Fayette in Jefferson County, and his organizing efforts extended into nearby Claiborne and Wilkinson.

The election of black candidates was heavily dependent on the proportion black of the voting-age population. Black candidates rarely received more than token levels of support from whites at the polls. We also know that the movement was more highly mobilized in the counties that had higher black populations, so it is important to determine whether civil rights activity remains an important factor when this and other factors are taken into consideration. We can find significant continuity in the organizations, leaders, and objectives in communities like Holmes County. Nevertheless, a more systematic test of the continuity of black political mobilization is warranted.

Table 8.3 presents the results from three separate OLS regression equations predicting the total number of county-level black elected officials. I have included several measures that might account for the election of black candidates, including early 1960s movement strength (Freedom

	County-level BEO, 1974	County-level BEO, 1979	County-level BEO, 1984
Freedom Summer volunteers	−.065	−.174	−.109
and staff, 1964	(−.009)	(−.048)	(−.030)
NAACP membership, 1966	.126	.188**	.217**
	(.090)	(.263)	(.299)
Violent Resistance Index,	−.211**	−.190*	−.188*
1960–69	(−.033)	(−.058)	(−.056)
Federal examiners, 1965–67	−.021	−.050	.057
	(−.078)	(−.348)	(.393)
Black candidates running for	.523***	.479***	.346***
office, 1967	(.338)	(.597)	(.426)
% vote for Whitley, 1966	.248**	.194*	.133
	(4.001)	(6.055)	(4.089)
Black voting-age population	.220**	.287***	.374***
as % of total, 1970	(2.340)	(5.908)	(7.585)
% Urban, 1970	.056	.043	.056
	(.004)	(.006)	(.008)
Constant	—	—	—
	(−1.195)***	(−2.320)**	(−2.573)**
R-squared	.701	.654	.633
Adj. R-squared	.667	.615	.592

* = p < .05; ** = p < .01; *** = p < .001 (one-tailed tests)

Note: The standardized coefficient is presented followed by the unstandardized coefficient in parentheses.

Summer), post–Voting Rights Act (VRA) movement organization (1966 NAACP membership), violent resistance from 1960–69, the presence of federal examiners, late 1960s electoral mobilization (black candidates running for office in 1967), electoral turnout measure (1966 Whitley campaign), the black voting-age population as a percentage of the total population in 1970, and the percentage urban.[1]

The late 1960s movement variable (NAACP) has a statistically significant and positive effect for 1979 and 1984, while the percentage vote for Clifton Whitley (1966) has a positive effect in 1974 and 1979. The relative size of the black voting-age population has a significant positive effect in all three models. The index of white violent resistance has a significant and negative impact on the number of county-level black elected officials for all three years. The two independent variables of percentage urban and presence of federal examiners do not have significant impacts on the number of black elected officials for any of these years.

The negative though nonsignificant effect of Freedom Summer results from the disproportionate impact of the southwest "Evers" counties (especially Jefferson and Claiborne), which can be treated as outliers because of the large residuals for each county. These are the only two counties in which the majority of county-level offices were held by blacks in 1984, and as noted above, they had no participation in Freedom Summer. A reanalysis of the three equations excluding Jefferson and Claiborne provides similar results; Freedom Summer has a positive but still nonsignificant effect.[2] These results confirm my earlier assertion that there was not one linear path leading to the election of black candidates.

The analyses presented in table 8.3 suggest that violent resistance played an important role in discouraging black office holding. This relationship is more interesting in light of the positive impact of violent resistance on the number of freedom votes cast in 1964 described in chapter 4. Over a long time frame, violent resistance plays a role in diminishing black acquisition of political power.

The most important finding reported in table 8.3 is the influence of the number of black candidates running for office in 1967 on the number of black elected officials in the 1970s and early 1980s. This is the most influential variable in the models for 1974 and 1979, and the second most influential variable in 1984. Overall, this pattern highlights the important role of the movement infrastructure and the development of local leaders in this period following the Voting Rights Act. Although few of these candidates were elected to office, the electoral effort surrounding their campaigns was an important connection between the civil rights organizing of the early 1960s and the acquisition of political power in the 1970s and 1980s. The influence of earlier black political mobilization and white violent resistance underscore the importance of studying the ongoing dynamics of movements and their consequences over a long time frame.

Refining the Links between Movements and Outcomes

This final segment of the quantitative analysis builds on the prior analysis to summarize the overall development of black political capacity in Mississippi. I present a path analysis for black elected officials in 1984. Previous discussion referred only to direct effects; path analysis allows for a consideration of the direct and indirect effects, providing a better model of the underlying causal processes. In addition, the path diagram nicely summarizes key points that emerged in the earlier models. These include (1) the transformation of the movement infrastructure to an electoral mobilization infrastructure in the 1967 elections and (2) the role of repression in diminishing the acquisition of political power.

The results of the path analysis are presented in figure 8.1.[3] In the path model, I use the number of black candidates for office in 1967 as an indicator of the electoral base in the county after the Voting Rights Act. Numbers on paths are standardized coefficients. The strongest direct effect on black elected officials is the relative size of the black voting-age population; this is followed closely by the number of black candidates for office in 1967. NAACP has a direct positive effect while white violence has a direct negative effect. Indirect effects mediated by black candidates are black voting-age population, Freedom Summer, NAACP membership in 1966, and white violence, in order of strength determined by the path coefficients. Indirect effects through NAACP are Freedom Summer and black voting-age population. White violence is positively impacted by Freedom Summer and percentage urban.[4] Finally, Freedom Summer is positively affected by both exogenous variables, urban and black voting-age population.

FIGURE 8.1: Path Model for Number of County-Level Black Elected Officials, 1984

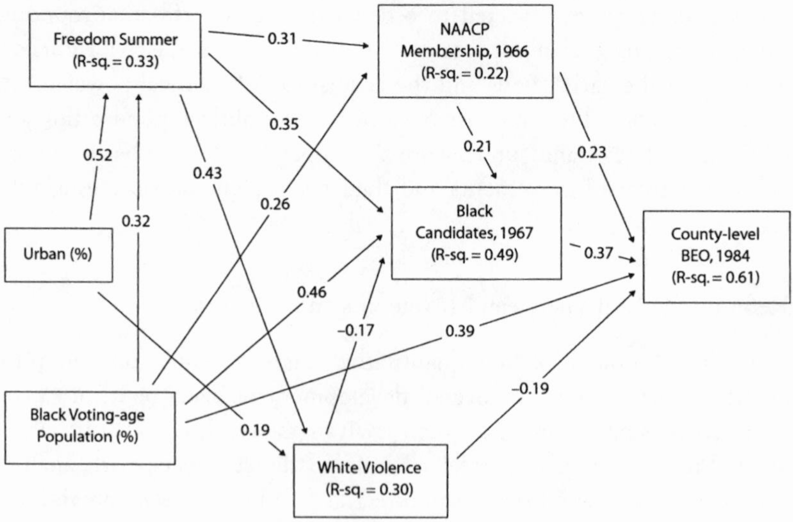

The path analysis demonstrates that the number of black candidates in 1967 is a key intervening variable transmitting effects of the movement base of the pre- and post-VRA period (Freedom Summer in 1964 and NAACP membership in 1966) to later black electoral success. The model specifies the transformation of the early movement base, which results in an infrastructure prepared to take advantage of new opportunities as they emerge in the 1970s and 1980s. The effects of Freedom Summer are mediated by NAACP membership and black candidates, and NAACP membership has both a direct and indirect effect through black candidates. This suggests that one of the ways that social movements generate social change is by producing a set of local organizations and networks. In this case, I call that cluster of organizations and networks the "electoral mobilization infrastructure."[5] In Mississippi the movement generated an independent structure by the late 1960s, which was positioned to take advantage of opportunities in the 1970s and 1980s. In addition, repression has negative direct and indirect effects on the number of black elected officials. Once again, the number of black candidates in 1967 is an important factor mediating the relationship between violence and black elected officials. One of the ways repression "works" is by reducing the number of black candidates for office.

The Impact of Black Politics

So far, this chapter has demonstrated the long-term impact of the civil rights movement on political participation and the election of black candidates. A further question remains: What impact has this participation had on the policy making and resource allocation of local political bodies? The pursuit of black political power was built on the assumption that black elected officials would be responsive to the demands of the black community and address the deeply entrenched inequities in the distribution of "public goods." All facets of southern politics reflected these inequalities.[6] As a result, newly elected black officials faced a tremendous burden of expectations, ranging from employment to paved roads.

This issue came into focus for me when I was doing some preliminary research in Mississippi for this study. I had traveled to Mississippi to collect archival materials and conduct interviews. I interviewed one of the long-term activists in Mississippi, Rims Barber, who told me a fascinating story about the early political career of Bennie Thompson—who is now the only black Congress member from Mississippi. Thompson had been a prominent activist at Tougaloo College, a hub of movement activity in Mississippi, and he later ran for city council in the small town of Bolton. In 1973 he was elected mayor (though the election was challenged vigorously in the courts by incumbent white elected officials), and among other things he tried to address one of the recurring problems in the town—the lack of adequate fire protection in the black community. Efforts were made to improve the quality of equipment and training. And, of course, the fire department began hiring blacks. These reforms seemed to have little impact on the ability of the fire department to protect homes in the black community. Ultimately, an engineer investigated and found that the water mains in the black neighborhoods were half the diameter of those in white neighborhoods. This, then, set in motion a much larger effort to secure federal funds to renovate the water system in Bolton so that an adequate and equitable water supply would serve both parts of the town. This account captures the dynamics of the civil rights struggle that are missing from the conventional history of the civil rights movement.[7] Of course, fire protection was only one of many arenas where racial inequalities had to be addressed. The case illustrates, on the one hand, some of the obstacles facing newly elected black officials, and it also exemplifies the increased responsiveness to black constituents by black elected officials. During the 1970s Thompson was successful at acquiring substantial federal funds to support other local improvements such as paved roads, public housing, and highway construction, and these efforts were part of a broader trend among black elected officials in the South. In 1979 Thompson observed that "the city halls are no longer places our black folks fear to come—old people come in and they kiss me. They are now a part of what's going on" (Johnson 1979; see also Goodman 1979).

The research by social scientists on this subject generally concludes that black "electoral participation does indeed make a difference, albeit a limited difference" on policy making (M. Morris 1984). The vast majority of the research has examined urban areas, finding impacts on employment, public services, parks, and recreation (see Eisinger 1982; Keech [1968] 1981). However, similar patterns have been found in the small towns of the South (Button 1982, 1989; Morrison 1987). James Button's study of six Florida communities compares different types of outcomes, "including police and fire protection, streets, parks and recreation, and employment," finding between 1960 and 1985 substantial improvement in each of these areas. However, there was variation among outcomes and across the towns. For example, greater gains were made in capital-intensive benefits such as parks or street paving than was the case for labor-intensive benefits such as police and fire protection. In addition, Button finds that towns that achieved black political dominance brought about a redistribution of public goods (1989).

Black elected officials may generate a further, unintended outcome by encouraging continued black political mobilization. Using the 1987 General Social Survey, Lawrence Bobo and Franklin Gilliam examine the impact of black office holding (which they call black empowerment) on black political participation. They find,

> first, that where blacks hold positions of political power, they are more active and participate at higher rates than whites of comparable socioeconomic status. Second, black empowerment is a contextual cue of likely policy responsiveness that encourages blacks to feel that participation has intrinsic value. . . . [B]lack empowerment . . . has broad and lasting consequences on how often, and why, blacks become active participants in the political process. (1990, 387)

Black political power can reinforce and sustain mobilization rather than leading to a demobilized and passive response. This finding parallels the Holmes County case, where small victories in the electoral arena were perceived as evidence of the efficacy of mobilization and fueled continued development and support of the movement infrastructure.

These positive assessments have been challenged by critics who view black elected officials as providing only symbolic gains but no real political influence for their constituencies (see, for example, R. Smith 1996). In Mississippi counties, black elected officials had an impact on the distribution of local government employment. Certain elected offices were especially efficacious. For example, an article on black politics in a Mississippi community newspaper noted that

> each Black supervisor will have control over his own budget [within the district of the county] and will hire his own workers. In addition, each will be able to appoint persons to key boards and commissions. However, all are in minority positions when it comes to the crucial decision-making process in which the Board of five determines such items as county mileage, county budget, industrial development, etc. The impact of Black persons participating in these decisions (even if outvoted every time) is potentially significant. It gives the Black community an 'entre' into these

important processes and a "legitimate" form for the presentation of its goals and ideals for the development of the land in which they live.[8]

We can assess the possible influence of the movement infrastructure, black political participation, and black office holding on black employment by local government. Table 8.4 presents data on black employment by local government, including measures of the percentage of local government employment held by blacks in 1970 and 1980. This table reports the total and percentage change in local government by blacks during this important decade. These measures of change provide the best indicators of the relationship between black political mobilization and the distribution of public resources. For example, notice that counties with sustained movement activity, higher voter turnout, and more black elected officials experienced much greater increases in the percentage of local government employment by blacks. These trends reflect real changes in the local political institutions in Mississippi that can be traced back to the earlier development of the civil rights movement. In additional analyses (not shown here) that control for each of these factors and the size of the black population, the number of black elected officials during the 1970s and the voter turnout by blacks have statistically significant and positive impacts on black employment by local governments. Measures of early 1960s civil rights mobilization do not have significant effects, but this is not surprising given the inclusion of more proximate measures of black mobilization. And, as we have already seen, the early movement was a key factor in the development of black political capacity of the 1970s. Although these are relatively simple measures of black gains (for example, we cannot tell whether these positions had greater responsibilities and salaries than the menial job blacks had been hired for in the past), they do provide striking support for the claim that black mobilization had much more than symbolic impacts at the local level. These measures of black public sector employment are only the most visible indicators of broader changes reflected most strongly in the counties that developed and sustained movement infrastructures.

However, this finding should not lead us to ignore limitations on the efficacy of black electoral mobilization. There have been specific and powerful obstacles to black political gains in the South, especially political efforts to address economic issues. These include the limited tax base of southern counties and municipalities, which is compounded by the long history of institutional racism (Button 1989; Morrison 1987). Moreover, there are the constraints inherent within electoral politics, such as the

TABLE 8.4: The Impact of Black Political Mobilization on Black Employment in Local Government

	Black Employment in Local Government				
County Characteristics	% of Total Local Government Employment, 1970	% of Total Local Government Employment, 1980	Total Change, 1980	% Change, 1970–80	Number of Counties
Level of Movement Activity					
Sustained	42.2	47.2	497.3	5.0	19
Episodic	41.4	42.8	189.9	1.4	27
None	27.2	29.1	175.3	1.9	35
Black Voter Turnout, 1970s					
High, 35% +	34.2	41.4	318.8	7.2	27
Medium, 25–35%	34.2	34.4	220.3	0.2	31
Low, 0–25%	38.7	38.6	229.5	−0.1	23
Black County Supervisors, 1974					
One or more	54.6	65.5	186.7	10.9	10
None	32.8	34.1	265.4	1.3	71
Black County Supervisors, 1979					
One or more	53.9	65.0	169.6	11.1	11
None	32.6	33.7	269.2	1.1	70
County-Level Black Elected Officials, 1974					
Two or more	57.0	66.4	227.1	9.4	9
One	48.1	52.2	222.2	4.1	5
None	31.7	33.1	262.0	1.4	67
County-Level Black Elected Officials, 1979					
Two or more	56.5	63.3	184.4	6.8	12
One	43.5	53.1	304.1	9.6	10
None	29.9	30.2	261.9	0.3	59
Total	35.5	38.0	255.7	2.5	81.0

Note: This table reports mean values for counties.

limited ability of local governments to influence the private sector and thereby generate broader economic gains. Nevertheless, there is substantial evidence that black political participation and black elected officials alter the distribution of public resources.

Conclusion

In this chapter, we have seen how obstacles to electoral impact worked, and we have seen the changes that resulted as these obstacles were dismantled. Both violence and vote-dilution tactics undermined the capacity of local movements and the long-term impacts of the movement. Strikingly, I find that as the legal obstacles to black office holding were undermined, activists were able to build on the prior infrastructure of the civil rights movement to win political office and make changes in local politics. Black elected officials were constrained in these efforts by limited resources and continuing opposition. However, the difference between counties that had black officeholders and those that did not suggests that there was real significance to these victories. With these findings concerning the long-term trajectories of Mississippi counties, we are reminded of the differences between Holmes County and Madison County reflected in the assessments of movement activists with a stronger sense of pride and collective efficacy in Holmes County compared to feelings of disappointment and sacrifice in Madison.

CHAPTER NINE

Conclusion: The Legacies of the Civil Rights Movement

I HAVE cast a broad net in this study to determine the patterns of change resulting from the civil rights movement in Mississippi. In this conclusion, I highlight key findings and their implications for the study of the civil rights movement and social movements more generally.

Most scholars assume that movements target change at the national level. While some movements do attempt to leverage change in federal law or policy, this strategy did not predominate during the civil rights movement nor is it the case for many social movements. Most movements seek change at a variety of levels, and the civil rights movement through its "local movement centers" attempted to transform the social structures of the South. Local movements did, in fact, shape an array of short-term and long-term outcomes in Mississippi.

Most commonly, activists and observers are interested in whether a movement succeeds. I have examined the intended and unintended impacts of the civil rights movement. In the mid-1970s, David Campbell and Joe Feagin observed that whether or not the movement produced changes in politics depends on "the standard of evaluation. . . . Small or inconsequential breakthroughs for some may be of great magnitude for others" (1975, 131). Campbell and Feagin's comments apply specifically to electoral politics, and they hold true for other arenas. Rather than the absolute magnitude of change, I have focused on the relative distribution of change across counties. The analysis I have presented shows that movements had effects where mobilization was sustained through an organizational infrastructure made up of diverse leaders and a complex leadership structure, multiple organizations, informal ties that cross geographic and social boundaries, and a resource base that draws substantially on contributions from their members for both labor and money. Given the obstacles facing the civil rights movement in Mississippi, the substantial and long-term impacts that local movements produced are even more noteworthy.

Continuity and Transformation in Three Mississippi Counties

In the first and most central case, Holmes County showed how a large movement base was transformed into highly visible political outcomes—most notably, large numbers of black elected officials. These are the cases that have received substantial national attention as the success stories of the civil rights movement (Morrison 1987). Mississippi counties that fit this model include Claiborne (Port Gibson), Coahoma (Clarksdale), Holmes (Lexington and Tchula), Jefferson (Fayette), and Marshall (Holly Springs).[1]

Holmes County represents one of the clearest cases of a successful movement county where blacks achieved significant political power. Holmes, located on the edge of the Mississippi Delta, exemplifies many of the economic problems that Delta counties shared during this period—a limited job base and high poverty. Among the early movement counties, Holmes is viewed as the one with the highest level of solidarity sustained by strong movement organizations into the 1970s and 1980s (Rural Organizing and Cultural Center 1991; Dittmer 1994). The Holmes County movement began in 1963 when a group of farmers from the Mileston area came to Greenwood to solicit the help of SNCC organizers in voter registration. Mileston was and continued to be an important base for the Holmes County movement. The community had an important cluster of black farmers who owned their land as the long-term legacy of a New Deal land-redistribution program. As many scholars have noted, landownership became an important base of economic autonomy and movement participation, especially for black men in the rural South (Payne 1995). The Holmes County movement was well established at the initiation of Freedom Summer in 1964, with a core group of local activists. Following Freedom Summer, Holmes County became the site of the strongest Mississippi Freedom Democratic Party organization in the state, and Mileston was the location of a community center used for a wide range of movement activity.

The Holmes movement focused a large amount of effort and resources on voter registration and later on campaigns by black candidates for local and state office. It is in this area that Holmes County has been unusually successful. This pattern was marked in an early victory in 1967 by Robert Clark in his campaign for a seat in the Mississippi legislature.

The second and third case studies focused on communities that diverged from the Holmes County pattern in two ways. Madison County began as one of the most highly mobilized counties in the Mississippi movement during the early 1960s. Here, the movement confronted organized white resistance in which all forms of repression were employed. Madison was one of the most violent counties in the state, and "legalistic" strategies were used with equal zeal. For examples, in order to preempt black political participation, the city of Canton used redistricting and annexations of white neighborhoods to thwart the efforts of black candidates and voters. The battle over redistricting and annexations continued from the period immediately after the Voting Rights Act through the early 1980s. Elections were frequently delayed because of pending litigation. Resistance and repression in Madison County undermined the movement base, making it difficult for campaigns to achieve even minor gains. As a result, litigation was the main tactic used by civil rights groups through the 1970s to challenge institutional inequalities. The level and effect of repression in Madison County is similar to other counties where blacks constituted a serious, but nondecisive, threat to white electoral dominance.

Like the second case study, the third examined a county with a small number of black elected officials at the county level. Bolivar County is a rural Delta county in which a large movement base and a large black population did not result in significant numbers of black elected officials. Several counties fit this model, including Washington (Greenville), Bolivar (Cleveland), and Sunflower (Indianola). I examined Bolivar County, which has a rich movement history that has not been the subject of scholarly research. The local economic structure presented a barrier to mobilization, and in the late 1960s the movement expanded through efforts to confront the poverty and economic dependence in the county. Bolivar shares many structural similarities with Holmes County in terms of poverty and a rural population, though a local movement never attained the same level of mobilization or political power.

Bolivar experienced a more fundamental change in the economic and social structures of the county than the other cases. Like the rest of the Delta, Bolivar County was shaped by the mechanization of farming, an impact that had far-reaching repercussions. Bolivar had a massive outmigration of blacks between 1960 and 1980, losing 6,325 persons, or 14.2 percent of the black population. The absolute decline was much less striking in Holmes County, but the relative decline was quite similar—16.2 percent. For the Delta as a whole, the 1960 population of 275,746 dropped to 208,738. The mechanization of farming and the decline in the black population was mirrored by the increased proportion of the population living in small towns. During this period, the decline of the traditional cotton economy resulted in the increased concentration of the population in small towns. One indicator of this trend is the decline of black farm laborers. In 1960 farm laborers constituted 46 percent of the black labor force in Bolivar County but dropped to 17 percent by 1970. The decline of the traditional cotton economy in counties like Bolivar loosened established mechanisms of social control, making the possibility of civil rights organizing more viable.[2] However, the lack of new economic opportunities constrained the movement's development and overall stability.

Movement Dynamics: Tactical Interaction and Repression

I find in all arenas that movement dynamics (the patterns of conflict between movements, their opponents, and authorities) have shaped the pattern of institutional change. None of the outcomes can be fully understood without examining the tactical interaction between the movement and its opposition. With poverty programs and electoral politics, there was a tight spiral in which mobilization and countermobilization were closely linked, each side responding to the strategies of the other. For electoral politics, this tactical interaction had a long time horizon, extending over two decades.

The conflicts over poverty programs were bounded by the rise and fall of the War on Poverty at the national level. However, the distribution of programs and the extent of movement influence were determined in large part by local struggles. With educational institutions, the interaction between mobilization and countermobilization fit Mayer Zald and Bert Useem's concept of a "loosely coupled tango" (1987). The notable pattern through the late 1960s and early 1970s was the sustained resistance by whites to desegregation and the effort to maintain control of educational institutions.

I have avoided some of the inaccurate and excessively optimistic conclusions about the movement's success by examining the multifaceted resistance to the civil rights movement. The forms of white countermobilization had varying impacts on the civil rights movement and its capacity to affect change. The overall pattern of resistance reflects a high level of tactical flexibility. For electoral politics, legal strategies (i.e., vote-dilution tactics) undermined black political power and shifted the battle to the courtroom. These effects occurred across the state. Economic reprisals for political participation were a further threat to the capacity of local movements. At the local level, violence aimed at the local movement undermined its long-term capacity to mobilize. This process diminished the ability of blacks to seize electoral opportunities once the legal barriers to black office holding had been dismantled. We see here the mutually reinforcing effects of very different resistance tactics.

White resistance to school desegregation passed through several phases. Following the *Brown* decision, white Mississippians formed organizations and passed legislation to maintain entirely segregated public schools. By the early 1960s, the legal foundations for freedom of choice plans were developed, which was followed by minimal changes at the local level. Finally, as court-ordered plans for full desegregation were being developed in the late 1960s, private all-white academies were formed. The strength of academies was greatest in movement counties and places where there was an organizational residue of the Citizens' Council. At times, white resistance had the unintended consequence of bringing other actors into the battle on the side of the civil rights movement. The Department of Justice was especially responsive to white violence, targeting areas where the movement met intense repression. In sum, there are two key issues for efforts to explain the consequences of movements: (1) the effect of repression on movements and (2) the effect of countermobilization on the overall pattern of change.

When comparing the influence of local movements on electoral politics, social policies, and school desegregation, we also see that the structure of federal intervention shapes the avenues and potential for movement influence. In electoral politics, movements had little direct influence on the assignment of federal examiners to oversee voter registration, but activists could organize around the presence of federal examiners to coordinate their efforts. The vote-dilution tactics of the Mississippi legislature presented civil rights groups with another strategic dilemma. The courts were institutionally open as a venue for challenge, but litigation often provides advantages to the powerful because court cases are both slow and costly. Civil rights attorneys were able to win important cases in federal courts, but the length of such battles prolonged the struggle for black political power.

The War on Poverty presented local and accessible venues for movements to target their struggles. Local movements invested considerable energy in creating programs like the Child Development Group of Mississippi, and activists attempted to influence the formation and policies of community action programs. Local whites often attempted to thwart black attempts to participate in the administration of poverty programs, but the Office of Economic Opportunity did come to see its mandate as facilitating the empowerment of blacks and the poor. Thus, the structure of policy implementation for the poverty programs facilitated direct mechanisms of influence for local civil rights movements.

The implementation of school desegregation unfolded quite differently than the development of poverty programs. Without any mechanism for community input, desegregation plans were developed through a tense but collaborative relationship between federal HEW officials and local school board authorities. In this context, civil rights groups had no mechanisms to influence the desegregation process. As a result, desegregation was least effective in the communities where the civil rights movement was strongest during the early 1960s. As described above, these communities also had the highest levels of resistance manifested in all-white private academies. With schools, whites were highly mobilized to defend segregated education, and federal intervention provided no institutional access for civil rights groups to counter the influence of local whites.

The implications of these relationships are clear. Movements shape the patterns of change in each of these arenas, but the direction of change is much more consistent with the aspirations of movement groups when state intervention provides meaningful points of leverage. Moreover, when state intervention provides institutional access to movement opponents, the prospects for direct movement influence diminishes significantly.

The Enduring Consequences of Movement Infrastructures

Resistance to the movement was severe, and we could not analyze dynamics or consequences of the civil rights movement without looking at resistance. Nevertheless, the most striking finding of this study is the impact of the civil rights movement itself on institutional outcomes.

In the early 1960s, the Mississippi movement focused on electoral mobilization through citizenship classes, voter registration, mock elections, and the formation of an independent political party, the Mississippi Freedom Democratic Party. These early efforts shaped the level of political participation through the early 1980s. Federal intervention was important, but the effects were smaller and less enduring than the movements. Through the late 1960s, as blacks faced vote-dilution tactics, local movements expanded their repertoire of skills in the electoral arena.

Often, the movement infrastructure included a voter's league or some other formal organization. The infrastructure always included an informal network of community activists who ran campaigns and mobilized voters.

The Mississippi movement mobilized most extensively for political participation, but its effects extended well beyond the electoral arena. Through the late 1960s, local movements attempted to generate economic changes in their communities. Remarkably, these relatively powerless local groups had substantial influence over the War on Poverty in Mississippi. In some cases, movements were able to directly administer and staff programs themselves. In other cases, local power holders administered poverty programs, effectively reducing the local movement's participation. In either case, movement counties received much higher levels of poverty program funding than the counties without a local movement.

The building of movement infrastructures was the underlying strategy of the Mississippi movement in the early 1960s, and this strategy had long-term consequences in Mississippi. This type of claim about movement influence is often asserted as a matter of fact. The results reported here demonstrate that an important determinant of the movement's ability to shape outcomes is its success in generating a local infrastructure.

Charles Payne has characterized "the themes of the community organizing tradition" as "the developmental perspective, an emphasis on building relationships, respect for collective leadership, for bottom-up change, the expansive sense of how democracy ought to operate in everyday life, the emphasis on building for the long haul, the anti-bureaucratic ethos, [and] the preference for addressing local issues" (1995, 364). This organizing approach contrasted with what Ella Baker characterized as the more common "mobilizing" approach using large numbers of people for short-term protest activity (Payne 1989). The community-organizing strategy with its long-term approach to social change characterized the movement in Mississippi. Mobilizing techniques were much less commonly used, and when used they were often employed to facilitate the work of community organizing such as citizenship and literacy classes, mass meetings, and freedom registration canvassing.

Mobilizing tactics, such as the campaigns in Birmingham or Selma, played an important role in the securing of federal initiatives such as the Civil Rights Act of 1964 and the Voting Rights Act of 1965.[3] However, the dramatic conflicts that these mobilizations created have obscured the less dramatic role of organizing and its relation to political outcomes in the history of the civil rights movement and the broader scholarship on social movements. The preponderance of movement activity targeted changes at the local level, where the "tripartite system of domination" circumscribed the lives of black southerners.

Theoretical Models of Movement Impact

In chapter 2, I outlined four models for analyzing the relationship between movements and outcomes. The disruption model suggests that movements can have momentary influence through threat and that organization building is antithetical to movement efficacy. The persuasion model contends that movement efficacy flows from communication that wins the support of sympathetic bystanders. Highly dramatic events and speeches are important ways that movements have broader influence. The negotiation model suggests that movements succeed as they move smoothly into the routine operations of the political process. In this model, it is the most moderate goals and tactics that have the greatest impact for social movements. Finally, I advanced a movement infrastructure model, building on key insights from research on social movements, democratic politics, and the policy process. Here, I focus on the elaboration of indigenous movement organizations that can pursue a variety of goals and that use "insider" and "outsider" tactics.

The disruption, persuasion, and negotiation models find partial support in this analysis of the Mississippi movement. For example, major campaigns using assertive tactics were important in Mississippi, as the disruption model suggests. In addition, local movements were able to use major events like the Freedom Vote to secure support from government actors and the broader public beyond Mississippi, as the persuasion model would expect. However, these models share three major limitations despite their obvious differences. First, the disruption and persuasion models underestimate the importance of organization as a link between movements and outcomes. Second, by suggesting that movements are influential through their mobilization of third parties who leverage government intervention, these models overemphasize the role of external actors. Third, each model inaccurately portrays the temporal process as a singular, momentary conflict. In contrast, I find at the local level protracted struggles with a long time horizon.

The negotiation model is correct to focus on the potential efficacy of "insider" tactics. Litigation and political campaigns were employed along with boycotts, demonstrations, and direct action. This model is also correct to emphasize the way in which outcomes are likely to cumulate incrementally over a long time period. However, there was not a linear transition "from protest to politics," from disruptive to routine strategies. In Mississippi the strategies noted above were intertwined in the early 1960s, and the tactics continued to be used simultaneously through the next two decades. Holmes County developed the strongest capacity to use both insider and outsider strategies.

Finally, I find strong support for the movement infrastructure model, which focuses closely on the long-term dynamics of movement building. The three central components of a movement's infrastructure are leadership, organizational structure, and resources. I have shown that strategies and tactics are shaped by the configuration of a movement's leadership, organization, and resource capacities. Leaders and organizations often carry particular repertoires of action and ideologies that influence the ability of movements to have lasting impacts. Infrastructures that allow the movement to employ multiple mechanisms of influence (including disruption, persuasion, and bargaining) will have the broadest impact because movements must pursue their objectives within a complex and changing environment. A movement infrastructure's autonomy and continuity are critical in accounting for the durability and influence of a movement. In the Mississippi movement, we witness a broader process of building long-term movement infrastructures. This is a strategy that many movements pursue, including many labor movements (Bronfenbrenner et al. 1998; Fantasia 1989; Griffin, Wallace and Rubin 1986; Voss and Sherman 2000), the environmental justice movement (Bullard 1990; Cable and Benson 1993), faith-based community organizations (Hart 2001; Warren 2001; Wood 2002), and many women's movements (Ferree and Martin 1995; Whittier 1995). As a result, the lessons of this case are relevant to a much broader array of movements. Moreover, the efforts of the Mississippi movement to engage in electoral politics or shape social policies are goals shared by many different social movements.

My findings conflict with those who argue that changes were minimal or short-lived. Some scholars assume that movements are efficacious and others assume that movements are inconsequential. This study directly challenges the argument that movements are inconsequential, and this research specifies the contexts within which movements are influential and the mechanisms through which they shape processes of change.

Indeed, some view federal agencies, courts, political parties, or economic elites as the agents driving institutional change. These groups did play important roles, but typically they acted in response to movement demands and the leverage brought to bear by the civil rights movement. The Mississippi movement attempted to forge independent structures for sustaining challenges to local inequities and injustices. In the face of resistance, movements built infrastructures and propelled changes in an array of local institutions, and those efforts have had an enduring legacy in Mississippi. Many citizens look to the civil rights struggle to find insights for contemporary movements. Yet popular accounts of the civil rights movement often point to the wrong lessons by emphasizing a top-down approach to social change. The lessons of the community-organizing tradition in Mississippi remain one of the movement's most important and underappreciated legacies.

Study Design

IN THIS appendix, I describe the research strategy that I have used to study the various impacts of the Mississippi civil rights movement. Building on the conceptualization of movement outcomes presented in chapter 2, I present a more detailed consideration of the empirical dilemmas for research on outcomes. This initial methodological discussion applies generally to studies of movement outcomes. In addition, I consider the Mississippi movement as a case study in terms of its strengths and limitations. The majority of the chapter focuses on the two components of the research design: the qualitative case studies and the quantitative data set of Mississippi counties. The analysis that flows from these two distinct research strategies is complementary. In fact, I argue that both are essential because each answers different types of questions about the potential impacts of movements on outcomes.

Broad Themes

Levels of Mobilization and Levels of Analysis

Like many social movements, the civil rights struggle included a combination of local, regional, and national organizations and campaigns. In this study, I give primary consideration to the local dimensions of mobilization, countermobilization, and impact. This focus is important for two reasons. First, the movement itself was based in local movement centers, despite the historiographical bias toward treating the movement as if it were a nationally coordinated movement "from above" (Morris 1984).[1] Second, by examining these smaller units, we can study the variation across the state. Here, James Button's assertion that there was local variation in mobilization and impact becomes a methodological point of leverage (1989). In an assessment of strategies for improving the explanatory power of case studies, Edwin Amenta (1991) suggests that analysis of "subunits" of the case has important advantages. His example is the distribution of New Deal programs across states. Lee Ann Banaszak (1996) follows the same strategy in her comparative study of the women's suffrage movements in the United States and Switzerland by examining state-level variation in the United States and canton-level variation in Switzerland. Obviously, for this design strategy to work, there must be variation and the subunits must be "meaningful." For example, the processes that take place within that unit must be consequential for explaining variation. With the civil rights movement, this is the case, and it turns out to be a useful strategy for examining movement outcomes in many other cases.

While keeping the primary focus on the local level, there are processes that must be examined at the state and national level to understand local movements and their consequences. These include the broader dynamics of movements, such as shifts in ideology, funding, or tactics, and changes in the opportunity structures that operate at these broader levels. For example, the collapse of COFO in the mid-1960s and the MFDP in the late 1960s originated at the state level, but these changes in movement organization impacted local movements. White resistance to black electoral power through vote-dilution tactics occurred in state legislatures as well as the municipal and county political bodies. Another example is the aggregate decline of the War on Poverty funding, which has important consequences at the local level. The rule of thumb used in this study is that I have examined these types of state and national processes when they impact on the local level in important ways. A more comprehensive explanation of the rise and decline of the War on Poverty or any other of these large-scale shifts is beyond the scope of this study.

Mobilization and Context

The questions examined in this study call for a research design that can capture the underlying dynamics of conflict and the variation from case to case. This includes the multiple actors who enter into the struggles with and against social movements. In short, the extensive collection of historical data is necessary before a balanced analysis can be made about the role of local organizing and other factors in producing social and political change. I have used two complementary research strategies for studying the movement in Mississippi, each of which corresponds to different sets of data and modes of analysis. They are as follows:

1. A quantitative county-by-county data set to examine three major groups of outcomes: (a) electoral politics, including participation and black office holding; (b) federal antipoverty programs; and (c) schools and desegregation.
2. A set of three case studies examining the variation in the patterns of movement development after 1965 at the county level. The case studies combine further archival research and informant interviews with local activists, politicians, and citizens.

The two research strategies allow for the combination of distinctive strengths found in each approach. The quantitative assessment of all Mississippi counties allows for a multivariate analysis with refined estimates of movement impact. The qualitative case studies allow us to situate these patterns in specific locales and explore the internal dynamics of the community in greater detail, especially the interplay between the movement organizations and the social infrastructure that sustains or undermines it.

The Outcome Arenas Studied

One of the major difficulties in studying the outcomes of social movements is determining exactly what outcomes to examine. This study centers on three major "outcome arenas"—electoral politics, federal poverty programs, and educational institutions. Each of these outcome arenas falls within the overall purview of local civil rights movements; however, the relative importance of each "goal" varied within the Mississippi movement as a whole and across local movements. From its origins in the early 1960s, electoral politics was the central focus of the Mississippi movement; as such, it represents a major and enduring goal, more than the other arenas. Underlying electoral politics and many of the other strategies pursued by the movement were a concern with the economic problems facing black Mississippians. The War on Poverty, then, was another arena in which local movements directed considerable energy. However, this is a more ambiguous case because movements were reluctant, fearing possible co-optation. Finally, with educational institutions, there was far less effort placed in attacking institutional inequalities in this arena.

Within each outcome arena, I have measured different types of outcomes at different points in time (following the theoretical argument

I make in chapter 2). By looking at many dependent variables, I can examine differences between outcomes (voter registration vs. black elected officials) and over time. Further, increasing the number of dependent variables in this way increases the overall reliability of the study, providing greater confidence in the theoretical conclusions (Campbell 1975).

Mississippi as a Case Study

Mississippi is well suited for a study of the consequences of the civil rights movement in the South. First, the historical significance of Mississippi alone makes it worthy of close examination. During the modern civil rights movement, Mississippi was a trailblazer in developing strategies of resisting the emergence of the movement. In the period after the Voting Rights Act, Mississippi once again developed new strategies for minimizing the political power of black Mississippians. Hence, Mississippi can be treated as a test case for the South as a whole.

Second, there is sufficient variation among counties on all of the key variables to allow for careful generalization to the civil rights movement in other parts of the South (including the extent of mobilization and countermobilization, the size of the black population, class structure, and urbanization). V. O. Key, in his classic study of southern politics (1949), argued that there were "many Souths." I argue similarly that Mississippi is not monolithic. Examining one state poses certain limitations, but it also has the methodological advantage of "holding constant" variation at the state level. This is especially useful given my primary interest in local patterns of conflict and change.

However, Mississippi's "exceptionalism" should be noted. First, the coordination of a statewide movement in the early 1960s and the wide array of strategies pursued by the movement make the Mississippi case unique. In most other states, the movement worked on a city-by-city basis[2] rather than coordinating and confronting racial inequality statewide as in Mississippi. In terms of the data available, this is a clear advantage because it means that comparable evidence can be used to examine varying levels of mobilization across the state. Second, the strategies used to resist the movement were more intense and more varied than in other areas.

Unit of Analysis

For the quantitative analysis and case studies, I use counties as the unit of analysis. There are three major reasons for using counties rather than municipalities. First, the movement mobilized at the county level in Mississippi. There was often variation in the county in terms of which areas had greater levels of participation in the movement. Fortunately, the case studies allow me to examine this variation. Nevertheless, counties were a primary organizational unit because they were the most important political unit in Mississippi containing, for example, the County Board of Supervisors, the most significant political body in local southern politics (see Black and Black 1987; and Krane and Shaffer 1992). This leads to a second reason for using counties as the unit of analysis—substantially important outcomes can be measured at the county level. Finally, a large body of political research uses counties as the unit of analysis dating back (at least) to Donald Matthews and James Protho's classic study *Negroes and the New Southern Politics* (1966). Following in this tradition, the results of this study can be compared to this broader body of research (see, for example, Alt 1994, 1995; Black and Black 1987; Colby 1986; Davis 1987; James 1988; Roscigno and Tomaskovic-Devey 1994; Salamon and Van Evera 1973; Stewart and Sheffield 1987; Timpone 1995 on electoral politics; Conlon and Kimenyi 1991 on schools; and Colby 1985 on poverty programs).

Counties are useful units. However, there are some measurement difficulties to be addressed especially with educational and poverty program variables. For schools, districts are the unit by which students and resources are distributed. In Mississippi many districts are contiguous with county boundaries. However, in some cases, there are multiple districts within the same county; (there is one multicounty district for Sharkey and Issaquena counties because of the low populations in these counties). For these multidistrict counties, data can be aggregated to the county level.[3] For the multicounty district, estimates can be determined using census reports for the school-age population for blacks and whites in each county. Multiple districts were not used primarily for the purposes of segregation; rather, racially separate schools were contained within each district. Typically, in a multidistrict county, there would be a district for the county seat and a rural school district. I have tested for possible bias by comparing the single and multidistrict counties.

With poverty programs, counties were again an important unit for distributing programs and resources. However, there were some statewide and multicounty programs. Where it is possible to make county-level estimates of the distribution of poverty program funds, I have done so. For a small number of cases, statewide programs cannot be disaggregated into county-level appropriations from the information included in the Office of Economic Opportunity reports.

There is one final methodological issue concerning the county data set. Hinds County includes the state capital, Jackson, and it is a statistical outlier on many variables. For this substantive and statistical rationale, I have excluded it from the quantitative date reported throughout the book.

Statewide Quantitative Data

In this section, I describe the quantitative data set with attention directed toward the analytic issues that have been addressed with the data. The specific variables and their sources are reported in appendix D. The richness of the data set described below allows me to examine hypotheses concerning movements, conflict, and change.

First, I describe the groups of outcome measures in detail. The first set of outcomes focuses exclusively on electoral politics with four groups of indicators: (1) voter registration; (2) votes cast for black candidates in statewide elections; (3) the number of black candidates in early elections; and (4) the number of county-level black elected officials for the years between 1974 and 1984 (before this point the numbers were too low to be meaningful at an aggregate level).

The second group of outcomes examines the expansion and distribution of public services in relation to the black community. Indicators of public services include community action programs (CAPs) and Head Start programs. Frances Fox Piven and Richard Cloward argue that political elites use public expenditures to diminish protest (1977; see also Colby 1985). Following a similar line of argument, John Dittmer argues that federal funding was initially directed toward the movement (in part because white politicians rejected the funding) but was shifted to "safer" hands as those resources became a base of power for community organizing (1993 and 1994; see also Quadagno 1994). This struggle played out over the funding for Head Start programs, and this case raises central issues concerning the constraints faced by local activists in dealing with federally funded programs. Collections of the Office of Economic Opportunity at the National Archives and Records Administration were consulted for documentation of CAP and Head Start programs in the state.

The third group of outcomes examines schools as an arena of conflict and includes measures of the extent of desegregation and the formation of private academies. The key indicator of desegregation is the dissimilarity index for selected years, and private academies are measured as the proportion of white school-age children attending these white-flight school.

This data provides the basis for analyzing how schools, as institutions, are shaped by the ongoing and historical residues of political conflict (see Andrews 2002).

There are two types of measures for the local movement: (1) indicators of local organizational strength and (2) indicators of the movement's capacity to mobilize the local community. Measures include the number of Freedom Summer volunteers, number of votes cast in the 1964 Freedom Vote (a mock election), number of Mississippi Freedom Democratic Party (MFDP—an independent movement-based political party) organizers in the county (1965), the number of COFO field-workers in the county prior to and following Freedom Summer, the number of NAACP members, and the amount of NAACP dues collected for the years between 1961 and 1970.

The intervention of the federal government, in this case the Justice Department, is measured by the presence of federal examiners and the number of people registered by federal examiners. This allows me to test to what extent factors external to the county impact on black electoral participation.

Measures of white resistance to the movement falls into four major categories: (1) organizations explicitly directed toward resisting the movement (e.g., Citizens' Council and Ku Klux Klan organizations); (2) violent actions taken by whites toward the movement to intimidate or stop local mobilizing; (3) the establishment of counterinstitutions to subvert the goals of the movement; and (4) "legal" resistance such as the changing of electoral procedures or boundaries.

For organizational measures, I use indicators of Citizens' Council and Ku Klux Klan organizations in the county. For the summer and fall of 1964, several indicators are used that measure white harassment and violence against civil rights workers, including threats, physical assault, and shots fired at civil rights workers; here, the relative impact of different resistance strategies can be assessed. For 1960 to 1969, I have used the number of attacks of civil rights workers compiled by David Colby (1987) from organizational records and newspapers.

Finally, I have compiled many variables measuring the local social structure. In order to account for variation in demographic and economic variables among the counties, data is available from census reports and city and county data books. I have compiled data on the income and occupational structure of blacks and whites in the county, urbanization, and absolute and relative size of the black and white population (and the voting-age population).

Community Studies

In this section, I discuss the logic of case selection, describe the three communities, review the types of data used, and outline the major questions that can be answered by the community studies. Many dimensions of the development and transformation of local movements are difficult, if not impossible, to measure quantitatively for all counties. The following issues are given primary consideration through the case studies: (1) early movement strength and early participant-leaders; (2) continuity or change in the movement base leading to late movement strength or internal factionalism; (3) a changing set of participants—in terms of class position, organizational affiliations, et cetera.; (4) external movement connections—links to national organizations and resources; (5) changing demographic basis and class structure; (6) role of federal funding of poverty programs; (7) federal intervention in electoral politics—federal examiners, Justice Department suits, et cetera; (8) violent repression by whites; and (9) non-violent resistance/opposition by whites.

I utilized the same mix of data sources for each case study. Informant interviews with key participants have helped to make up for a sparse literature on the period after 1965. The interview list was constructed to tap different target groups. Major groups include movement activists from different points in time and with different organizational affiliations. In addition, elected officials and community leaders were interviewed. I employed a uniform interview protocol that focused on the level and forms of political conflict. Interview data was supplemented with a review of local weekly newspapers. Last, archival sources (described in appendix B) were examined to formulate profiles of the "movement infrastructure" that developed in the early and mid-1960s. These profiles have been assembled based on published historical work and archival research with the SNCC, CORE, and NAACP papers and the manuscript and oral history collections at Tougaloo College.

The community studies significantly strengthen the research design by focusing on the same set of outcomes (electoral politics, education, and social policies) while extending the range of data. On the question of movement strategy and infrastructure, the community studies include data about tactics that cannot be captured for all Mississippi counties, such as the formation of community centers (in Holmes and Madison), rural health clinics (Bolivar), and farming and manufacturing cooperatives (Bolivar and Holmes). It is noteworthy that the movement strategies listed here are both characteristics of mobilization and outcomes. Further, the community studies provide additional insight into the strategies used by whites toward the movement, such as the redrawing of electoral boundaries (Parker, Colby, and Morrison 1994). Last, the community studies shed light on the ways in which local social structure shaped political mobilization and consequently changes in local institutions.

Data Sources

The research for this study was derived from four major sources: (1) archival collections of participants, civil rights organizations, and government agencies; (2) informant interviews; (3) newspapers; and (4) reports and documentation of various organizations and agencies such as the United States Commission on Civil Rights. Let me describe each in turn, highlighting the limitations and strengths of each.

Archival Collections

By far, the most valuable source of data for this study was the archival collections that document mobilization at the local level. The major collections consulted for this study are listed in appendix B. Nevertheless, one limitation of the archival collections is the almost exclusive documentation of major civil rights organizations (e.g., CORE and SNCC) and the early 1960s; this limitation is reflected in the historical scholarship. However, for the period from 1965 to 1970, extensive documentation is available in smaller collections. For an understanding of the Mississippi movement during this period, one of the most valuable collections is the Civil Rights Litigation Records at Tougaloo College. In addition to the original documents, there is a set of 170 microfilm reels, including the case and office files for the major civil rights legal organizations working in Mississippi. The activities of many local movements find their way into the Litigation Records. To paraphrase one of the activists interviewed for this study, there were civil rights lawyers behind every bush back then. The collections of various organizations were examined, including SNCC, CORE, NAACP, CDGM, and the MFDP. The Freedom Information Service Archives was another particularly valuable collection for the post–Voting Rights Act period. In addition, the collections of many individuals are available and were examined, including Fannie Lou Hamer, Ed King, Rims Barber, Charles Horowitz, and James Loewen. In addition to these movement sources, I have examined the documents of various government agencies, including the Office of Economic

Opportunity, the Department of Justice, and the United States Commission on Civil Rights.

Interviews

Informant interviews provided another source of documentation that was especially important for the community studies. In each community, I conducted open-ended interviews with key participants. Individuals were selected who could comment on specific areas of the local movement and community history. In other words, I attempted to interview individuals representing different periods and organizations. A uniform interview protocol was used to provide comparable information about the internal dynamics and trajectory of local movements. Topics covered in the open-ended interview were key organizations, leadership, internal conflicts, major tactics, repression, early electoral campaigns, and participation in the War on Poverty. However, I tailored the interview to the respondent's experience and expertise, such as Head Start, the history of litigation in the community, or a specific movement organization. Using interviews to establish a community history is a difficult task, and researchers face a number of potential problems. The most important problem is the limitations of memory over an expanded time frame. This was especially acute for my study, where I was interested in establishing sequencing and detailed accounts of major events such as boycotts.

The interviews also provided data on the relations between different organizations, a (retrospective) account of the high and low points of mobilization, and the forms of repression and their effects. I conducted the interview research in tandem with the other research for this study. Like all forms of data, the interviews are strengthened when they are scrutinized in relation to other forms of data. For example, prior to conducting the interviews, a preliminary profile and history was established for each community based on archival research and prior studies. If a respondent discussed an event or organization that I did not already have documentation on, I returned to the archival collections and local newspapers to search for independent confirmation and further documentation on a particular time period or organization.

In addition to the interviews I collected, I have drawn on interviews that have been conducted by prior researchers. These include the Tom Dent Oral History Collection conducted in the late 1970s and early 1980s, the Civil Rights Documentation Project at Howard University, and Stanford University's Project South Oral History Collection of taped meetings, discussions, and interviews from 1965. Because many of these interviews were conducted in the 1960s and 1970s, they help address the memory problem in my interviews. In addition, some of the recordings are with individuals who have since died or of meetings that obviously cannot be re-created.

Newspapers

Like interviews, newspapers come with particular strengths and limitations. Newspapers were used for a number of different reasons. When reporters interviewed key informants, they can be used much as the interviews noted above to assess the ideas and tactics of key actors in the midst of conflict. In the case of Mississippi, local newspapers have to be treated with special care because they can vary widely between towns depending on the local editor. For example, in Holmes County the *Lexington Advertiser* reported extensively on movement activity, going as far as announcing meetings of the MFDP and NAACP. In Madison and Bolivar counties, local newspapers were openly hostile to the movement. In both cases, the newspapers reported infrequently on the movement. The newspapers also participated in openly repressing the movement. The *Bolivar Commercial* listed the names of parents sending their children to formerly all-white schools, inviting economic pressure and violence on these families. The *Madison County Herald* listed the names of individuals who had registered to vote in the past week as an act of intimidation. Neither paper reported movement activity beyond vague rumors. For example, in the mid-1960s, the *Bolivar Commercial* reported a rumor that civil rights activists were working in Shaw. More common were diatribes in response to events covered in the national press. The *Bolivar Commercial* pursued the "outside agitator" theory by blaming organizations like the Delta Ministry (a group sponsored by the National Council of Churches) or "Yankee" lawyers for any local activity. In short, the Madison and Bolivar papers were not helpful sources for news on major campaigns (which were generally not reported) during the 1960s. For Bolivar County, the *Delta Democrat Times* from Greenville in nearby Washington County reported on movement activity. For example, the Shelby school boycott of 1968 generated numerous articles in the *Delta Democrat Times,* in contrast to the *Bolivar Commercial*, which only commented on the boycott after it ended.

For this study, I have collected extensive newspaper coverage for each of the three cases. Part of that coverage was collected from newspaper clippings in the subject files at the Mississippi Department of Archives and History (MDAH) under a broad range of topics. These subject files proved particularly helpful for the period from 1970 to 1985. By this period the major newspapers in the state, the *Clarion-Ledger* and the *Jackson Daily News*, began to report on black politics and protest more systematically. The subject files also include articles from regional and local newspapers and articles from the *Jackson Advocate* (a black-owned newspaper), the *New Orleans Times-Picayune*, the *Memphis Commercial Appeal*, and the *Washington Post*. These files, though limited, were helpful in establishing a baseline of major protest events, political battles, and litigation within each of the communities. I followed up on key events reported in state or regional newspapers (e.g., a boycott sponsored by the United League of Holmes County in 1978) by examining local newspapers and by interviewing central actors.

In addition to the subject files, I made intensive investigation of local newspapers for selected points in time. I conducted a review of newspapers in each community during the following periods: Freedom Summer, the implementation of freedom of choice school desegregation, poverty program implementation, the formation of CAP boards, and full-scale school desegregation (for this period a search was also conducted of the *New York Times*, which reported widely on the *Alexander v. Holmes* decision and the implementation of school desegregation). In addition, searches were conducted for other periods of local mobilization and local elections.

A final methodological point on the use of newspapers: generally speaking, newspapers report on events, but not on organizations, or only incidentally on organizations as sponsors of events. For example, the *Delta Democrat Times* covered in minute detail the school boycott in Shelby during the spring and summer of 1968. The coverage was especially detailed concerning legal developments such as the curfew. The Shelby Educational Committee was noted as a sponsor of the boycott, but little investigation was made concerning the origin or development of this organization. An organization like the North Bolivar County Farm Cooperative never received substantial coverage in the local or regional press. The important point is that these limitations in the data, unless duly noted and addressed, can lead to analytic errors. The most serious error is to reproduce the notion that the civil rights movement was a series of "events" without addressing the underlying organizational developments in particular locales.

Reports and Government Documents

The last source of documentation of the Mississippi movement is reports and data generated by government agencies and other organizations. These include reports by the United States Commission on Civil Rights, the Joint Center for Political Studies, and congressional hearings. More familiar sources such as census documents are used frequently, especially for the quantitative data set; and reports published by the state of Mississippi were used for education, election returns, and other county-level data. Many of these state documents are located at the Information Services Library of Jackson State University.

Archival Collections

Amistad Research Center—Tulane
University, New Orleans
Tom Dent Oral History Collection

Freedom Information Service, Jackson,
Mississippi (maintained by Ms. Jan
Hillegas)
Civil Rights Collection

Howard University, Washington, D.C.
Civil Rights Documentation Project, Oral
History Collection

Information Services Library; Jackson State
University (formerly affiliated with the
Research and Development Center),
Jackson, Mississippi
Collection of government publications and
reports

Library of Congress, Washington, D.C.
NAACP Papers

Mississippi Department of Archives and
History (MDAH), Jackson, Mississippi
Association of Citizens' Councils Papers
Attorney General A. E. Sumner Papers
Council of Federated Organizations Papers
Fannie Lou Hamer Papers
Mississippi Freedom Democratic Party
Papers
Project South Oral History Collection,
Stanford University
Subject Files

National Archives and Records
Administration (NARA)
Office of Economic Opportunity
(Community Service Administration),
Department of Justice

Schomburg Center for the Study of Black
Culture, New York
CORE Papers
Ruth Schein Papers
SNCC Papers

State Historical Society of Wisconsin
(SHSW), Madison, Wisconsin
Alvin Oderman, 1965–66 Papers
Amzie Moore Papers
Charles Howard Baer Papers
Child Development Group of Mississippi
Papers
COFO, Shaw Office, 1964–65
CORE Mississippi, 4th Congressional District
Papers
Eugene Nelson, 1964 Papers
Freedom Information Service Papers,
1962–67
Harriet Tanzman Papers
Jake Freisen, 1964–67 Papers
Jerry Tecklin, 1964 Papers
Joann Ooiman Robinson Papers
Lee Bankhead Papers
Lise Vogel Papers
Madison Measure for Measure Papers

Michael Grossman Papers
Stuart Ewen Papers

Tamiment Library, New York University, New York
Mississippi Freedom Labor Union
(subject file)

Tougaloo College, Jackson, Mississippi
Charles Horowitz Papers
Civil Rights Litigation Papers

Ed King Papers
James Loewen Papers
James McRee Papers
Rims Barber Papers
Tom Dent Oral History Collection

University of Southern Mississippi, Hattiesburg, Mississippi
Oral History Collection

List of Interviews

Conducted by Author

Canton/Madison County
Rims Barber, Jackson, June 5, 1996
Ed Blackmon, Canton, June 19, 1996
John Brown, Canton, July 8, 1996
Robert Chinn, Canton, June 27, 1996
J. L. McCullough, Madison County,
  July 22, 1996
Wilbert Robinson, Canton, July 22, 1996
Shirley Simmons, Canton, July 22, 1996

Bolivar County
Velma Bartley, Shaw, June 14, 1996
Owen Brooks, Greenville, June 13, 1996
Milburn Crowe, Mound Bayou,
  July 17, 1996
Robert Gray, Shelby, July 19, 1996
Otha Reed, Shelby, June 13, 1996
L. M. Reynolds, Shelby, June 13, 1996
Lillie Robinson, Cleveland, July 18, 1996
Kermit Stanton, Shelby, June 13, 1996
J. Y. Trice, Rosedale, June 14, 1996
Ellis Turnage, Cleveland, July 18, 1996

Holmes County
Rev. Booker, Lexington, July 29, 1996
Walter Bruce, Pickens, July 19, 1996
Eddie Carthan, Tchula, July 29, 1996
Bernice Montgomery Johnson, Jackson,
  June 20, 1996

**Tom Dent Oral History Collection, Amistad
Research Center, Tulane University and
Tougaloo College**
Owen Brooks
Ed Brown
Program Honoring C. O. Chinn
Charlie Cobb
Dave Dennis
Annie Devine (see also "Annie Devine
  Remembers" article in *Freedomways*)
Mary Hightower
An Evening with Anne Moody
Jesse Morris (with Willie Peacock)
Jerome Smith
Matt Suarez
Tougaloo Symposium, Annie Devine

Civil Rights Documentation Project,
Moorland-Spingarn Research Center,
Howard University
Owen Brooks
Annie Devine
Muhammad Kenyatta
George Raymond
Matteo Suarez
Hollis Watkins

Stanford Oral History Project
Cleveland, white volunteer interview
Annie Devine interview
Susan Lorenzi interview/canvassing
MFLU Bull Session, Shaw
MFLU meeting, Cleveland
Mileston Bull Session (typed notes/Xerox)p

Descriptions of Major Variables and Sources

Variable Name	Variable Description	Source
Movement Variables		
Freedom Summer staff and volunteers	Number of Freedom Summer volunteers working in county, summer 1964	SNCC Papers, A:XV:197, reel 39, Schomburg Center for the Study of Black Culture
Freedom Votes, 1964	Number of freedom votes cast in mock election, November 1964	Freedom Information Services Archives, General Files, Jackson, Mississippi
MFDP, 1965	Number of MFDP staff/contact persons in county	"FDP Projects by County and Contacts," August 23, 1965, Ed King Papers, 11:579, Tougaloo College
NAACP, 1966	Number of members in NAACP, 1966	"Mississippi State Conference 1956–1972," NAACP Papers, III C 75, Library of Congress
Countermovement Variables		
Freedom Summer resistance	Number of incidents of physical attack on civil rights workers, June–August 1964	Holt (1965, 207–52); McAdam (1988, 257–82)
Violent resistance index	Number of incidents of attack/ assault on civil rights workers, 1960–69	Compiled by Colby (1987, 45–46)
Ku Klux Klan	Presence of organization in county, ca. 1964	House Hearings, Activities of the Ku Klux Klan, 1965

Variable Name	Variable Description	Source
Citizens' Council	Presence of organization in county, January 1956	*The Citizen* (monthly publication), 1956
Electoral Politics Federal examiners	Presence or absence of federal examiners in county	United States Commission on Civil Rights (1968, 244–47, table 9)
Registered black voters, 1960	Number of black registered voters, 1960	United States Commission on Civil Rights (1961, 272–75)
Registered black voters, 1967	Number of black registered voters, 1967	United States Commission on Civil Rights (1968, 244–47, table 9)
Black candidates, 1967	Black candidates running for office in 1967 county and state elections	MFDP microfilm collection, reel 2, MDAH; and Rims Barber Papers, box 1, file 7, Tougaloo College
Black candidates, 1971	Black candidates running for office in 1971 county and state elections	Rims Barber Papers, box 1, file 7, Tougaloo College
Whitley vote, 1966	Average of votes cast for Clifton Whitley in the Democratic primary and general election for governor, August and November 1966	*Mississippi Official and Statistical Register* (1968–72, 439, 442)
Evers vote, 1971	Votes cast for Charles Evers in general election for governor, 1971	*Mississippi Official and Statistical Register* (1972–76, 455)
Racial turnout disparity, 1966	Proportion white turnout (votes for white candidates divided by white voting-age population) minus proportion black turnout (votes for Whitley divided by black voting-age population).	*Mississippi Official and Statistical Register* (1968–72, 439, 442)
Racial turnout disparity, 1971	Proportion white turnout (votes for white candidates divided by WVAP) minus proportion black turnout (votes for Evers divided by BVAP).	*Mississippi Official and Statistical Register* (1972–76, 455)

Variable Name	Variable Description	Source
Black voter turnout, 1970s	Votes cast for black candidates in statewide elections in 1971, 1975, and 1978 divided by three times the black voting-age population in 1979.	*Mississippi Official and Statistical Register* (1968–72, 1972–76, 1976–80)
County-level BEO, 1974	Total county-level black elected officials, 1974	*National Roster of Black Elected Officials* (1974, vol. 4, 117–28)
County-level BEO, 1979	Total county-level black elected officials, 1979	*National Roster of Black Elected Officials* (1979, vol. 9, 128–39)
County-level BEO, 1984	Total county-level black elected officials, 1984	*National Roster of Black Elected Officials* (1984, vol. 14, 213–31)
Schools		
Students attending white academies	Number of students attending white academies, grades K–12, selected years	*Nonpublic Schools,* Department of Education, State of Mississippi
White school-age children	Number of white school-age children (ages 5–17), 1970	U.S. Bureau of the Census, *1970 Census of Population, General Social and Economic Characteristics,* table 35
Proportion black among school-age children	Proportion calculated based on 1970 census data for ages 5–17	U.S. Bureau of the Census, *1970 Census of Population, General Social and Economic Characteristics,* table 35
Dissimilarity index	Dissimilarity index of segregation, 1968, 1970, 1972, 1978	U.S. Department of Health, Education, and Welfare, *Directory of Public Elementary and Secondary Schools in School Districts,* multiple years
Poverty Programs		
CDGM, 1965	Presence of CDGM project in county, summer 1965	Reported in Greenberg (1969)
CAP grants, 1965–68	Total CAP grants for 1965–68	Budget Reports located in multiple files by organization, Region IV, Mississippi, box 14, Grant Profiles, 1965–1972, Policy Research Division, Office of Operations, OEO, RG 381, NARA

Variable Name	Variable Description	Source
CAP grants, 1969–71	Total CAP grants for 1969–71	Budget Reports located in multiple files by organization, Region IV, Mississippi, box 14, Grant Profiles, 1965–1972, Policy Research Division, Office of Operations, OEO, RG 381, NARA
Urban, 1960	Percentage population urban, 1960	U.S. Bureau of the Census, *County and City Data Book* (1967, 182, 192)
Urban, 1970	Percentage population urban, 1970	U.S. Bureau of the Census, *County and City Data Book* (1977, 258, 270)
Black voting-age population, 1960	Total black persons of voting age, 1960	United States Commission on Civil Rights (1968, 244–47, table 9)
Black voting-age population, 1970	Total black persons of voting age, 1970	U.S. Bureau of the Census, *General Population Characteristics, 1970*, table 35
Black voting-age population, 1980	Total black persons of voting age, 1980	Printed in *Handbook of Selected Data for Mississippi* (1983), from the 1980 Census
Landowner concentration, 1969	Proportion of farm acreage owned by owners of 500 or more acres.	U.S. Bureau of the Census, *Census of Agriculture* (1972)
Black occupational vulnerability, 1970	Proportion of black voting-age population unemployed or employed as local government workers, farm laborers, tenants, and domestic laborers	U.S. Bureau of the Census, *1970 Census of the Population*, multiple tables
Black occupational autonomy, 1970	Proportion of black voting-age population who own farms, nonagricultural self-employed, federal government employees, and employed in manufacturing	U.S. Bureau of the Census, *1970 Census of the Population*, multiple tables
Black median family income, 1970	Black median family income	U.S. Bureau of the Census, *1970 Census of the Population*
Poverty, 1970	Proportion of households earning under $3,000 in 1960	U.S. Bureau of the Census, *1970 Census of the Population, County and City Data Books* (1967)

Notes

Chapter One

1. Numerous studies have attempted to determine the impact of key court decisions and legislative changes, including Davidson and Grofman (1994) on the Voting Rights Act, Grofman (2000) on the 1964 Civil Rights Act, and Rosenberg (1991) on major Supreme Court decisions.

2. Over the past four decades, leading scholars have reviewed the relevant literature on social movements and have noted the limited amount of systematic research on outcomes (Diani 1997; Eckstein 1965; Giugni 1998; Marx and Wood 1975; McAdam, McCarthy, and Zald 1988; Tarrow 1998). Burstein, Einwohner, and Hollander observe that "the field of social movements grew tremendously in the 1970s and 1980s, but the study of movement outcomes did not. . . . [The result is] that we still know very little about the impact of social movements on social change" (1995, 276). In the past five to ten years, this has been a growth area, and in chapter 2, I discuss recent trends in studies of movement impact in detail.

Chapter Two

1. For elaborations and critiques of Gamson, see Goldstone (1980a; 1980b), Mirowsky and Ross (1979), and Steedly and Foley (1979). These articles are reprinted in an appendix to the second edition (1990) of Gamson's study.

2. See, for example, Davidson and Grofman's edited volume *Quiet Revolution in the South* (1994). Also, Amenta, Caruthers, and Zylan's (1992) research on the Townsend movement shows regional variations in mobilization and impact on old-age policies; as does Katzenstein (1987) in her essay on women's movements in the United States and Europe.

3. Rochon (1998) claims that there are greater methodological difficulties for research on political impact than cultural impact. I argue that the challenges are the same, and both require systematic research to determine whether and, if so, how movements are influential.

4. Perhaps the one area where there is some conceptual and operational standardization for the object of explanation is in research using media-reported data on collective action events.

5. Nevertheless, this difference has little to do with general methodological or analytic problems.

6. David Snow suggested the broad contours of this point.

7. This may be one of the ways that unionization campaigns differ from other forms of contentious politics.

8. The literature responding to Piven and Cloward's thesis is quite extensive; see the 1993 edition of their *Regulating the Poor* for a bibliography. Two important critiques from movement scholars are Gamson and Schmeidler's "Organizing the Poor" (1984) and Morris's *The Origins of the Civil Rights Movement* (1984). See also Piven and Cloward's responses in (1984) and (1992).

9. These models of movement influence are connected to methodological strategies. For example, Rucht and Neidhardt argue that media-reported protest is a meaningful barometer of all protest: "Insofar as we are interested in those protests which are an input for the political system, media-reported protests have a higher validity than the whole range of actual protests" (1998, 77).

10. For more detailed discussion of movement organization, see Conell and Voss (1990), Minkoff (1995), Schwartz (1976), Schwartz and Paul (1992), and Staggenborg (1988).

11. For other general discussions of repression, see Balbus (1973), Gurr (1986), and Marx (1979).

12. For examples from the civil rights movement, see Parker, *Black Votes Count* (1990), and Barkan, "Legal Control of the Southern Civil Rights Movement" (1984). On the labor movement, see, for example, Fantasia (1989) and Griffin, Wallace, and Rubin (1986).

13. Other cases of vote manipulation and intimidation can be found in Berry (1973) and Salamon (1972a), and reports of the United States Commission on Civil Rights (1968, 1975, 1981).

14. Scholars attempting to define countermovements have confronted a number of difficulties. In particular, there is a tendency to conflate conservative movements with countermovements and assume that countermovements are by definition "reactionary." Stepping around this problem, Meyer and Staggenborg argue that "a 'countermovement' is a movement that makes contrary claims simultaneously to those of the original movement" (1996, 1630). However, the distinction becomes insignificant if the movement and countermovement persist over an extended period of time. In such cases, we should abandon the movement/countermovement label and analyze "opposing movements" (1632–33).

15. In McAdam's (1982) early formulation of political process theory, he distinguished three broad sets of factors: (1) the structure of political opportunities, (2) indigenous organizational strength, and (3) cognitive liberation. In a sense, I have collapsed the last two as primarily endogenous factors, leaving the first as the set of exogenous factors that shape the contours of mobilization.

16. McAdam's (1996) synthesis points to the same four factors.

17. Political process theory provides a useful approach to examining the role of formal political institutions in movement dynamics, but scholars often treat the state as the only aspect of a movement's broader context that is consequential. As Gamson and Meyer (1996) observe, the political opportunity structure often serves as a "sponge" standing in for the other elements of the environment within which movements unfold. For many movements, including the civil rights movement, this focus on the state makes sense, but economic, social, and cultural characteristics of a movement's environment are also influential (Gamson and Meyer 1996; McCammon et al.

2002; Schwartz 1976). These elements of the broader context are examined in the empirical discussion of the Mississippi movement.

Chapter Three

1. For more comprehensive treatments, see John Dittmer (1994) and Charles Payne (1995). I rely on the extensive scholarly research on the Mississippi movement as well as numerous biographies and autobiographies of key participants and observers. See the citations throughout this chapter for further suggestions.

2. For a thorough and exceptional study of Mississippi blacks during the Jim Crow era, see McMillen (1989).

3. Charles M. Sherrod, "Non-Violence," n.d., folder 161, Litigation Records, Tougaloo College.

4. Ibid.

5. Ibid.

6. See Belfrage (1965), Harris (1982), Holt (1965), McAdam (1988), McCord (1965), Mills (1992), and Mills (1993).

7. See Payne (1995) for an account of the internal debate.

8. The events at Atlantic City are documented in many studies of the movement. See, for example, Carson (1981). On the MFDP, see McLemore (1971) and Romaine (1970).

9. During the same period, Alabama changed from 13.4 to 19.3 percent, Louisiana from 27.8 to 31.7, South Carolina from 22.9 to 37.3, Tennessee from 49.8 to 69.4, and Texas from 26.7 to 57.7 (Lawson 1976, 284).

10. See Simpson (1982).

11. See Carson (1981); Payne (1995); and "Mississippi: Structure of the Movement, Present Operations, and Prospects for this Summer," Jerry Tecklin Papers, 1:5, State Historical Society of Wisconsin (hereinafter SHSW); "Federal Programs Report: Summer Progress—Winter Plans," COFO, August 1964, Ed King Papers, Tougaloo College.

12. See Dittmer (1994), Greenberg (1969), and Payne (1995).

Chapter Four

1. See McMillen (1989) for a historical study of the Mississippi blacks during Jim Crow.

2. "Outline of Mississippi Project Areas," Ruth Schein Papers, folder 2, Schomburg Center.

3. "Outline of Mississippi Project Areas," Ruth Schein Papers, folder 2, Schomburg Center. The trends I describe are based on Colby (1987), McMillen (1989), and the "Outline of Mississippi Project Areas." In quantitative analyses of violence against the movement, I find that movement strength is the most important predictor of the level of violence.

4. The report is included in *Hearings before the United States Commission on Civil Rights, Volume 1, Voting*, held in Jackson, Mississippi, February 16–20, 1965.

5. The 1964 Freedom Vote was the second "mock" election. The 1963 Freedom Vote was for the positions for governor and lieutenant governor, and the 1964 Freedom Vote was for positions in the U.S. House of Representatives and formed part of the evidentiary base for the MFDP's challenge to the seating of the white candidates elected in the "regular" election.

6. The correlation between violence and Freedom Votes is 0.89, and this relationship holds up under more stringent specifications (see the regression analysis for Freedom Votes in Andrews 1997).

7. See appendix A for a full description of the logic of case selection.

8. Interview with Jerome Smith, August 28, 1983, Tom Dent Collection, Tougaloo College.

9. Rural Organizing and Cultural Center, *Minds Stayed on Freedom* (1991, 32); the Rural Organizing and Cultural Center is a local movement organization in Holmes County that sponsored a project where teenagers in the community conducted oral histories with movement veterans. It stands alone as a model of conducting and writing history "from the bottom up."

10. Payne (1995) argues that landownership explains the higher level of participation by men in the Holmes County movement compared to other counties where women typically formed the backbone of the movement.

11. Estimates based on 1964 *Census of Agriculture*, U.S. Bureau of the Census (1965). Letter, June 26, 1964, Eugene Nelson Papers, State Historical Society of Wisconsin (hereinafter SHSW).

12. Rural Organizing and Cultural Center, Minds Stayed on Freedom (1991, 151); the Turnbow incident is described in Carson (1981), Dittmer (1994), and Payne (1995).

13. Rural Organizing and Cultural Center, *Minds Stayed on Freedom* (1991, 70); report, Susan Lorenzi, September 26, 1966, Alvin Oderman Papers, SHSW; interview with Mary Hightower, August 20, 1978, Tom Dent Collection, Tougaloo College.

14. Weekly report, October 16–25, 1964, CORE Papers, reel 23:228; "Mileston Opens Community Center," *The Student Voice*, October 28, 1964, p. 3, copy in Freedom Information Service Archives, folder "FDP—Freedom Vote 1964"; letters to parents from Eugene Nelson, multiple dates during Freedom Summer, Eugene Nelson Papers, SHSW; "Constitution of the Holmes County Community Center," December 5, 1965, Litigation Records, Tougaloo College; Holmes County Community Center Newsletter, Fall 1966, Ed King Papers, 11:607, Tougaloo College.

15. Letters to parents from Eugene Nelson, July 18 and August 2, 1964, Eugene Nelson Papers, SHSW.

16. "The following are names . . . ," SNCC Papers, 65:185; Salamon (1972b); Hartman Turnbow testimony, Congressional Record, June 16, 1964, pp. 14008–9.

17. Interview with Mary Hightower, August 20, 1978, Tom Dent Collection, Tougaloo College.

18. Henry Lorenzi, "Some Thoughts on the Future of the Holmes County Movement," May 1967, Litigation Records, reel 85, folder "Holmes County, Milton Olive," Tougaloo College.

19. Rural Organizing and Cultural Center, *Minds Stayed on Freedom* (1991, 29, 139).

20. Madison County FDP, "Organizing for an ASC election," CORE papers, Fourth Congressional District, reel 1:2, SHSW; see also Dittmer (1994, 333–35); Sue Lorenzi, "News-Sheet on the Lorenzi's—Holmes Co., Miss.," August 27, 1966, Alvin Oderman Papers, SHSW.

21. In 1960 the census reports that there were 8,757 nonwhites eighteen years old or over, and that there were 8,219 in 1970.

22. David Emmons, "Black Politics in the South—Holmes County, Mississippi: Robert Clark and the Politics of Intimacy," MFDP Records, reel 3, item 6, Mississippi Department of Archives and History (hereinafter MDAH); "Key List Mailing #6," MFDP, January 22, 1966, Ed King Papers, 12:641, Tougaloo College; interview with Ed Brown, July 2, 1979, Tom Dent Collection, Tougaloo College.

23. "Holmes County Community Center, Annual News Letter, December 1967," Litigation Records, reel 85, folder "Holmes County, Milton Olive," Tougaloo College; Sue Lorenzi, "News-Sheet on the Lorenzi's—Holmes Co., Miss.," August 27, 1966, Alvin Oderman Papers, SHSW; First Annual Report, Holmes County Community Center, SNCC Papers, reel 65, folder 183.

24. "Key List Mailing #6," MFDP, January 22, 1966, Ed King Papers, 12:641, Tougaloo College; memo, "Harassment of Negroes in Holmes County during the summer of 1966 by law enforcement officers and justices of the peace," Reiss to Aronson, Ray, Bronstein, and Lorenzi, August 12, 1966, Litigation Records, reel 85, folder "Holmes County, General Files," Tougaloo College.

25. "We Are the Majority Race" (33-page booklet describing local movement), Holmes MFDP, Civil Rights Litigation Records, reel 169, Tougaloo College; see also Henry Lorenzi, "Some Thoughts on the Future of the Holmes County Movement," May 1967, Litigation Records, reel 85, folder "Holmes County, Milton Olive," Tougaloo College; Lorenzi's memo to be circulated within the movement documented a wide range of assets of the Holmes movement; report, Susan Lorenzi, September 26, 1966, Alvin Oderman Papers, SHSW.

26. "Statement of the Holmes County Community Center Association . . . ," Litigation Records, reel 85, folder "Holmes County, Milton Olive"; Holmes County Community Center Newsletter, Fall 1966, Ed King Papers, 11:607, Tougaloo College; "Summary of Central Mississippi, Inc.," Litigation Records, reel 85, folder "Holmes County, Milton Olive," Tougaloo College; Sue Lorenzi, "News-Sheet on the Lorenzi's—Holmes Co., Miss.," August 27, 1966, Alvin Oderman Papers, SHSW.

27. A further indicator of the long-term viability of the Holmes movement is that there is still an MFDP organization in the county that endorses candidates and engages in protest campaigns; interview with Walter Bruce, July 29, 1996.

28. See Meier and Rudwick (1973) and Moody (1968) for descriptions of this early period.

29. Letter, Dave Dennis to Jim McCain, August 8, 1963, CORE Papers, reel 22.

30. *Madison County Herald (MCH)*, June 20, 1963. Lists of "Applicants for Registration to Vote" were published in the MCH periodically throughout 1963 and 1964.

31. Debbie Bernstein, "Canton Project History," p. 2, February 28, 1965, CORE Papers, reel 10.

32. Memo, "Mississippi in Motion," Dennis to McCain, October 19, 1963, CORE Papers, reel 22.

33. Interview with Matt Suarez, July 31, 1977, Tom Dent Collection, Tougaloo College.

34. "A Review of the Mississippi Civil Rights Movement: Then and Now" [tape recording], November 9, 1978, Tougaloo Symposium, Tom Dent Collection, Tougaloo College.

35. McComb was one of the few places with higher levels of violence, especially a series of bombings. See Harris (1992).

36. "Canton Police Arrest Gunman, Set Trial for June Shooting," *Mississippi Free Press* [hereafter *MFP*], July 6, 1963.

37. See Meier and Rudwick (1976) for a broader analysis of boycotts within the African American protest tradition.

38. "Canton Fights Back," *MFP*, January 25, 1964; the role of mass meetings is thoroughly analyzed by Morris (1984).

39. "Slowdown Shows Plan," *MFP*, March 7, 1964; "Negro Queue in Mississippi Is Symbol of Frustration," New York Times, March 2, 1964, p. 20; interview with Ed Blackmon, June 19, 1996.

40. "Freedom Day in Canton," *MFP*, February 29, 1964.

41. "Canton Fights Back," *MFP*, January 25, 1964.

42. "2625 Canton Students Stay Home from School," *MFP*, March 14, 1964; field report, Edward S. Hollander, March 9, 1964, SNCC Papers, 38:92.

43. Field report, Edward S. Hollander, March 9, 1964, SNCC Papers, 38:92.

44. Ibid.

45. Debbie Bernstein, "Canton Project History," February 28, 1965, CORE papers, reel 10, Schomburg Center.

46. An early study by Killian and Grigg, *Racial Crisis in America* (1964), documents the use of biracial committees throughout the urbanized and upper South as a delaying mechanism.

47. "Outline of Mississippi Project Areas," n.a., n.d., Ruth Schein Papers, Schomburg Center; "Citizens Council Reorganized Here; Racial Demonstration Discounted," *MCH*, February 27, 1963; *COFO et al. v. L. A. Rainey et al.*, COFO Records, *MDAH*; "The Mississippi Power Structure," Poor People's Corporation Papers, 2:4, SHSW.

48. *COFO et al. v. L. A. Rainey et al.*, COFO Records, MDAH; Dittmer (1994, 222); another legalistic strategy was used during a boycott in Clarksdale in 1961 when leaders were charged with "conspiring to withhold trade from downtown merchants," *MFP*, December 16, 1964.

49. "Canton Policemen Beat Two Youths," *MFP*, February 15, 1964.

50. Ibid.; see also "Freedom Day in Canton," *MFP*, February, 29, 1964, which reports on further efforts to pressure black merchants.

51. Walter Wittman, "Partial Summary of Depositions at Canton, Madison County, on February 8, 9, 10, 1965," SNCC Papers, 65:224.

52. "List of Volunteers and Staff," SNCC Papers, A:XV:197, reel 39, Schomburg Center; Colby (1985, 45–46); Dittmer (1994, 255).

53. Another pattern took place in Bolivar (described below) where the increased staff allowed COFO to expand into new communities. For example, during Freedom Summer a strong local movement was initiated in the Bolivar County town of Shaw, which is described below.

54. COFO solicited reports from all project offices during the fall of 1964. These reports are an extremely valuable source for documenting the dilemmas facing local projects after Freedom Summer and Atlantic City. Major problems included the flow of communication and resources from the state COFO office and internal staff problems. The reports also document the diversity of projects being pursued by local movements. Large (but probably incomplete) collections of these reports can be found in the Charles Horowitz Papers, box 2, folder 33, Tougaloo College; and the Stuart Ewen Papers, box 1, folder 1, SHSW.

55. Madison and Rankin Counties [Special Project Report], n.d. [Fall 1964], Charles Horowitz Papers, box 2, folder 33, Tougaloo College.

56. Mary Brumder, Holmes County [Special Project Report], November 21, 1964, Charles Horowitz Papers, box 2, folder 33, Tougaloo College.

57. See documentation in the Joann Oiman Robinson Papers, SHSW.

58. Statement by George Raymond, January 7, 1965, Joann Oiman Robinson Papers, 1:7, SHSW; letter from George Raymond, January 9, 1965, Robinson Papers, 1:7, SHSW; "Report for Madison County," June 2, 1965, Robinson Papers, 1:3, SHSW; flyer, "ASC Ballot," Robinson Papers, 1:7, SHSW; "The Madison County Citizen," May 1, 1965, Robinson Papers, 1:8, SHSW; see also United States Commission on Civil Rights, *Hearings before the United States Commission on Civil Rights: Volume II, Administrations of Justice, February 16–20, 1965*.

59. "Incidents . . . Democratic Primary Election, June 7, [1966]," SNCC Papers, 41:22. These and other incidents are described in Washington Research Project, *The Shameful Blight: The Survival of Racial Discrimination in Voting in the South* (1972). Other documentation of vote manipulation and intimidation can be found in Berry (1973), Salamon (1972a), and reports of the United States Commission on Civil Rights (1968, 1975, 1981).

60. Interview with Ed Blackmon, June 19, 1996.

61. "A Review of the Mississippi Civil Rights Movement: Then and Now" [tape recording], November 9, 1978, Tougaloo Symposium, Tom Dent Collection, Tougaloo College.

62. Interview with Ed Blackmon, June 19, 1996; "Suit Claims Blacks Denied City Services," *MCH*, February 13, 1975; "Police Charged with Hiring Discrimination," *MCH*, June 5, 1975; "Racial Bias Charges in Fire Department," *MCH*, June 12, 1975; "Report Threatens Revenue Funds," *MCH*, August 11, 1977; "Canton Faces Cutoff of Revenue Sharing Funds," *MCH*, December 15, 1977; "Canton's Revenue Sharing Funds Are Cut Off," *MCH*, January 12, 1978; "U.S. Court Schedules Canton Election Suit," *MCH*, March 16, 1978; "Hospital Is Target of NAACP Complaint," *MCH*, April 6, 1978.

63. Interview with Annie Devine by Tom Dent, August 17, 1976, Tom Dent Collection, Tougaloo College.

64. See Dollard (1937) and Powdermaker ([1939] 1968) for studies of nearby Sunflower County during the Jim Crow era. See also McMillen (1989).

65. "Staff Reports," Commission on the Delta Ministry, October 1965, Ed King Papers, 12:622, Tougaloo College.

66. Communications to Jesse Morris from the Mound Bayou Project, n.d. [Fall 1964], Charles Horowitz Papers, box 2, folder 33, Tougaloo College.

67. Notes on Freedom Day, n.a., July 16, 1964, Lise Vogel Papers, SHSW (also in Jerry Tecklin Papers, box 1, folder 7, SHSW, with list of registrants).

68. Letter, Bonnie Guy to "Friends," July 18, 1964, Lise Vogel Papers, SHSW.

69. Project report, Mary Sue Gellatly, n.d., COFO Papers, Shaw, Mississippi, SHSW; Shaw weekly report, Mary Sue Gellatly, September 19, 1964; September 26, 1964; September 28, 1964; October 2, 1964; October 17, 1964; October 28, 1964; COFO Papers, Shaw, Mississippi, SHSW; Shaw weekly report, Mary Sue Gellatly, September 26, 1964, COFO Papers, Shaw, Mississippi, SHSW.

70. Project report, Mary Sue Gellatly, March 20, 1965, COFO Papers, Shaw, Mississippi, SHSW.

71. "Shaw, Mississippi: New Sounds in the Delta" [transcript of radio broadcast], 1965, Ed King Papers, 11:564, Tougaloo College; See also Findlay (1993); Hilton (1969); Lise Vogel Papers, SHSW; and MFLU subject file, Tamiment Library, New York University.

72. "COFO News—Incident Summary," February 27–March 2, 1965, Charles Baer Papers, 1:2, SHSW.

73. See Dittmer (1994, chap. 16), and Greenberg (1969).

74. *Examination of the War on Poverty, Staff and Consultant Reports*, U.S. Senate Committee on Labor and Public Welfare on Community Action Program: Interpretative Analysis, Vol. 4, September 1967.

75. "A Brief History of the Shelby Problems," n.a., September 1968, Rims Barber Papers, 6:254, Tougaloo College; untitled one-page report ("A biracial group has been formed . . ."), n.a., n.d., Rims Barber Papers, 6:254, Tougaloo College; "Shelby—Boycott of Schools," n.a., n.d., Rims Barber Papers, 6:254, Tougaloo College; press release, "Federal Courts Bring Victory to Shelby Blacks," Delta Ministry, May 31, 1968, Rims Barber Papers, 6:254, Tougaloo College; "Black School Crisis in Mississippi," n.a., n.d. [1969], Rims Barber Papers, 6:254, Tougaloo College; "Our School Sure Need Changing," n.a., n.d. [1967], Rims Barber Papers, 6:254, Tougaloo, College; selected articles from the Memphis Commercial Appeal and the Delta Democrat Times can be found in Rims Barber Papers, 6:254, Tougaloo College.

76. Interview with Robert Gray, July 19, 1996; "Shelby Mayor Robert Gray—The New Black Elected Official," *Jackson Advocate*, March 15-21, 1979, p. 1B.

77. On the Delta Health Center, see Dorsey (1977) and Huttie (1973).

78. "The Agricultural Co-operative as a Possible Means of Providing Food for Needy Persons," 1967 [?], Charles Baer Papers, 1:6, SHSW; "Future for Mound Bayou Rests with Compassionate Strangers," *Boston Sunday Globe*, January 18, 1976, Charles Baer Papers, 1:6, SHSW; Rutherford Associates, "Food Processing in the Mississippi Delta," October 1, 1970, Charles Baer Papers, 1:4, SHSW; see Redding (1992) and Schwartz (1976) for similar efforts during the Populist movement.

Chapter Five

1. See Lawson (1976, 1985) and Scher and Button (1984) for overviews of the Voting Rights Act. Some of the scholarship on the Voting Rights Act has been directly linked to congressional

debates over renewal of the act (e.g., in 1971, 1975, 1981). Here, researchers have been interested in demonstrating the gains made under vigorous enforcement and the need for further efforts to protect black voting rights.

2. Using the number of black elected officials as an indicator of black electoral influence is sometimes criticized as an overly crude indicator (Swain 1993). However, the persistence of racial bloc voting provides some confidence in the validity of the indicator in aggregated data.

3. As another point of comparison, Parker, Colby, and Morrison (1994) report that 12.2 percent of all elected offices in Mississippi were held by blacks in 1989.

4. Rather than measuring repression directly, Salamon and Van Evera (1973) measure vulnerability to economic coercion, taking the proportion of the black population in selected occupations, such as domestic workers.

5. Hartman Turnbow testimony, *Congressional Record*, June 16, 1964, pp. 14008–9.

6. "Ex-Sheriff in Holmes Testifies," January 4, 1964, p 1A, newspaper not listed, Mississippi Department of Archives and History (hereinafter MDAH) Subject Files—Holmes County.

7. "Federal Court Orders Holmes Registrar Not to Discriminate," *Lexington Advertiser*, September 30, 1965, p. 1; *United States of America v. Henry B. McLellan et al.*, Litigation Records, reel 99, folder "Holmes County Community Hospital," Tougaloo College.

8. Announcement of federal registrars in towns on April 6 and April 13, 1968, "around the state," April 5, 1968, FIS Mississippi Newsletter, Horowitz Papers, Tougaloo College; "United States Commission on Civil Rights Staff Report, May 13, 1969, Municipal Elections in Mississippi," June 3, 1969, Horowitz Papers, box 3, folder 52, Tougaloo College.

9. "Mississippi: How Negro Democrats Fared." MFDP Records, reel 1.

10. Holmes County Community Center Newsletter, Fall 1966, Ed King Papers, 11:607, Tougaloo College.

11. Report ("6:15 a.m. Wednesday, November 8 [1967] while waiting at the Jackson Municipal Airport"), Jerry Gutman, Litigation Records, reel 83, folder "Elections, Complaints," Tougaloo College; letter, Parker to Bronstein, November 15, 1967, Litigation Records, reel 83, folder "Elections, Complaints," Tougaloo College; letter, Steinman to Lewis, November 9, 1967, Litigation Records, reel 83, folder "Elections, Complaints," Tougaloo College.

12. David Emmons, "Black Politics in the South—Holmes County, Mississippi: Robert Clark and the Politics of Intimacy," MFDP Records, reel 3, item 6, MDAH; Sue Lorenzi, "News-Sheet on the Lorenzi's—Holmes Co., Miss.," August 27, 1966, Alvin Oderman Papers, State Historical Society of Wisconsin (hereinafter SHSW); Rural Organizing and Cultural Center, *Minds Stayed on Freedom* (1991, 129).

13. "Incidents . . . Democratic Primary Election, June 7th," General Elections, Litigation Records, reel 83, Tougaloo College; Alan Boles, "Shoot-Out Threatened at Mississippi Poll," *Yale Daily News*, November 8, 1967, Elections Results Project, 1967, Litigation Records, reel 83, Tougaloo College; "7 Win Problems Lower Vote," November 10, 1967, Horowitz Papers, Tougaloo College; "More Election Day News," November 10, 1967, Horowitz Papers, Tougaloo College.

14. "Holmes County Has Been in Politics from the Beginning," *The Drummer*, April 30, 1971.

15. This is true at least for the counties where the movement operated. Arguably, the movement could have had an impact on communities without a local movement, although it would be very difficult to determine whether or not this type of impact occurred.

16. See U.S. Commission on Civil Rights, *The Voting Rights Act: The First Months* (1965), for a detailed description of the role of federal examiners.

17. I measured the presence or absence of federal examiners in the county. Examiners provided a parallel registration process that was intended to eliminate discrimination. The Voter Education Project report (and other researchers) used the total number of blacks listed by federal examiners as an indicator of the effect of examiners. This conflates the outcome (number of registered blacks) with the facilitative role played by examiners and overestimates the effect of examiners.

18. Although direct effects of examiners were limited, there may have been indirect effects. For example, the presence of examiners may have moderated the resistance of examiners in other counties. If this were true, then the cross-sectional estimates would underestimate the overall impact of examiners.

19. A second reason for moving to other outcome measures is that the data on voter registration is the least reliable measure of political participation. Voter registration records are not kept by race, so the data used are estimates of various kinds either by local registrars or self-reported in census data. Even aggregate data on voter registration tends to be inaccurate because registrars fail to purge records on a regular basis for deaths, migration, and felony conviction (Lichtman and Issacharoff 1991).

20. Clifton Whitley ran for the U.S. Senate in the Democratic primary in August and in the general election as an independent candidate. Voter turnout in these two elections is highly correlated ($r = 0.797$), so I have used an average of the two as an indicator of mid-1960s black electoral mobilization.

21. "Racial bloc voting" refers to the tendency in biracial elections for whites to vote for white candidates and blacks for black candidates. In legal cases concerning discriminatory redistricting, racial bloc voting research has been important for establishing the discriminatory effect of at-large election systems.

22. These counties had no Freedom Summer projects. By 1966 Claiborne County had 1,316 adult members of the NAACP; Jefferson and Wilkinson had 924 and 889, respectively.

23. The two variables (the size and proportion of the black voting-age population) cannot be entered into the same equation without generating multi-colinearity. In table 5.2, the dependent variables require a control for the absolute size of the black electorate. In tables 5.3 and 5.4, the dependent variables require a control for the relative size of the black electorate.

24. Thomas A. Johnson, "Leaders of Mississippi's Black Activists Confident of the Future," *New York Times*, January 11, 1970, p. 57.

Chapter Six

1. Major histories of the War on Poverty include Katz (1986), Patterson ([1986] 1994), Piven and Cloward ([1971] 1993), and Quadagno (1994). See also Brown and Erie (1981), Fried-

land (1976), Friedman (1977), Greenstone and Peterson ([1973] 1976), and Miller and Rein (1965).

2. Specific agencies were sometimes referred to as Community action agencies (CAA); to avoid confusion, I have used CAP throughout the chapter.

3. The only book-length study of CDGM is Greenberg's *The Devil Has Slippery Shoes* (1969), based on her experience as an OEO staff member who worked closely with CDGM. See also Dittmer (1994) and Payne (1995).

4. Interview with Bernice Johnson, June 20, 1996.

5. Scott to Haddad, July 5, 1965, file "CDGM 1965, Head Start—Mississippi," box 108, RG 381, National Archives and Record Administration (NARA).

6. Inspection Report, CDGM Area B, July 30, 1966, file "Mississippi," box 108, RG 381, NARA.

7. Scott to Haddad, July 5, 1965, file "CDGM 1965, Head Start—Mississippi," box 108, RG 381, NARA; Haaser to May, March 3, 1966, file "Head Start, Mississippi, CDGM, January–August 1966," box 83B, RG 381, NARA; Sugarman quoted in Dittmer (1994, 372).

8. For an overview, see evidence and testimony included in *Examination of the War on Poverty, Hearings before the Subcommittee on Employment, Manpower, and Poverty of the Committee on Labor and Public Welfare*, U.S. Senate, 90th Congress, 1st Session, part 2, Jackson, MS, April 20, 1967 (754–63).

9. The two dependent variables are the total CAP grants for 1965–68 and 1969–71; budget reports in multiple files by organization, Region IV, Mississippi, box 14, Grant Profiles, 1965–72, Policy Research Division, Office of Operations, Office of Economic Opportunity, RG 381, NARA. I have handled the problem of multicounty projects in two ways. First, I divided the budget evenly among the counties covered by the CAP. For the second estimation, I divided the budget among the counties proportional to the number of households with an income below $3,000 in a county. Both estimates produced similar results. I have reported the analysis using the "proportional" estimates. Because participation in programs was based on economic eligibility, this latter strategy is a better, if not perfect, approximation of the distribution. There were eighteen CAPs in Mississippi from 1965–71; eight were multicounty agencies.

10. MFDP is measured by the number of staff/contact persons in the county; "FDP Projects by County and Contacts," August 23, 1965, file "FDP—General Mississippi Summer, 1965 (579)," box 11, Ed King Papers, Tougaloo College.

11. U.S. House Committee on Un-American Activities, Activities of Ku Klux Klan Organizations in the U.S. (Washington, DC: GPO, 1965); "MS Citizens' Council Map," *The Citizen*, January 1956; data on violence were compiled by Colby (1987).

12. Sloan to Bozman, October 14, 1966, file "Southeast Region, 1966," box 2, Regional Organizational Subject Files, 1966–69, CAP Office, Records of the Director, RG 381, NARA.

13. Governors could veto poverty programs unless they were administered through a college or university. Some programs, such as CDGM, were administered through historically black colleges to avoid this problem. Other programs were sponsored by universities outside the South such as the Tufts Delta Health Center in Bolivar County.

14. Memo from Dean to Shriver, February 24, 1966, file "Southeast Region, 1966," box 2, RG 381, NARA.

15. Dean to Shriver, February 24, 1966, file "Southeast Region, 1966," Regional Organizational Subject Files, 1966–69, CAP Office, Records of the Director, 2:381, NARA; Westgate to Gonzales, attached to memo from Gonzales to Bozman and Hausler, December 11, 1965, Administrative, Mississippi, State Files, 1965–68, CAP Office, Records of the Director, 5:381, NARA.

16. Westgate to Gonzales, attached to memo from Gonzales to Bozman and Hausler, December 11, 1965, Administrative, Mississippi, State Files, 1965-68, CAP Office, Records of the Director, 5:381, NARA.

17. "Holmes County Community Newsletter," Fall 1966, Ed King Papers, box 11, file 607, Tougaloo College; "Anti-Poverty Program Discussed," *Lexington Advertiser,* February 24, 1966, p. 1; "Holmes CAP Advisory Group," *Lexington Advertiser,* March 10, 1966, p. 1; Salamon (1972b).

18. "An Outline of Important Events," box 2, file 8, Moore Papers, SHSW; "Chronological History," box 3, file 1, Moore Papers, SHSW.

19. Estimating the size of the movement organization is difficult. The "Outline of Important Events" cited above reports "approximately 7,000 signatures" on the petition, providing one indicator. "Bolivar County CAP Unites Races for Common Purpose," *Delta Democrat Times,* October 5, 1966, p. 11, included in letter from Davis to Berry, October 10, 1966, Administrative, Mississippi, State File, 1965–68, CAP Office, Records of the Director, 12:381, NARA; Seward to May, March 17, 1966, file "Mississippi—OEO Program (Compilation) 1966, January–March," 40:381, NARA; petition from Reverend Story to President Johnson included in report May to Sugarman, March 3, 1966, file "Mississippi—OEO Program (Compilation) 1966, January–March," 40:381, NARA; "Minutes of the Proceedings, St. Peter's Rock M. B. Church," January 19, 1966, box 2, file 8, Moore Papers, SHSW.

20. "Resident Participation," Bolivar County CAP, Inc., box 2, file 6, Moore Papers, SHSW; Bartley letter, March 13, 1966, box 2, file 8, Moore Papers, SHSW; ACBC to Shriver and Sloan, 1966, box 2, file 8, Moore Papers, SHSW; "A Report of the Meeting Held with CAP," March 22, 1966, box 2, file 8, Moore Papers, SHSW.

21. Berry to May, March 31, 1966, file "Mississippi—OEO Program (Compilation) 1966, January–March," 40:381; Seward to May, March 17, 1966, file "Mississippi—OEO Program (Compilation) 1966, January–March," box 40:381, NARA; *Examination of the War on Poverty,* U.S. Senate, 90th Congress, 1st Session, vol. IV (Washington, DC: GPO, 1967), pp. 1185–97; Berry to Long, Smith, and Moore, April 14, 1966, box 3, file 1, Moore Papers, SHSW.

22. Kirk to Berry, January 13, 1967, Administrative, Mississippi, State File, 1965–68, CAP Office, Records of the Director, 5:381, NARA; Sloan to Shriver and Harding, December 30, 1966, file "Southeast Region, 1966," Regional Organizational Subject Files, 1966–69, CAP Office, Records of the Director, 2:381, NARA.

23. Sloan to Shriver, November 8, 1966, file "Southeast Region, 1966," box 2, Regional Organizational Subject Files, 1966–69, CAP Office, Records of the Director, RG 381, NARA.

24. Ibid.; R. Martin to E. May, July 27, 1967, file "Mississippi—OEO Program (Compilation) 1967, January–December," box 40, RG 381, NARA.

25. R. Martin to E. May, July 27, 1967, file "Mississippi—OEO Program (Compilation) 1967, January–December," box 40, RG 381, NARA.

Chapter Seven

1. These processes are also noteworthy because much of the research on resistance to school desegregation has focused on urban and northern school districts. There is a vast literature on desegregation; see, for example, Hochschild (1984), James (1989), Orfield (1994), Rossell (1983), Rossell and Crain (1982), and Smock and Wilson (1991).

2. For studies examining the impact of the Mississippi movement on electoral politics, see Andrews (1997), Colby (1986), and Stewart and Sheffield (1987); on social policies, see Quadagno (1994) and Colby (1985).

3. For detailed accounts of the court case and implementation, see Parker (1987), Rosenberg (1991), and Wirt (1970).

4. Data reported in "Negroes in Desegregated Schools in Mississippi, Autumn, 1966," Rims Barber Papers, box 6, folder 253, Tougaloo College.

5. Memo from Marian E. Wright and Henry M. Aronson, Litigation Records, folder "Carthan," reel 138, Tougaloo College.

6. Sue Lorenzi, Stanford Oral History Project, Mississippi Department of Archives and History.

7. *State of Mississippi v. Thomas Bartley,* Litigation Records, reel 7, folder "Bartley," Tougaloo College.

8. "Abstract from Answers to Interrogatories," *Cowan et al. v. Bolivar County School Board,* Litigation Records, reel 141, folder "Cowan et al.," Tougaloo College.

9. "School Year '65–'66, Canton, Mississippi," Michael Grossman Papers, State Historical Society of Wisconsin (hereinafter SHSW).

10. "Boycott Victory," in *Freedom Flame,* Shaw Mississippi Student Union, August 5, 1964, Litigation Records, reel 141, folder "Cowan et al.," Tougaloo College; "Petition to the School Board of Bolivar County from Parents of Shaw School Students," 1965, Litigation Records, reel 141, folder "Cowan et al.," Tougaloo College; "School Integration 1965 Canton, Mississippi and Differences between White and Negro Schools in the City of Canton," Bobbie Ruth Chinn, Mary Catherine, and Carl Taylor, Michael Grossman Papers, SHSW; Viola McGee, "School Desegregation Report for Cleveland," Litigation Records, reel 141, folder "Cowan et al.," Tougaloo College.

11. Three of the districts included in the *Alexander* case "were brought against three county school boards of education which controlled only transportation systems" (Munford 1973, 14).

12. "Bolivar County Whites Rally to Protest Order on Schools," *Memphis Commercial Appeal,* May 31, 1969, Litigation Records, reel 93, folder "Desegregation, General," Tougaloo College.

13. "Preliminary Fact-Finding Report of NEA Staff Team on School Desegregation in Mississippi," Litigation Records, reel 93, folder "Desegregation, General," Tougaloo College.

14. Ibid.

15. Data from U.S. Department of Health, Education and Welfare, *Directory of Public Elementary and Secondary Schools in Selected Districts*, Office of Civil Rights, 1968 and 1972; see also details from court case against Madison County Board of Education (1974), Rims Barber Papers, box 7, folder 289, Litigation Records, Tougaloo College.

16. "Preliminary Fact-Finding Report of NEA Staff Team on School Desegregation in Mississippi," Litigation Records, reel 93, folder "Desegregation, General," Tougaloo College.

17. "Comparison of Attendance of Pupils in the Various School Districts of the State before and after the Dates of Court Ordered Desegregation Thereof," State Department of Audit, Jackson, Mississippi, Litigation Records, reel 93, folder "Desegregation, General," Tougaloo College.

18. Data from *Coffey v. Educational Finance Commission*, reported in Carroll (1981, 134).

19. *Thelma Head et al. v. Randolph Thrower et al.*, Litigation Records, reel 93, folder "Desegregation, General," Tougaloo College.

20. "Leads on Private School Support," Rims Barber Papers, box 6, folder 243, Tougaloo College.

21. "School Involvement Project," James Loewen Papers, box 14, Tougaloo College.

22. "Mississippi Advances Bills to Aid Whites Fleeing Public Schools," *New York Times*, March 8, 1970, sec. 1, p. 30.

23. See the following dissertations for background on the MPSA: Carroll (1981), Mathis (1975), and Sansing (1971). As noted earlier, movements often change their goals over the course of their development. In the case of the Citizens' Council, it is both interesting and revealing that the primary goal of the organization had shifted in slightly over ten years from a thorough defense of segregated public institutions to a rearguard attempt to establish private institutions.

24. There has been substantial research on the impact of law (see Rosenberg 1991). One of the major constraints of law as a mechanism of change is that court orders often lack an effective institution to oversee and enforce decisions. The *Alexander* decision may be unique because of the extensive interaction between HEW, the Justice Department, and the courts. Hence, it would be inaccurate to attribute the effects of the Alexander decision measured in the models to "the courts" exclusively. Rather, there was a coordinated federal effort in these counties greater than was present in other locales.

25. With academies, the relationship between percentage black and academy attendance is linear, but with segregation there is a threshold corresponding to majority black.

26. A variation on Olzak et al.'s competition theory argues that white resistance is not targeted at all African Americans (or the total proportion within a population). Rather, middle- and working-class white resistance is targeted toward poor and working-class African Americans; this argument suggests that whites are less motivated by racial prejudice than class prejudice (see Bullock and Rodgers 1976; and Conlon and Kimenyi, 1991). To the extent that white responses are motivated against contact with poor blacks and not against contact with poor whites, we could argue that class and race dynamics are at play. Class-based variants of competition theory suggest that whites' resistance is greatest to poor blacks. I expect greater support for academies where the number of black households in poverty constitutes a greater proportion of a county's population.

27. There is substantial evidence that movement leadership in antibusing movements had an "elite" base (Mottl 1980; Zald and Useem 1987).

Chapter Eight

1. To maintain consistency across the different models, I use the 1970 measures for percentage urban and percentage black voting-age population in all of the remaining models including the path analysis. Compared to the 1970 indicators, the 1980 measures of these variables produce nearly identical effects, so no significant bias is introduced into the later models. For example, the correlation between the 1970 and 1980 black voting-age populations is over 0.98.

2. I have not excluded these counties from table 8.3 or the following path analysis because the empirical analysis without these counties generates the same substantive conclusions.

3. The path coefficients are determined by a reanalysis using only statistically significant variables. As in table 8.3, the number of black candidates in 1967 (rather than 1971) is used in the path analysis to emphasize the earliest point in the development of the electoral infrastructure. I treat Freedom Summer as an independent variable predicting white violence even though some of the violence occurred before Freedom Summer. This decision is based on the observation that violence was most often responsive to movement activity. In his study of white violence, Colby (1987) makes a similar decision, treating an index of civil rights activity as an independent variable predicting white violence.

4. The black voting-age population does not have a direct effect on white violence because the relationship is curvilinear.

5. The electoral mobilization infrastructure resembles the idea of "abeyance structures" advanced by Taylor (1989) to refer to the organizations that link two periods of mass mobilization. However, electoral infrastructures link widespread mobilization to a period of later success in electoral politics.

6. For recent studies that examine the persistence of these inequalities, see Colclough (1988), Falk and Rankin (1992), Lichter (1989), and Tomaskovic-Devey and Roscigno (1996).

7. On the background and career of Bennie Thompson, see Morrison (1987). Button's study (1989) of six Florida towns also documents the disparities in fire protection and the efforts of civil rights groups and black elected officials to address these disparities.

8. "How Much Power Do We Now Have," *The Drummer*, November 24–30, 1971.

Chapter Nine

1. In grouping the counties, I have relied on the historical literature and several aggregate indicators, including Charles Baer's (1970) index of movement strength for 1961–65 as an indicator of the level of early movement activity in a county.

2. See Dollard (1937) and Powdermaker ([1939] 1968) for studies of nearby Sunflower County, which was very similar to Bolivar County.

3. See Morris (1993) and Garrow (1978).

Appendix A

1. See Payne's essay at the end of *I've Got the Light of Freedom* (1995) and Carson's essay "Civil Rights Reform and the Black Freedom Struggle" (1986) for more thorough developments of this idea. For historical analyses that focus on local patterns of mobilization, see Ceselski (1994), Chafe (1980), Dittmer (1994), Eskew (1997), and Norrell (1985).

2. The SCLC's strategy reflected this pattern by focusing on particular cities, for example, Birmingham, Selma, and Chicago. Even SNCC's work outside Mississippi was focused on one town rather than statewide.

3. Studies examining school desegregation and politics in urban areas have followed a similar strategy of aggregating across school districts to compare cities to each other.

References

Abney, Glenn. 1974. "Factors Related to Negro Voter Turnout in Mississippi." *Journal of Politics* 37:1057–63.

Alford, Robert, and Roger Friedland. 1975. "Political Participation and Public Policy." *Annual Review of Sociology* 1:429–79.

Alt, James E. 1994. "The Impact of the Voting Rights Act on Black and White Voter Registration in the South." In *Quiet Revolution in the South: The Impact of the Voting Rights Act, 1965–1990*, edited by C. Davidson and B. Grofman, 351–77. Princeton: Princeton University Press.

———. 1995. "Race and Voter Registration in the South." In *Classifying by Race*, edited by P. E. Peterson, 313–32. Princeton: Princeton University Press.

Amenta, Edwin. 1991. "Making the Most of a Case Study: Theories of the Welfare State and the American Experience." *International Journal of Comparative Sociology* 32:172–94.

Amenta, Edwin, Bruce Caruthers, and Yvonne Zylan. 1992. "A Hero for the Aged? The Townsend Movement, the Political Mediation Model, and US Old Age Policy, 1934–1950." *American Journal of Sociology* 98:308–39.

Amenta, Edwin, Kathleen Dunleavy, and Mary Bernstein. 1994. "Stolen Thunder? Huey Long's 'Share Our Wealth,' Political Mediation, and the Second New Deal." *American Sociological Review* 59:678–702.

Amenta, Edwin, Drew Halfmann, and Michael P. Young. 1999. "The Strategies and Context of Social Protest: Political Mediation and the Impact of the Townsend Movement in California." *Mobilization* 4:1–23.

Amenta, Edwin, and Michael P. Young. 1999. "Making an Impact." In *How Social Movements Matter*, edited by M. Giugni, D. McAdam, and C. Tilly, 22–41. Minneapolis: University of Minnesota Press.

Amenta, Edwin, and Yvonne Zylan. 1991. "It Happened Here: Political Opportunity, the New Institutionalism, and the Townsend Movement." *American Sociological Review* 56:250–65.

Aminzade, Ronald. 1992. "Historical Sociology and Time." *Sociological Methods & Research* 20:456–80.

Aminzade, Ronald, Jack A. Goldstone, and Elizabeth Perry. 2001. "Leadership Dynamics and Dynamics of Contention." In *Silence and Voice in the Study of Contentious Politics*, edited by R. Aminzade et al., 126–54. Cambridge: Cambridge University Press.

Andrews, Kenneth T. 1997. "The Impacts of Social Movements on the Political Process: A Study of the Civil Rights Movement and Black Electoral Politics in Mississippi." *American Sociological Review* 62:800–19.

———. 2001. "Social Movements and Policy Implementation: The Mississippi Civil Rights Movement and the War on Poverty, 1965–1971." *American Sociological Review* 66:71–95.

———. 2002. "Movement-Countermovement Dynamics and the Emergence of New Institutions." *Social Forces* 80:911–36.

Arnez, Nancy. 1978. "Implementation of Desegregation as a Discriminatory Process." *Journal of Negro Education* 47:28–45.

Baer, Charles. 1970. "New Black Politics in Mississippi." Ph.D. diss., Northwestern University, Evanston, IL.

Balbus, Isaac D. 1973. *The Dialectics of Legal Repression: Black Rebels before the American Criminal Courts.* New Brunswick, NJ: Transaction Books.

Banaszak, Lee Ann. 1996. *Why Movements Succeed or Fail: Opportunity, Culture and the Struggle for Woman Suffrage.* Princeton: Princeton University Press.

Barkan, Steven. 1984. "Legal Control of the Southern Civil Rights Movement." *American Sociological Review* 49:552–65.

Belfrage, Sally. 1965. *Freedom Summer.* New York: Vintage Press.

Benford, Robert D., and Scott A. Hunt. 1992. "Dramaturgy and Social Movements: The Social Construction and Communication of Power." *Sociological Inquiry* 62:36–55.

Berry, Jason. 1973. *Amazing Grace: With Charles Evers in Mississippi.* New York: Saturday Review Press.

Bigart, Homer. 1969. "Citizens Councils in Schools Drive." *New York Times,* June 12, 29, p. 1.

Black, Earl, and Merle Black. 1987. *Politics and Society in the South.* Cambridge: Harvard University Press.

Bloom, Jack M. 1987. *Class, Race and the Civil Rights Movement.* Bloomington: Indiana University Press.

Bobo, Lawrence, and Franklin D. Gilliam Jr. 1990. "Race, Sociopolitical Participation, and Black Empowerment." *American Political Science Review* 84:377–93.

Brockett, Charles. 1991. "The Structure of Political Opportunities and Peasant Mobilization in Central America." *Comparative Politics* 23:253–74.

———. 1993. "A Protest Cycle Resolution of the Repression/Popular-Protest Paradox." *Social Science History* 17:457–84.

Bronfenbrenner, Kate, Sheldon Friedman, Richard W. Hurd, Rudolph A. Oswald, and Ronald Seeber. 1998. *Organizing to Win: New Research on Union Strategies.* Ithaca, NY: Cornell University Press.

Brown, Michael K., and Steven P. Erie. 1981. "Blacks and the Legacy of the Great Society: The Economic and Political Impact of Federal Social Policy." *Public Policy* 29:299–330.

Browning, Rufus P., Dale R. Marshall, and David H. Tabb. 1984. *Protest Is Not Enough: The Struggle of Blacks and Hispanics for Equality in Urban Politics.* Berkeley: University of California Press.

Bullard, Robert. 1990. *Dumping in Dixie: Race, Class, and Environmental Quality.* Boulder: Westview Press.

Bullock, Charles S., and Harrell R. Rodgers Jr. 1976. "Coercion to Compliance: Southern School Districts and School Desegregation." *Journal of Politics* 38:987–1011.

Burstein, Paul. 1979. "Public Opinion, Demonstrations and the Passage of Antidiscrimination Legislation." *Public Opinion Quarterly* 43:157–72.

————. 1985. *Discrimination, Jobs, and Politics: The Struggle for Equal Employment Opportunity in the United States since the New Deal*. Chicago: University of Chicago Press.

————. 1991a. "Legal Mobilization as a Social Movement Tactic: The Struggle for Equal Employment Opportunity." *American Journal of Sociology* 96:1201–25.

————. 1991b. "'Reverse Discrimination' Cases in the Federal Courts: Legal Mobilization by a Countermovement." *Sociological Quarterly* 32:511–28.

————. 1993. "Explaining State Action and the Expansion of Civil Rights: The Civil Rights Act of 1964." *Research in Political Sociology* 6:117–37.

————. 1999. "Social Movements and Public Policy." In *How Social Movements Matter*, edited by M. Giugni, D. McAdam, and C. Tilly, 3–21. Minneapolis: University of Minnesota Press.

Burstein, Paul, Rachel Einwohner, and Jocellyn Hollander. 1995. "The Success of Social Movements: A Bargaining Perspective." In *The Politics of Social Protest: Comparative Perspectives on State and Social Movements*, edited by J. C. Jenkins and B. Klandermans, 275–95. Minneapolis: University of Minnesota Press.

Burstein, Paul, and William Freudenburg. 1978. "Changing Public Policy: The Impact of Public Opinion, Antiwar Demonstrations, and War Costs on Senate Voting on Vietnam War Motions." *American Journal of Sociology* 84:99–122.

Burton, Michael G. 1984. "Elites and Collective Protest." *Sociological Quarterly* 25:45–66.

Button, James. 1978. *Black Violence*. Princeton: Princeton University Press.

————. 1982. "Southern Black Elected Officials: Impact on Socioeconomic Change." *Review of Black Political Economy* (Fall): 29–45.

————. 1989. *Blacks and Social Change: Impact of the Civil Rights Movement in Southern Communities*. Princeton: Princeton University Press.

Cable, Sherry, and Michael Benson. 1993. "Acting Locally: Environmental Injustice and the Emergence of Grass-roots Environmental Organization." *Social Problems* 40:464–77.

Cagin, Seth, and Philip Dray. 1988. *We Are Not Afraid*. New York: Bantam Books.

Campbell, David, and Joe R. Feagin. 1975. "Black Politics in the South: A Descriptive Analysis." *Journal of Politics* 37:129–59.

Campbell, Donald. 1975. "'Degrees of Freedom' and the Case Study." *Comparative Politics Studies* 8:178–93.

Carroll, Terry Doyle. 1981. "Mississippi Private Education: An Historical, Descriptive, and Normative Study." Ed.D. diss., University of Southern Mississippi, Hattiesburg.

Carson, Clayborne. 1981. *In Struggle: SNCC and the Black Awakening of the 1960's*. Cambridge: Harvard University Press.

————. 1986. "Civil Rights Reform and the Black Freedom Struggle." In *The Civil Rights Movement in America: Essays*, edited by Charles W. Eagles, 19–32. Jackson: University Press of Mississippi.

Cecelski, David S. 1994. *Along Freedom Road: Hyde County, North Carolina, and the Fate of Black Schools in the South*. Chapel Hill: University of North Carolina Press.

Chafe, William. 1980. *Civilities and Civil Rights: Greensboro, North Carolina, and the Black Struggle for Freedom*. New York: Oxford University Press.

Chevigny, Paul G. 1965. "A Busy Spring in the Magnolia State." In *Southern Justice*, edited by Leon Friedman, 13–34. Cleveland: Meridian Books.

Chong, Dennis. 1991. *Collective Action and the Civil Rights Movement*. Chicago: University of Chicago Press.

Citizens' Councils of America. 1956. "Mississippi Citizens' Council Map." *The Citizens' Council*. (June): 6.

Clemens, Elisabeth. 1993. "Organizational Repertoires and Institutional Change: Women's Groups and the Transformation of U.S. Politics, 1890–1920." *American Journal of Sociology* 98:755–98.

———. 1997. *The People's Lobby: Organizational Innovation and the Rise of Interest Group Politics in the United States, 1890–1925.* Chicago: University of Chicago Press.

———. 1998. "To Move Mountains: Collective Action and the Possibility of Institutional Change." In *From Contention to Democracy*, edited by Marco Giugni, Doug McAdam, and Charles Tilly, 109–24. Lanham, MD: Rowman and Littlefield.

Cobb, James C. 1992. *The Most Southern Place on Earth: The Mississippi Delta and the Roots of Regional Identity.* New York: Oxford University Press.

Cohen, Jean. 1985. "Strategy or Identity: New Theoretical Paradigms and Contemporary Social Movements." *Social Research* 52:663–16.

Colby, David. 1985. "Black Power, White Resistance, and Public Policy: Political Power and Poverty Program Grants in Mississippi." *Journal of Politics* 47:579–95.

———. 1986. "The Voting Rights Act and Black Registration in Mississippi." *Publius: The Journal of Federalism* 16:123–37.

———. 1987. "White Violence and the Civil Rights Movement." In *Blacks in Southern Politics*, edited by L. Moreland, R. Steed, and T. Baker, 31–48. New York: Praeger.

Colclough, Glenna. 1988. "Uneven Development and Racial Composition in the Deep South: 1970–1980." *Rural Sociology* 53:73–86.

Conell, Carol, and Kim Voss. 1990. "Formal Organizations and the Fate of Social Movements: Craft Association and Class Alliance in the Knights of Labor." *American Sociological Review* 55:255–69.

Conlon, John R., and Mwangi S. Kimenyi. 1991. "Attitudes toward Race and Poverty in the Demand for Private Education: The Case of Mississippi." *Review of Black Political Economy* 20:5–22.

Costain, Anne N. 1981. "Representing Women: The Transition from Social Movement to Interest Group." *Western Political Quarterly* 34:100–13.

———. 1992. *Inviting Women's Rebellion: A Political Process Interpretation of the Women's Movement.* Baltimore: John Hopkins University Press.

Cowart, Andrew. 1969. "Anti-Poverty Expenditures in the American States." *Midwest Journal of Political Science* 13:219–36.

Cress, Daniel M., and David Snow. 2000. "The Outcomes of Homeless Mobilization: The Influence of Organization, Disruption, Political Mediation, and Framing." *American Journal of Sociology* 105:1063–104.

Cunnigen, Donald. 1987. "Men and Women of Goodwill: Mississippi's White Liberals." Ph.D. diss., Harvard University, Cambridge.

Davenport, Christian, ed. 2000. *Paths to State Repression: Human Rights Violations and Contentious Politics.* Lanham, MD: Rowman and Littlefield.

Davidson, Chandler. 1984. "Minority Vote Dilution: An Overview." In *Minority Vote Dilution*, edited by C. Davidson, 1–23. Washington, DC: Howard University Press.

Davidson, Chandler, and Bernard Grofman. 1994. *Quiet Revolution in the South: The Impact of the Voting Rights Act, 1965–1990.* Princeton: Princeton University Press.

Davis, Theodore. 1987. "Blacks' Political Representation in Rural Mississippi." In *Blacks in Southern Politics*, edited by L. Moreland, R. Steed, and T. Baker, 149–59. New York: Praeger.

Delaney, John T., Paul Jarley, and Jack Fiorito. 1996. "Planning for Change: Determinants of Innovation in U.S. National Unions." *Industrial and Labor Relations Review* 49:597–614.

Dent, Tom. 1997. *Southern Journey: A Return to the Civil Rights Movement*. New York: William Morrow.

Diani, Mario. 1997. "Social Movements and Social Capital." *Mobilization* 2:129–47.

Dittmer, John. 1985. "The Politics of the Mississippi Movement: 1954–1964." In *The Civil Rights Movement in America: Essays*, edited by C. W. Eagles, 65–93. Jackson: University Press of Mississippi.

———. 1993. "The Transformation of the Mississippi Movement, 1964–1968: The Rise and Fall of the Freedom Democratic Party." In *Essays on the American Civil Rights Movement*, edited by W. Marvin Dulaney and Kathleen Underwood, 9–43. College Station: Texas A&M University Press.

———. 1994. *Local People: The Struggle for Civil Rights in Mississippi*. Urbana: University of Illinois Press.

Dollard, John. 1937. *Caste and Class in a Southern Town*. New Haven: Yale University Press.

Dorsey, L. C. 1977. *Freedom Came to Mississippi*. New York: Field Foundation.

Earl, Jennifer. 2003. "Tanks, Tear Gas, and Taxes: Toward a Theory of Movement Repression." *Sociological Theory* 21:44–68.

Eckstein, Harry. 1965. "On the Etiology of Internal Wars." *History and Theory* 4:133–63.

Edwards, Bob, and Sam Marullo. 1995. "Organizational Mortality in a Declining Social Movement: The Demise of Peace Movement Organizations in the End of the Cold War Era." *American Sociological Review* 60:908–27.

Eisinger, Peter. 1973. "The Conditions of Protest Behavior in American Cities." *American Political Science Review* 67:11–28.

———. 1982. "Black Employment in Municipal Jobs: The Impact of Black Political Power." *American Political Science Review* 76:380–92.

Eskew, Glenn T. 1997. *But for Birmingham: The Local and National Movements in the Civil Rights Struggle*. Chapel Hill: University of North Carolina Press.

Evans, Sara M. 1980. *Personal Politics: The Roots of Women's Liberation in the Civil Rights Movement and the New Left*. New York: Vintage.

Falk, William W., and Bruce H Rankin. 1992. "The Cost of Being Black in the Black Belt." *Social Problems* 39:299–313.

Fantasia, Rick. 1989. *Cultures of Solidarity: Consciousness, Action and Contemporary American Workers*. Berkeley: University of California Press.

Ferree, Myra Marx, and Patricia Yancey Martin. 1995. "Doing the Work of the Movement: Feminist Organizations." In *Feminist Organizations: Harvest of the New Women's Movement*, edited by M. M. Ferree and P. Y. Martin, 3–23. Philadelphia: Temple University Press.

Findlay, James F. 1993. *Church People in the Struggle: The National Council of Churches and the Black Freedom Movement, 1950–1970*. New York: Oxford University Press.

Fireman, Bruce, and William Gamson. 1979. "Utilitarian Logic in the Resource Mobilization Perspective." In *The Dynamics of Social Movements: Resource Mobilization, Social Control, and Tactics*, edited by M. Zald and J. McCarthy, 8–44. Cambridge: Winthrop.

Fording, Richard. 1997. "The Conditional Effect of Violence as a Political Tactic." *American Journal of Political Science* 41:1–29.

Forman, James. 1972. *The Making of Black Revolutionaries: A Personal Account*. New York: Macmillan.

Frey, Scott R., Thomas Dietz, and Linda Kalof. 1992. "Characteristics of Successful American Protest Groups: Another Look at Gamson's Strategy of Social Protest." *American Journal of Sociology* 98:36–87.

Friedland, Roger. 1976. "Class Power and Social Control: The War on Poverty." *Politics and Society* 6:459–89.

Friedman, Lawrence M. 1977. "The Social and Political Context of the War on Poverty: An Overview." In *A Decade of Federal Antipoverty Programs: Achievements, Failures and Lessons*, edited by R. H. Haveman, 21–47. New York: Academic Press.

Gale, Richard. 1986. "Social Movements and the State: The Environmental Movement, Countermovement and Government Agencies." *Sociological Perspectives* 29:202–40.

Gamson, William. [1975] 1990. *The Strategy of Social Protest*. Belmont: Wadsworth.

Gamson, William, and David S. Meyer. 1996. "Framing Political Opportunity." In *Comparative Perspectives on Social Movements: Political Opportunities, Mobilizing Structures, and Cultural Framings*, edited by D. McAdam, J. D. McCarthy, and M. N. Zald, 275–90. Cambridge: Cambridge University Press.

Gamson, William, and Emilie Schmeidler. 1984. "Organizing the Poor." *Theory and Society* 13:587–99.

Ganz, Marshall. 2000. "The Paradox of Powerlessness: Leadership, Organization, and Strategy in the Unionization of California Agriculture, 1959–1977." *American Journal of Sociology* 105:1003–62.

Garrow, David. 1978. *Protest at Selma: Martin Luther King, Jr. and the Voting Rights Act of 1965*. New Haven: Yale University Press.

Gelb, Joyce. 1987. "Social Movement 'Success': A Comparative Analysis of Feminism in the United States and the United Kingdom." In *The Women's Movements of the United States and Western Europe*, edited by M. F. Katzenstein and C. M. Mueller, 267–89. Philadelphia: Temple University Press.

———. 1995. "Feminist Organization Success and the Politics of Engagement." In *Feminist Organizations: The Harvest of the New Women's Movement*, edited by M. M. Ferree and P. Y. Martin, 128–34. Philadelphia: Temple University Press.

Gerlach, Luther P., and Virginia M. Hine. 1970. *People, Power, Change: Movements of Social Transformation*. Indianapolis: Bobbs-Merrill.

Giugni, Marco. 1998. "Was It Worth the Effort? The Outcomes and Consequences of Social Movements." *Annual Review of Sociology* 24:371–93.

Goldstone, Jack. 1980a. "Mobilization and Organization: Reply to Foley and Steedly and Gamson." *American Journal of Sociology* 85:1426–32.

———. 1980b. "The Weakness of Organization: A New Look at Gramson's *The Strategy of Social Protest*." American Journal of Sociology 85:1017–42.

Goldstone, Jack, and Charles Tilly. 2001. "Threat (and Opportunity)" In *Silence and Voice in the Study of Contentious Politics*, edited by R. Aminzade et al., 179–94. Cambridge: Cambridge University Press.

Goodman, George, Jr. 1979. "Black Mayors in the South Are Learning How to Get Federal Grants." *New York Times*. September 3, sec 1, p. 5.

Graham, Fred. 1970. "Federal Judges Rule Out Benefit for Segregated Private 'Academies.'" *New York Times*, January 14, sec. 1, p. 1.

Grant, Joanne. 1998. *Ella Baker: Freedom Bound*. New York: John Wiley and Sons.

Greenberg, Polly. 1969. *The Devil Has Slippery Shoes: A Biased Biography of the Child Development Group in Mississippi*. London: Macmillan.

Greenstone, J. David, and Paul E. Peterson. [1973] 1976. *Race and Authority in Urban Politics: Community Participation in the War on Poverty.* Chicago: University of Chicago Press.

Griffin, Larry J., Michael E. Wallace, and Beth A. Rubin. 1986. "Capitalist Resistance to the Organization of Labor Before the New Deal: Why? How? Success?" *American Sociological Review* 51:147–67.

Grofman, Bernard, ed. 2000. *Legacies of the 1964 Civil Rights Act.* Charlottesville, VA: University Press of Virginia.

Gurr, Ted Robert. 1986. "Persisting Patterns of Repression and Rebellion: Foundations for a General Theory of Political Coercion." In *Persistent Patterns and Emerging Structures in a Waning Century,* edited by M. P. Karns, 149–68. New York: Praeger Special Studies for the International Studies Association.

Haines, Herbert H. 1984. "Black Radicalization and the Funding of Civil Rights: 1957–1970." *Social Problems* 32:31–43.

Hampton, Harry, and Steve Fayer. 1990. *Voices of Freedom: An Oral History of the Civil Rights Movement from the 1950s through the 1980s.* New York: Bantam Books.

Handler, Joel F. 1978. *Social Movements and the Legal System: A Theory of Law Reform and Social Change.* New York: Academic Press.

Harris, David. 1982. *Dreams Die Hard.* New York: St. Martin's.

Hart, Stephen. 2001. *Cultural Dilemmas of Progressive Politics: Styles of Engagement among Grassroots Activists.* Chicago: University of Chicago Press.

Harvey, Anna L. 1998. *Votes without Leverage: Women in American Electoral Politics, 1920–1970.* Cambridge: Cambridge University Press.

Helfgot, Joseph. 1974. "Professional Reform Organizations and the Symbolic Representation of the Poor." *American Sociological Review* 39:475–91.

Hester, Kathryn. 1982. "Mississippi and the Voting Rights Act: 1965–1982." *Mississippi Law Journal* 52:803–76.

Hilton, Bruce. 1969. *The Delta Ministry.* New York: Macmillan.

Hochschild, Jennifer. 1984. *The New American Dilemma: Liberal Democracy and School Desegregation.* New Haven: Yale University Press.

Holt, Len. 1965. *The Summer that Didn't End.* New York: William Morrow.

Huttie, Joseph. 1973. " 'New Federalism' and the Death of a Dream in Mound Bayou, Mississippi." *New South,* 20–29.

Irons, Jennifer. 2002. "From Segregation to Moderation: Legitimacy Struggle and Political Discursive Change." University of Arizona, unpublished ms.

Isaac, Larry, and Lars Christiansen. 2002. "How the Civil Rights Movement Revitalized Labor Militancy." *American Sociological Review.* 67:722–46.

James, David R. 1988. "The Transformation of the Southern Racial State: Class and Race Determinants of Local-State Structures." *American Sociological Review* 53:191–208.

———. 1989. "City Limits on Racial Equality: The Effects of City-Suburb Boundaries on Public School Desegregation, 1968–1976." *American Sociological Review* 54:963–85.

James, David R., and Karl E. Taueber. 1985. "Measures of Segregation." *Sociological Methodology* 15:1–32.

Jenkins, J. Craig. 1983. "Resource Mobilization Theory and the Study of Social Movements." *Annual Review of Sociology* 9:527–53.

Jenkins, J. Craig, and Craig M. Eckert. 1986. "Channeling Black Insurgency: Elite Patronage and Professional Social Movement Organizations in the Development of the Black Movement." *American Sociological Review* 51:812–29.

Johnson, Thomas A. 1979. "Mississippi's Black Mayors Intensify Efforts to Influence Elections." *New York Times*. February 2, sec. 1, p. 10.

Joint Center for Political Studies. Selected Volumes. *National Roster of Black Elected Officials*. Washington, DC: Joint Center for Political Studies.

Jones, Mack. 1976. "Black Officeholding and Political Development in the Rural South." *Review of Black Political Economy* 6:375–407.

Joubert, Paul E., and Ben M. Crouch. 1977. "Mississippi Blacks and the Voting Rights Act of 1965." *Journal of Negro Education* 46:157–67.

Katz, Michael. 1986. *In the Shadow of the Poorhouse: A Social History of Welfare in America*. New York: Basic Books.

Katznelson, Ira. 1981. *City Trenches: Urban Politics and the Patterning of Class in the United States*. New York: Pantheon Books.

Katzenstein, Mary F. 1987. "Comparing the Feminist Movements of the United States and Western Europe: An Overview." In *The Women's Movements of the United States and Western Europe: Consciousness, Political Opportunity and Public Policy*, edited by M. F. Katzenstein and C. M. Mueller, 3–20. Philadelphia: Temple University Press.

———. 1990. "Feminism within American Institutions: Unobtrusive Mobilization in the 1980s." *Signs* 16:27–54.

———. 1998. *Faithful and Fearless: Moving Feminist Protest Inside the Church and Military*. Princeton: Princeton University Press.

Keech, William R. [1968] 1981. *The Impact of Negro Voting: The Role of the Vote in the Quest for Equality*. Westport, CT: Greenwood Press.

Kernell, Sam. 1973. "Comment: A Re-evaluation of Black Voting in Mississippi." *American Political Science Review* 67:1307–18.

Key, V. O. 1949. *Southern Politics in State and Nation*. New York: Knopf.

Killian, Lewis, and Charles Grigg. 1964. *Racial Crisis in America: Leadership in Conflict*. Englewood Cliffs, NJ: Prentice-Hall.

Kimmeldorf, Howard. 1988. *Reds and Rackets: The Making of Radical and Conservative Unions on the Waterfront*. Berkeley: University of California Press.

Kinder, Donald R., and Lynn M. Sanders. 1996. *Divided by Color: Racial Politics and Democratic Ideals*. Chicago: University of Chicago Press.

King, Mary. 1987. *Freedom Song: A Personal Story of the 1960s Civil Rights Movement*. New York: Morrow.

Kitschelt, Herbert P. 1986. "Political Opportunity Structures and Political Protest: Anti-Nuclear Movements in Four Democracies." *British Journal of Political Science* 16:57–85.

Klandermans, Bert. 1997. *The Social Psychology of Protest*. Cambridge, Eng.: Blackwell.

Koopmans, Ruud. 1997. "Dynamics of Repression and Mobilization: The German Extreme Right in the 1990s." *Mobilization* 2:149–65.

Kornhauser, William. 1959. *The Politics of Mass Society*. New York: Free Press.

Krane, Dale, and Stephen D. Shaffer. 1992. *Mississippi Government and Politics: Modernizers versus Traditionalists*. Lincoln: University of Nebraska Press.

Kriesi, Hanspeter, Ruud Koopmans, Jan WIllem Duyvendak, and Marco Giugni. 1995. *New Social Movements in Western Europe: A Comparative Analysis*. Minneapolis: University of Minnesota Press.

Laumann, Edward O., and David Knoke. 1987. *The Organizational State: Social Choice in National Policy Domains*. Madison: University of Wisconsin Press.

Lawson, Steven F. 1976. *Black Ballots: Voting Rights in the South, 1944–1969*. New York: Columbia University Press.

———. 1985. *In Pursuit of Power: Southern Blacks and Electoral Politics, 1965–1982*. New York: Columbia University Press.

Lewis, John, and Michael D'Orso. 1998. *Walking with the Wind: A Memoir of the Movement*. New York: Simon & Schuster.

Lichbach, Mark Irving. 1987. "Deterrence or Escalation?: The Puzzle of Aggregate Studies of Repression and Dissent." *Journal of Conflict Resolution* 31:266–97.

Lichter, Daniel T. 1989. "Race, Employment Hardship, and Inequality in the American Nonmetropolitan South." *American Sociological Review* 54:436–46.

Lichtman, Allan, and Samuel Issacharoff. 1991. "Black/White Voter Registration Disparities in Mississippi: Legal and Methodological Issues in Challenging Bureau of Census Data." *Journal of Law and Politics* 7:525–57.

Lieberman, Robert. 1995. "Race, Institutions, and the Administration of Social Policy." *Social Science History* 19:511–42.

Lieberson, Stanley. 1980. *A Piece of the Pie: Black and White Immigrants since 1880*. Berkeley: University of California Press.

Lipsky, Michael. 1968. "Protest as a Political Resource." *American Political Science Review* 62:1144–58.

Lo, Clarence Y. H. 1982. "Countermovements and Conservative Movements in the Contemporary U.S." *Annual Review of Sociology* 8:107–34.

Loewen, James. 1981. "Continuing Obstacles to Black Electoral Success in Mississippi." *Civil Rights Research Review* 9:24–39.

———. 1990. "Racial Bloc Voting and Political Mobilization in South Carolina." *Review of Black Political Economy* 19:23–37.

Lofland, John. 1993. "Theory-bashing and Answer-improving in the Study of Social Movements." *American Sociologist* 24:37–58.

Lohmann, Susanne. 1993. "A Signaling Model of Informative and Manipulative Political-Action." *American Political Science Review* 87:319–33.

Luker, Kristin. 1984. *Abortion and the Politics of Motherhood*. Berkeley: University of California Press.

MacLeod, Jay. 1991. "Introduction: Racism, Resistance and the Origins of the Holmes County Movement." In *Minds Stayed in Freedom: The Civil Rights Struggle in the Rural South, An Oral History*, 1–20. Boulder: Westview Press.

Maguire, Dairmund. 1993. "Protestors, Counterprotestors, and the Authorities." *Annals of the American Academy of Political and Social Sciences* 528:101–13.

Mansbridge, Jane J. 1986. *Why We Lost the ERA*. Chicago: University of Chicago Press.

———. 1994. "Politics of Persuasion." In *The Dynamics of American Politics*, edited by L. C. Dodd and C. Jillison, 298–310. Boulder, CO: Westview Press.

Markoff, John. 1997. "Peasants Help Destroy an Old Regime and Defy a New One: Some Lessons from (and for) the Study of Social Movements." *American Journal of Sociology* 102:1113–42.

Marx, Anthony. 1992. *Lessons of Struggle: South African Internal Opposition, 1960–1990*. Oxford: Oxford University Press.

Marx, Gary. 1979. "External Efforts to Damage or Facilitate Social Movements: Some Patterns, Explanations, Outcomes, and Complications." In *The Dynamics of Social Movements: Resource*

Mobilization, Social Control, and Tactics, edited by M. Zald and J. McCarthy, 94–125. Cambridge: Winthrop.

Marx, Gary T., and James L. Wood. 1975. "Strands of Theory and Research in Collective Behavior." *Annual Review of Sociology* 1:363–428.

Mathis, Kenneth W. 1975. "An Historical and Status Survey of Member Schools of the Mississippi Private School Association." Ed.D. diss., University of Mississippi, Oxford.

Matthews, Donald R., and James W. Protho. 1966. *Negroes and the New Southern Politics*. New York: Harcourt, Brace and World.

McAdam, Doug. 1982. *Political Process and the Development of Black Insurgency, 1930–1970*. Chicago: University of Chicago Press.

———. 1983. "Tactical Innovation and the Pace of Insurgency." *American Sociological Review* 48:735–54.

———. 1988. *Freedom Summer*. Oxford: Oxford University Press.

———. 1996. "Conceptual Origins, Current Problems, Future Directions." In *Comparative Perspectives on Social Movements: Political Opportunities, Mobilizing Structures, and Cultural Framings*, edited by D. McAdam, J. D. McCarthy, and M. N. Zald, 23–40. New York: Cambridge University Press.

———. 1999. *Political Process and the Development of Black Insurgency, 1930–1970*. 2nd ed. Chicago: University of Chicago Press.

McAdam, Doug, John McCarthy, and Mayer Zald. 1988. "Social Movements." In *Handbook of Sociology*, edited by N. Smelser, 695–737. Newbury Park, CA: Sage.

McAdam, Doug, and David A. Snow. 1997. *Social Movements: Readings on Their Emergence, Mobilization, and Dynamics*. Los Angeles: Roxbury.

McAdam, Doug, and Yang Su. 2002. "The War at Home: Antiwar Protest and Congressional Voting, 1965 to 1973." *American Sociological Review* 67:696–721.

McAdam, Doug, Sidney Tarrow, and Charles Tilly. 1996. "To Map Contentious Politics." *Mobilization* 1:17–34.

———. 2001. *Dynamics of Contention*. Cambridge: Cambridge University Press.

McCammon, Holly J. 1993. "From Repressive Intervention to Integrative Prevention: The U.S. State's Legal Management of Labor Militancy, 1881–1978." *Social Forces* 71:569–601.

McCammon, Holly J., Karen E. Campbell, Ellen M. Granberg, and Christine Mowery. 2002. "How Movements Win: Gendered Opportunity Structures and U.S. Women's Suffrage Movements, 1866 to 1919." *American Sociological Review* 66:49–70.

McCarthy, John, David Britt, and Mark Wolfson. 1991. "The Institutional Channeling of Social Movements." *Research in Social Movements, Conflict and Change* 13:45–76.

McCarthy, John, and Mayer Zald. 1977. "Resource Mobilization and Social Movements: A Partial Theory." *American Journal of Sociology* 82:1212–41.

McCord, William. 1965. *Mississippi: The Long, Hot Summer*. New York: W. W. Norton.

McCrary, Peyton. 1990. "Racially Polarized Voting in the South: Quantitative Evidence from the Courtroom." *Social Science History* 14:507–31.

McLemore, Leslie Burl. 1971. "The Mississippi Freedom Democratic Party: A Case History of Grass-Roots Politics." Ph.D. diss., University of Massachusetts, Amherst.

McMillen, Neil. 1971. *The Citizens' Council: Organized Resistance to the Second Reconstruction, 1954–1964*. Urbana: University of Illinois Press.

———. 1989. *Dark Journey: Black Mississippians in the Age of Jim Crow*. Urbana: University of Illinois Press.

Meier, August, and Elliott Rudwick. 1973. *CORE, a Study in the Civil Rights Movement, 1942–1968*. New York: Oxford University Press.

———. 1976. "The Origins of Nonviolent Direct Action in Afro-American Protest: A Note on Historical Discontinuities." In *Along the Color Line: Explorations in the Black Experience*, edited by August Meier, 307–404. Urbana: University of Illinois Press.

Melucci, Alberto. 1989. *Nomads of the Present: Social Movement and Individual Needs in Contemporary Society*. Philadelphia: Temple University Press.

Meyer, David S. 1990. *A Winter of Discontent: The Nuclear Freeze and American Politics* New York: Praeger.

Meyer, David S., and Suzanne Staggenborg. 1996. "Movements, Countermovements, and the Structure of Political Opportunity." *American Journal of Sociology* 101:1628–60.

Meyer, David S., and Nancy Whittier. 1994. "Social Movement Spillover." *Social Problems* 41:277–99.

Miller, S. M., and Martin Rein. 1965. "The War on Poverty: Perspectives and Prospects." In *Poverty as a Public Issue*, edited by Ben Seligman, 272–320. New York: Free Press.

Mills, Kay. 1993. *This Little Light of Mine: The Life of Fannie Lou Hamer*. New York: Dutton.

Mills, Nicolaus. 1992. *Like a Holy Crusade: Mississippi 1964—the Turning of Civil Rights Movement in America*. Chicago: Ivan R. Dee.

Minkoff, Debra C. 1993. "The Organization of Survival: Women's and Racial-Ethnic Voluntarist and Activist Organizations, 1955–1985." *Social Forces* 71:887–908.

———. 1995. *Organizing for Equality: The Evolution of Women's and Racial-Ethnic Organizations in America, 1955–1985*. New Brunswick, NJ: Rutgers University Press.

———. 1997. "The Sequencing of Social Movements." *American Sociological Review* 62:779–99.

Mirowsky, John, and Catherine Ross. 1979. "Protest Group Success: The Impact of Group Characteristics, Social Control and Context." *Sociological Focus* 14:177–92.

"Mississippi Advances Bills to Aid Whites Fleeing Public Schools." 1970. *New York Times*, March 8, sec. 1, p. 30.

Moody, Anne. 1968. *Coming of Age in Mississippi*. New York: Laurel.

Morris, Aldon. 1981. "Black Southern Student Sit-in Movement: An Analysis of Internal Organization." *American Sociological Review* 46:744–67.

———. 1984. *The Origins of the Civil Rights Movement: Black Communities Organizing for Change*. New York: Free Press.

———. 1993. "Birmingham Confrontation Reconsidered." *American Sociological Review* 58:621–36.

Morris, Aldon, and Cedric Herring. 1987. "Theory and Research in Social Movements: A Critical Review." *Annual Review of Political Science* 2:137–98.

Morris, Aldon, and Carol Mueller. 1992. *Frontiers in Social Movement Theory*. New Haven: Yale University Press.

Morris, Milton D. 1984. "Black Electoral Participation and the Distribution of Public Benefits." In *Minority Vote Dilution*, edited by Chandler Davidson, 271–85. Washington, DC: Howard University Press.

Morrison, Minion K. C. 1987. *Black Political Mobilization: Leadership, Power, and Mass Behavior*. Albany: State University of New York Press.

Moses, Bob. 1970. "Mississippi: 1961–2." *Liberation* 14:8–17.

Moses, Robert P. 2001. *Radical Equations: Civil Rights From Mississippi to the Algebra Project*. Boston: Beacon Press.

Mottl, Tahi L. 1980. "The Analysis of Countermovements." *Social Problems* 27:620–35.

Mueller, Carol McClung. 1978. "Riot Violence and Protest Outcomes." *Journal of Political and Military Sociology* 6:46–63.

Munford, Luther. 1973. "White Flight from Desegregation in Mississippi." *Integrated Education* 11:12–26.

Murray, Richard, and Arnold Velditz. 1977. "Race, Socioeconomic Status, and Voting Participation." *Journal of Politics* 39:1064–72.

———. 1978. "Racial Voting Patterns in the South: An Analysis of Major Elections from 1960 to 1977 in Five Cities." *Annals of the American Academy of Political and Social Science* 439:29–39.

Norrell, Robert J. 1985. *Reaping the Whirlwind: The Civil Rights Movement in Tuskegee.* New York: Alfred A. Knopf.

Oberschall, Anthony. 1973. *Social Conflict and Social Movements.* Englewood Cliffs, NJ: Prentice-Hall.

O'Connor, Robert E. 1998. "Race and Head Start Participation: Political and Social Determinants of Enrollment Success in the States." *Social Science Quarterly* 79:595–606.

Offe, Claus. 1985. "New Social Movements: Challenging the Boundaries of Institutional Politics." *Social Research* 59:817–68.

Olivier, Johan L. 1991. "State Repression and Collective Action in South Africa, 1970–84." *South African Journal of Sociology* 22:109–17.

Olson, Mancur. 1965. *The Logic of Collective Action: Public Goods and the Theory of Groups.* Cambridge: Harvard University Press.

Olzak, Susan. 1992. *The Dynamics of Ethnic Competition and Conflict.* Stanford: Stanford University Press.

Olzak, Susan, Suzanne Shanahan, and Elizabeth West. 1994. "School Desegregation, Interracial Exposure, and Antibusing Activity in Contemporary Urban America." *American Journal of Sociology* 100:196–241.

Opp, Karl-Deiter, and Wolfgang Roehl. 1990. "Repression, Micromobilization, and Political Protest." *Social Forces* 69:521–47.

Orfield, Gary. 1994. "School Desegregation after Two Generations: Race, Schools, and Opportunity in Urban Society." In *Race in America: The Struggle for Equality*, edited by Herbert Hill and James E. Jones, 234–62. Madison: University of Wisconsin Press.

Parker, Frank. 1987. "Protest, Politics, and Litigation: Political and Social Change in Mississippi, 1965 to Present." *Mississippi Law Journal* 57:677–704.

———. 1990. *Black Votes Count: Political Empowerment in Mississippi after 1965.* Chapel Hill: University of North Carolina Press.

Parker, Frank, David C. Colby, and Minion K. C. Morrison. 1994. "Mississippi." In *Quiet Revolution in the South: The Impact of the Voting Rights Act, 1965–1990*, edited by C. Davidson and B. Grofman, 136–54. Princeton: Princeton University Press.

Parker, Frank, and Barbara Phillips. 1981. *Voting in Mississippi: A Right Still Denied.* Washington, DC: Lawyer's Committee for Civil Rights Under Law.

Patterson, James. [1986] 1994. *America's Struggle against Poverty.* 2nd ed. Cambridge: Harvard University Press.

Paul, Shuva, Sarah Mahler, and Michael Schwartz. 1997. "Mass Action and Social Structure." *Political Power and Social Theory* 11:45–99.

Payne, Charles. 1989. "Ella Barker and Models of Social Change." *Signs* 14:885–99.

————. 1995. *I've Got the Light of Freedom: The Organizing Tradition and the Mississippi Freedom Struggle*. Berkeley: University of California Press.

Peterson, Paul E., and J. David Greenstone. 1977. "Racial Change and Citizen Participation: The Mobilization of Low-Income Communities through Community Action." In *A Decade of Federal Antipoverty Programs: Achievements, Failures and Lessons*, edited by R. H. Haveman, 241–78. New York: Academic Press.

Piven, Frances Fox, and Richard Cloward. 1977. *Poor People's Movements*. New York: Pantheon Books.

Piven, Frances Fox, and Richard Cloward. 1984. "Disruption and Organization: A Reply to William A. Gamson and Emilie Schmeidler." *Theory and Society* 13:587–99.

————. 1992. "Normalizing Collective Protest." In *Frontiers in Social Movement Theory*, edited by Aldon Morris and Carol Mueller, 301–25. New Haven: Yale University Press.

————. [1971] 1993. *Regulating the Poor: The Functions of Public Welfare*. Rev. ed. New York: Vintage Books.

Powdermaker, Hortense. [1939] 1968. *After Freedom: A Cultural Study in the Deep South*. New York: Atheneum.

Quadagno, Jill. 1992. "Social Movements and State Transformation: Labor Unions and Racial Conflict in the War on Poverty." *American Sociological Review* 57:616–34.

———— 1994. *The Color of Welfare: How Racism Undermined the War on Poverty*. Oxford: Oxford University Press.

Ragin, Charles C. 1989. "The Logic of Comparative Method and the Algebra of Logic." *Journal of Quantitative Anthropology* 1:373–98.

Raines, Howell. 1977. *My Soul Is Rested: The Story of the Civil Rights Movement in the Deep South*. New York: Penguin.

Rasler, Karen. 1996. "Concessions, Repression, and Political Protest in the Iranian Revolution." *American Sociological Review* 61:132–52.

————. 2000. "Mobilization, Opportunity Structure, and Polity Responsiveness: The Role of Repression in the Intifada." In *Paths to State Repression*, edited by Christian Davenport, 173–192. Lanham, MD: Rowman and Littlefield.

Redding, Kent. 1992. "Failed Populism: Movement-Party Disjuncture in North Carolina, 1890–1900." *American Sociological Review* 57:340–52.

Reed, Roy. 1969. "Full Integration Worries and Angers Mississippi." *New York Times*, November 24, sec. 1, p. 1.

————. 1970. "Mississippi Banks Assisting Segregated Schools." *New York Times*, August 27, sec. 1, p. 26.

Robnett, Belinda. 1996. "African-American Women in the Civil Rights Movement, 1954–1965: Gender, Leadership, and Micromobilization." *American Journal of Sociology* 101:1661–93.

Rochon, Thomas R. 1998. *Culture Moves: Ideas, Activism, and Changing Values*. Princeton: Princeton University Press.

Rochon, Thomas R., and Ikuo Kabashima. 1998. "Movement and Aftermath: Mobilization of the African American Electorate, 1952–1992." In *Politicians and Party Politics*, edited by J. Geer. Baltimore: Johns Hopkins University Press.

Rochon, Thomas R., and Daniel A. Mazmanian. 1993. "Social Movements and the Policy Process." *Annals of the American Academy of Political and Social Sciences* 528:75–156.

Romaine, Anne Cook. 1970. "The Mississippi Freedom Democratic Party through August 1964." M.A. thesis, University of Virginia, Charlottesville.

Roscigno, Vincent J., and Donald Tomaskovic-Devey. 1994. "Racial Politics in the Contemporary South: Toward a More Critical Understanding." *Social Problems* 41:585–607.

Rosenberg, Gerald N. 1991. *The Hollow Hope: Can Courts Bring about Social Change?* Chicago: University of Chicago.

Rosenstone, Steven J., and John Mark Hansen. 1993. *Mobilization, Participation, and Democracy in America.* New York: Macmillan.

Rosenthal, Jack. 1970. "A White Academy Gets Public Texts." *New York Times,* September 5, sec. 1, p. 1.

Rossell, Christine. 1983. "Desegregation Plans, Racial Isolation, White Flight and Community Response." In *The Consequences of School Desegregation,* edited by Christine Rossell and Willis Hawley, 13–57. Philadelphia: Temple University Press.

Rossell, Christine, and Robert L. Crain. 1982. "The Importance of Political Factors in Explaining Northern School Desegregation." *American Journal of Political Science* 26:772–96.

Royce, Edward. 1985. "The Origins of Southern Sharecropping: Explaining Social Change." *Current Perspectives in Social Theory* 6:279–99.

Rucht, Dieter, and Friedhelm Neidhardt. 1998. "Methodological Issues in Collecting Protest Event Data." In *Acts of Dissent: New Developments in the Study of Protest,* edited by D. Rucht, R. Koopmans, and F. Neidhardt, 65–89. Berlin: Edition Sigma.

Rupp, Leila J., and Verta Taylor. 1987. *Survival in the Doldrums: The American Women's Rights Movement, 1945 to the 1960s.* New York: Oxford University Press.

Rural Organizing and Cultural Center. 1991. *Minds Stayed on Freedom: The Civil Rights Struggle in the Rural South, an Oral History.* Boulder: Westview Press.

Sabatier, Paul. 1975. "Social Movements and Regulatory Agencies: Toward a More Adequate—and Less Pessimistic—Theory of 'Clientele Capture.'" *Policy Sciences* 6:301–42.

Salamon, Lester. 1972a. "Mississippi Post-Mortem: The 1971 Elections." *New South* 27:43–47.

———. 1972b. "Protest Politics and Modernization in the American South: Mississippi as a Developing Society." Ph.D. diss., Harvard University, Cambridge.

———. 1973. "Leadership and Modernization: The Emerging Black Political Elite in the American South." *Journal of Politics* 35:615–46.

———. 1979. "The Time Dimension in Policy Evaluation: The Case of New Deal Land-Reform Experiments." *Public Policy* 27:129–83.

Salamon, Lester, and Stephen Van Evera. 1973. "Fear, Apathy and Discrimination: A Test of Three Explanations of Political Participation." *American Political Science Review* 67:1288–306.

Sansing, James Allen. 1971. "A Descriptive Survey of Mississippi's Private Segregated Elementary and Secondary Schools in 1971." Ed.D. diss., Mississippi State University, Starkville.

Santoro, Wayne. 1999. "From Protest to Politics." Unpublished ms., Department of Sociology, Vanderbilt University.

Scher, Richard, and James Button. 1984. "Voting Rights Act: Implementation and Impact." In *Implementation of Civil Rights Policy,* edited by Charles S. Bullock III and Charles M. Lamb, 20–54. Monterey, CA: Brooks/Cole.

Schumaker, Paul D. 1975. "Policy Responsiveness to Protest Group Demands." *Journal of Politics* 37:488–521.

Schwartz, Michael. 1976. *Radical Protest and Social Structure: The Southern Farmers' Alliance and Cotton Tenancy, 1880–1890.* New York: Academic Press.

Schwartz, Michael, and Shuva Paul. 1992. "Resource Mobilization versus the Mobilization of People: Why Consensus Movements Cannot Be Instruments of Social Change." In *Frontiers* in *Social Movement Theory*, edited by Aldon Morris and Carol Mueller, 205–23. New Haven: Yale University Press.

Scott, James C. 1985. *Weapons of the Weak: Everyday Forms of Peasant Resistance*. New Haven: Yale University Press.

———. 1989. *Domination and the Arts of Resistance: Hidden Transcripts*. New Haven: Yale University Press.

Sewell, William H. 1996. "Three Temporalities: Toward an Eventful Sociology." In *The Historic Turn in the Human Sciences*, edited by T. J. McDonald, 245–80. Ann Arbor: University of Michigan Press.

Silver, James W. 1964. *Mississippi: The Closed Society*. New York: Harcourt, Brace & World.

Simpson, William. 1982. "The Birth of the Mississippi 'Loyalist Democrats' (1965–1968)." *Journal of Mississippi History* 44:27–45.

Sinsheimer, Joseph. 1989. "The Freedom Vote of 1963: New Strategies of Racial Protest in Mississippi." *Journal of Southern History* 55:217–44.

Smelser, Neil. 1962. *Theory of Collective Behavior*. New York: Free Press.

Smith, Christian. 1996. *Resisting Reagan: The U.S. Central America Peace Movement*. Chicago: University of Chicago Press.

Smith, Robert C. 1996. *We Have No Leaders: African Americans in the Post–Civil Rights Era*. Albany: State University of New York Press.

Smock, Pamela J., and Franklin D Wilson. 1991. "Desegregation and the Stability of White Enrollments: A School-Level Analysis, 1968–84." *Sociology of Education* 64:278–92.

Snyder, David, and William R. Kelly. 1979. "Strategies for Investigating Violence and Social Change: Illustrations from Analyses of Racial Disorders and Implications for Mobilization Research." In *The Dynamics of Social Movements: Resource Mobilization, Social Control, and Tactics*, edited by M. Zald and J. McCarthy, 212–37. Cambridge: Winthrop.

Southern Education Reporting Service. 1964. *Statistical Summary, State by State of School Segregation-Desegregation in the Southern and Border Area from 1954 to the Present*. Nashville, TN: Southern Education Reporting Service.

Staggenborg, Suzanne. 1988. "The Consequences of Professionalization and Formalization in the Pro-Choice Movement." *American Sociological Review* 53:585–606.

———. 1995. "Can Feminist Organizations Be Effective?" In *Feminist Organizations: Harvest of the New Women's Movement*, edited by M. M. Ferree and P. Y. Martin, 339–55. Philadelphia: Temple University Press.

Steedly, Homer, and John Foley. 1979. "The Success of Protest Groups: Multivariate Analyses." *Social Science Research* 8:1–15.

Stepan-Norris, Judith, and Maurice Zeitlin. 1995. "Union Democracy, Radical Leadership, and the Hegemony of Capital." *American Sociological Review* 60:829–50.

Stewart, Joseph, and James F. Sheffield. 1987. "Does Interest Group Litigation Matter? The Case of Black Political Mobilization in Mississippi." *Journal of Politics* 49:780–98.

Swain, Carol M. 1993. *Black Faces, Black Interests: The Representation of African Americans in Congress*. Cambridge: Harvard University Press.

Tarrow, Sidney. 1991. *Struggle, Politics, and Reform: Collective Action, Social Movements, and Cycles of Protest*. Ithaca: Cornell University Press.

———. 1993. "Social Protest and Policy Reform: May 1968 and the Loi d'Orientation in France." *Comparative Political Studies* 25:579–607.

———. 1994. *Power in Movement: Social Movements, Collection Action, and Politics*. Cambridge: Cambridge University Press.

————. 1996a. "Social Movements in Contentious Politics: A Review Article." *American Political Science Review* 90:874–83.

————. 1996b. "States and Opportunities: The Political Structuring of Social Movements." In *Comparative Perspectives on Social Movements: Political Opportunities, Mobilizing Structures, and Cultural Framings*, edited by D. McAdam, J. D. McCarthy, and M. N. Zald, 41–61. New York: Cambridge University Press.

————. 1998. *Power in Movement: Social Movements, Collection Action, and Politics.* 2nd ed. Cambridge: Cambridge University Press

Taylor, Garth. 1986. *Public Opinion and Collective Action: The Boston School Desegregation Conflict.* Chicago: University of Chicago Press.

Taylor, Verta. 1989. "Social Movement Continuity: The Women's Movement in Abeyance." *American Sociological Review* 54:761–75.

Tilly, Charles. 1978. *From Mobilization to Revolution.* New York: McGraw Hill.

————. 1999. "From Interactions to Outcomes in Social Movements." In *How Social Movements Matter*, edited by M. Giugni, D. McAdam, and C. Tilly, 253–70. Minneapolis: University of Minnesota Press.

Timpone, Richard. 1995. "Mass Mobilization or Government Intervention?: The Growth of Black Registration in the South." *Journal of Politics* 57:425–43.

————. 1997. "The Voting Rights Act and Electoral Empowerment: The Case of Mississippi." *Social Science Quarterly* 78:177–85.

Tomaskovic-Devey, Donald, and Vincent J. Roscigno. 1996. "Racial Economic Subordination and White Gain in the U.S. South." *American Sociological Review* 61:565–89.

Turner, Ralph, and Lewis Killian. [1957, 1972] 1987. *Collective Behavior.* Englewood Cliffs, NJ: Prentice-Hall.

United States Bureau of the Census. 1969. *Census of Agriculture, Mississippi.* Part 33, sec. 1, vol. 1. Washington, DC: Government Printing Office.

U.S. Commission on Civil Rights [USCCR]. 1961. *Voting.* Washington, DC: Government Printing Office.

————. 1965. *The Voting Rights Act: The First Months.* Washington, DC: Government Printing Office.

————. 1968. *Political Participation.* Washington, DC: Government Printing Office.

————. 1969. *Federal Enforcement of School Desegregation: A Report.* Washington, DC: Government Printing Office.

————. 1975. *The Voting Rights Act: Ten Years Later.* Washington, DC: Government Printing Office.

————. 1981. *The Voting Rights Act: Unfilled Goals.* Washington, DC: Government Printing Office.

Useem, Bert. 1980. "Solidarity Model, Breakdown Model, and the Boston Anti-Busing Movement." *American Sociological Review* 45:357–96.

Verba, Sidney, and Norman H. Nie. 1972. *Participation in America: Political Democracy and Social Equality.* New York: Harper & Row.

Verba, Sidney, Kay Lehman Schlozman, and Henry E. Brady. 1995. *Voice and Equality: Civic Voluntarism in American Life.* Cambridge: Harvard University Press.

Voss, Kim, and Rachel Sherman. 2000. "Breaking the Iron Law of Oligarchy: Union Revitalization in the American Labor Movement." *American Journal of Sociology* 106: 303–49.

Voter Education Project of the Southern Regional Council. 1966. *The Effects of Federal Examiners and Organized Registration Campaigns on Negro Voter Registration*. Atlanta, GA: Southern Regional Council.

Walker, Jack L. 1991. *Mobilizing Interest Groups in America: Patrons, Professions and Social Movements*. Ann Arbor: University of Michigan Press.

Warren, Mark R. 2001. *Dry Bones Rattling: Community Building to Revitalize Democracy* Princeton: Princeton University Press.

Washington Research Project. 1972. *The Shameful Blight: The Survival of Racial Discrimination in Voting in the South*. Washington, DC: Washington Research Project.

Webb, Keith, Ekkart Zimmerman, Michael Marsh, Anne-Marie Aish, Christina Mironesco, Christopher Mitchell, Leonardo Morlino, and James Walston. 1983. "Etiology and Outcomes of Protest." *American Behavioral Scientist* 26:311–31.

Whittier, Nancy. 1995. *Feminist Generations: The Persistence of the Radical Women's Movement*. Philadelphia: Temple University Press.

Wilson, C. J. 1973. "Voices From Mississippi." *New South*, 62–71.

Wilson, James B. 1965. "Municipal Ordinances, Mississippi Style." In *Southern Justice*, edited by Leon Friedman, 35–42. Cleveland: Meridian Books.

Wirt, Frederick. 1970. *Politics of Southern Equality: Law and Social Change in a Mississippi County*. Chicago: Aldine.

———. 1997. *We Ain't What We Was: Civil Rights in the New South*. Durham, NC: Duke University Press.

Wood, Richard L. 2002. *Faith in Action: Religion, Race, and Democratic Organizing* Chicago: University of Chicago Press.

Woodruff, Nan Elizabeth. 1994. "Mississippi Delta Planters and Debates over Mechanization, Labor and Civil Rights in the 1940s." *Journal of Southern History* 60:263–84.

Woodward, C. Vann. 1955. *The Strange Career of Jim Crow*. London: Oxford University Press.

Wooten, James. 1970a. "A Protest by Parents." *New York Times*. January 8, sec, 1, p. 1.

———. 1970b. "US Forms Panel for Mississippi." *New York Times*, January 1, sec. 1, p. 21.

———. 1970c. "Exodus Seen as a Threat to the System on Eve of Integration Move." *New York Times*, January 5, sec. 1, p. 1.

Zald, Mayer N., and Bert Useem. 1987. "Movement and Countermovement Interaction: Mobilization, Tactics, and State Involvement." In *Social Movements in an Organizational Society: Collected Essays*, edited by M. N. Zald and J. D. McCarthy, 247–72. New Brunswick, NJ: Transaction.

Zinn, Howard. 1965. SNCC: *The New Abolitionists*. Boston: Beacon Press.

Index

Bolivar County Community Action Program, Inc. (BCCAP), 148–50
Bolivar County Improvement Association, 100
boycotts: of buses, 44; in Holmes County, 86, 89; laws against, 94; in Madison County, 75, 91–93; in Shelby, 103–6, 159–60
Bradford, John, 100–101
bridge leaders, 23–24
Brockett, Charles, 35
Brooks, Owen, 100
Brown, Ed, 86
Browning, Rufus P., 28
Brown v. Board of Education, 155–56
Burstein, Paul, 27
bus boycotts, 44
busing, 170
Button, James, 18, 20, 37, 186, 201

Campbell, David, 191
Campbell, Foote, 92
candidates, for election. *See* political candidates
Canton (Madison County): city council election system, 98, 176; employment discrimination by, 99; private academies, 164, 165; school desegregation, 159; voter registration, 89–90
CAPS. *See* community action programs
Caraway, William, 177
Carmichael, Stokely, 52
Carroll, Terry, 164
Carson, Clayborne, 4–5, 9
Caruthers, Bruce, 18
causal issues, 20–21. *See also* methodology
CDGM. *See* Child Development Group of Mississippi
Central Mississippi, Inc. (CMI), 89, 146–47
Chaney, James, 31, 54–55
Child Development Group of Mississippi (CDGM): in Bolivar County, 103, 148–49; vs. CAPS, 150–51; federal funding of, 151; history of, 60–61, 139–40; in Holmes County, 141; integration issues, 152; investigations and audits of, 141–42; number of counties with projects, 140; white opposition to, 61, 141. *See also* Head Start

Chong, Dennis, 2
churches, 100
Citizens' Council: and *Brown v. Board of Education*, 155–56; county comparison, 70, 78; expansion of, 34; founding of, 44; funding of, 45; intimidation tactics, 44; of Madison County, 93, 94; measurement of, 207; and private academy formation, 165–66, 169, 236n23; response to early NAACP campaigns, 43; and Sovereignty Commission, 31
citizenship classes, 55, 102
Civil Rights Commission: black teacher survey, 68; on federal examiner in Holmes County, 118; on harassment of black candidates, 119; and OEO, 152; school desegregation, 158; voter registration data, 72, 121, 127
civil rights movements, time frame applied to, 9. *See also* Mississippi civil rights movement, development of
civil rights workers, 32–33
Clark, Robert, 88, 121, 123
clergy, 23, 66, 80
Cleveland (Bolivar County), 42, 100, 101, 103, 161
Cloward, Richard, 26, 29, 206
CMI. *See* Central Mississippi, Inc.
COFO. *See* Council of Federated Organizations
Colby, David, 95, 207
community action programs (CAPS): administration of, 139; board selection issues, 145–46; in Bolivar County, 103, 148–50; vs. CDGM, 150–51; formation and funding of, 142–45; Governor Johnson's funding veto, 152; in Holmes County, 88–89, 146–48; measurement of, 233n9, objective of, 138; poverty program process, 60. *See also* Head Start
community centers, 81–82, 86, 101, 102
community organizing approach, 47–49, 91
community studies, as part of research design, 6–7, 203, 208–9
competition theory, 169–70, 236n26
Congressional Challenge (1965), 85
congressional districts, 59, 113, 174, 175–76

King, Mary, 1
Ku Klux Klan, 31, **70**, **78**, 83, 207

labor unions, 25, 100, 102–3
Langford, Cliff, 148
Latin American peasant mobilization, 35
law enforcement, 31, 87, 90–91, 94
Lawson, Steven, 45–46
lawsuits: congressional districts, 99, 175;
   determining the impact of, 223n1; difficulties of, 195; election rules, 176–77,
   179; employment discrimination by cities,
   99; school desegregation, 161
leadership, 22, 23–24, 25, 27, 86
Lee, George, 43
Lee, Herbert, 31, 50
Leflore County, 66
legal barriers: boycotts, 94; political participation, 113; political power, 59, 174–77;
   school desegregation, 156; voter registration, 44
legal challenges. *See* lawsuits
legislature, of Mississippi: blacks in, **178**;
   Freedom Summer response, 51; "massive
   resistance" legislation, 31–32; post–
   Voting Rights Act legislation, 59; school
   desegregation, 156; school funding,
   164, 165
Levin, Tom, 139
Lewis, Daisy, 81, 82, 88, 120–21, 147
Lewis, John, 1
Lexington (Holmes County), 165
Lexington Advertiser, 147
Lichbach, Marc, 34
Lipsky, Michael, 26–27
literacy requirements, 109
litigation. *See* lawsuits
Loewen, James, 32, 98, 165
Lorenzi, Henry, 84, 88, 122
Lorenzi, Susan, 81, 122, 158
Lowenstein, Allard, 53
Loyalist Democrats, 73, 119
lynchings, **70**, **78**

MacLeod, Jay, 79, 87
Madison County: Board of Supervisors
   positions, 76; boycotts, 75, 91–93;

demographic profile, 77, **78**; movement
   development, 89–99, 193; voter
   registration, 89, 90, 92
Madison County Herald, 94
Madison County Union for Progress
   (MCUP), 99
Mansbridge, Jane, 17
MAP. *See* Mississippi Action for Progress
maps, of counties, 8, **67**
Marshall, Dale Rogers, 28
Matthews, Donald, 112, 205
mayors, number of black, **178**
Mazmanian, Daniel, 28
McAdam, Doug, 37, 77, 224nn15–16
McCammon, Holly, 16
McComb (Pike County), 49–50, 227n35
McLellan, Henry, 117
McMillen, Neil, 34, 225n2
MCUP. *See* Madison County Union for
   Progress
Meredith, James, 156
methodology: causal issues, 20–22, 223n3;
   civil rights activity measurement, 68;
   voter registration influence, 127
Meyer, David, 33–34
MFDP. *See* Mississippi Freedom Democratic
   Party
MFLU. *See* Mississippi Farm Labor Union
Mileston, 79, 81
ministers, 23, 66, 80
Minkoff, Debra, 23
Mississippi, as a case study, 204
Mississippi Action for Progress (MAP),
   61, 142
Mississippi civil rights movement, develop-
   ment of: early (1954–60), 42–45;
   1961–65, 45–57; after 1965, 57–62. *See
   also specific entries*
Mississippi Farm Labor Union (MFLU), 100,
   102–3
Mississippi Freedom Democratic Party
   (MFDP): and CDGM, 139; county
   comparison, **78**; formation of, 55; Freedom
   Vote campaign, 56; Holmes County, 81, 84,
   87–88, 100, 103, 122, 146, 227n27; importance of, 57; legal challenge of congressional
   districts, 175; measurement of, 207

voter registration: in Bolivar County, 100, 101, 102; gains after 1965, 58–59; in Holmes County, 80, 83, 85, 114–18, 121; Kennedy administration's goals, 15; legal barriers, 44; in Madison County, 89, 90, 92; MFDP campaigns, 55; movement vs. non-movement counties, 125, 127–28; NAACP campaigns, 43; number of blacks registered, 56, 69, 72, 78, 111; problems with data, 232n19; SNCC campaigns, 49–50; and Voting Rights Act, 109–10; white countermobilization, 18, 112, 131–34

voter turnout, 125, 126, 128–30, 131–34, 189, 232n20

Votes without Leverage (Harvey), 17

voting: intimidation at polling places, 32, 97, 98, 121; "racial bloc voting," 129, 231n2, 232n21; registrars' obstacles, 53; skimming of black vote, 32; Supreme Court's interpretation of, 176

Voting Rights Act (1965): discriminatory intent elimination (1982), 177; federal oversight over elections, 58; interpretation of, 176; overview of, 230–31n1; and political participation, 108–14; and political power, 179; public opinion, 27

War on Poverty, 59–61, 136–39, 153–54, 195–96, 202. *See also* antipoverty programs; Child Development Group of Mississippi (CDGM); community action programs (CAPS)

Washington, George, 94–95

Watkins, Hollis, 54

Westgate, Bob, 146

Whitaker, R. L., 119

"white flight," 170

white opposition, 30–33. *See also* counter-movements; repression

Whitley, Clifton, 120, 126, 129, 130, 133, 182, 232n20

Why We Lost the ERA (Mansbridge), 17

Williams, Jewel, 97

Winstonville (Bolivar County), 100–101

Wirt, Frederick, 158, 159

women's movements, 16–17, 223n2. *See also* Equal Rights Amendment (ERA); suffrage movement

Woodward, C. Vann, 44

Wright, Marian, 157

Young, Michael, 17, 21

Zald, Mayer, 33, 194

Zylan, Yvonne, 18